I0797056

MY WORK AMONG THE FREEDMEN

A Nation Divided: Studies in the Civil War Era

Orville Vernon Burton and Elizabeth R. Varon, *Editors*

My Work among the Freedmen

The Civil War and Reconstruction Letters of Harriet M. Buss

EDITED BY

Jonathan W. White and Lydia J. Davis

University of Virginia Press
CHARLOTTESVILLE AND LONDON

University of Virginia Press

Printed in the United States of America on acid-free paper

First published 2021

1 3 5 7 9 8 6 4 2

Library of Congress Cataloging-in-Publication Data

Names: Buss, Harriet M., 1825 or 1826–1895, author. | White, Jonathan W., editor. | Davis, Lydia J., editor.
Title: My work among the freedmen : the Civil War and Reconstruction letters of Harriet M. Buss / edited by Jonathan W. White, Lydia J. Davis.
Other titles: Nation divided.
Description: Charlottesville : University of Virginia Press, [2021] | Series: A nation divided: studies in the Civil War era | Includes bibliographical references and index.
Identifiers: LCCN 2020058442 (print) | LCCN 2020058443 (ebook) | ISBN 9780813946634 (hardcover) | ISBN 9780813946641 (ebook)
Subjects: LCSH: Buss, Harriet M., 1825 or 1826–1895—Correspondence. | Women teachers—United States—19th century—Correspondence. | Women, White—United States—19th century—Correspondence. | Freedmen—United States. | African American students—Southern States—History—19th century. | Teaching—Social aspects—Southern States. | Southern States—Race relations—History—19th century. | LCGFT: Personal correspondence.
Classification: LCC LA2317.B77 A3 2021 (print) | LCC LA2317.B77 (ebook) | DDC 371.10082—dc23
LC record available at https://lccn.loc.gov/2020058442
LC ebook record available at https://lccn.loc.gov/2020058443

Cover photo: Liberty County schoolchildren, 1890 (Courtesy of Hargrett Rare Book and Manuscript Library, University of Georgia Libraries); *background:* Shutterstock/Katrien1 and pixabay/Coffee

For Nathan and Elizabeth Busch,
who have built a very special academic home
in Christopher Newport University's
Center for American Studies

CONTENTS

ILLUSTRATIONS

FOREWORD

HARRIET BUSS fits the quintessential definition of the Yankee schoolmarm decried by Dunning School scholars. William Archibald Dunning, a Columbia University historian, significantly influenced popular understandings of the Reconstruction era through his writings and training of professional historians. Under the guise of objectivity, the Dunning School characterized Reconstruction as a mistake. Scholars also promoted as fact that ill-prepared, uneducated, and corrupt African Americans wreaked havoc on the region and the nation while Southern white race traitors (labeled "scalawags") and vengeful Northern white Americans ("carpetbaggers") abetted them during the "tragic era," as one scholar titled his 1929 history. Their scholarly publications allowed Harriet Buss, her contributions to African American education, and her letters of correspondence to become lost to history. She became one of the nameless Yankee schoolteachers who invaded the defeated South, except to W. E. B. Du Bois and other African American scholars committed to Carter G. Woodson's black history movement.[1]

Harriet Buss was more than the Dunning School caricature. She was an outspoken, single Massachusetts native who received an education at a reputable state normal school. After teaching at several antebellum institutions, Buss responded to the Civil War humanitarian crisis posed by African American refugees seeking freedom amid a war zone. The civilian Yankee invader labored in the slave refugee camps of the Port Royal Experiment discussed in Willie Lee Rose's pioneering *Rehearsal for Reconstruction* and later clarified by revisionist historians.

Buss's work, however, proved more than a novel adventure undertaken by some missionaries. While other white women typically lasted one season, Buss persisted. She taught in the slave refugee camps of the South Carolina Low Country, in the Freedmen's Bureau schools in Norfolk, Virginia, and at a Raleigh, North Carolina, HBCU in its formative years. As a result, she had a lasting impact on the development of postwar African American public schools. Her tenure reflected motivations that were more akin to those of African American educators who came south than to those of the majority of her white counterparts. She expanded the economic opportunities and social capital of her students, and in the process, she cultivated educated citizens and leaders. Importantly, Buss's many letters home, more than her formal reports to the supporting agencies, offer valuable insights.

Buss embodied a politics that made the Reconstruction project viable but drew the ire and violent wrath of white supremacists. As a single woman, she took risks by working on the Southern African American educational frontier. Yet she did not need the protection of white men. Instead, she empowered African Americans in three Southern states. She equipped black men and women with the tools, language, and activist spirit necessary for their struggle for full inclusion in the national body politic as educated and equal citizens. Her failing health forced a break in her service following the Civil War refugee crisis. She found employment in the interim; however, she remained unsatisfied. She quickly returned to the Southern educational field, where her work brought her more than a paycheck. Her Southern African American students provided professional and personal nourishment as well as income. Teaching them, she was no longer hungry, physically or spiritually, as she had been when she taught in Illinois and Massachusetts. She found fulfillment, joy, and hope as an active social justice reformer committed to remaking the postwar nation.

Beyond the on-the-ground educational developments, Buss's letters shed light on how the Civil War transformed Northern white women's employment opportunities and informed the diverse racialized, classist, and gendered political understandings of the national Reconstruction project. Buss bridged white and black, Northern and Southern, and gendered religious and political communities within a rich and diverse network. While inquiring on Sterling, Massachusetts, affairs, she offered unfiltered commentary on the real conditions of freedpeople and corrected media reports shaping policy and national attitudes on Reconstruction. She solicited needed supplies as well as possible opportunities for her students among her own overlapping familial, educational, and religious circles. She forged genuine relationships with the future politician Robert Smalls, Henry Tupper, and others committed to African American education and to building an inclusive, more just postwar nation. By bridging race, gender, and region, she helped to lay the foundation for African American public schools and present-day Shaw University.

Her letters also reveal the real challenges posed by the Ku Klux Klan and Southern white derailers of Reconstruction as well as the failure of federal leadership. Her anger against Southern white instigators of racial violence is palpable when she writes in a November 1868 letter, "When

I read the accounts of the rebel outrages in Louisiana, Mississippi, Alabama, Georgia, and other southern localities, I feel as if I would like to be *Commander-in-Chief* of the Military for a time." Buss's frustration with President U. S. Grant and the waning national commitment to the Reconstruction educational project is made clear when she proclaims: "I dislike Grant now, and hope Sumner will carry the day." Buss's frank assessment, agency, and experiences as an educator in the African American schools make plain the politics of erasure by Dunning scholars, who deemed her archival traces and positionality inconvenient. While revisionist scholars have overturned Dunning interpretations, the recovery of Buss and her critical voice is an important intervention of the sesquicentennial reassessment of Reconstruction.

Epitomized in her common letter closing "with love, Hattie," this compelling collection of letters reintroduces readers to Harriet Buss as a significant interlocutor who helps us to understand the motivations, experiences, and achievements of white Northern women who labored on the Southern educational frontier. Buss's experiences, commentary, and fierce commitment force us to reassess the growth of African American education, the extent to which the Civil War expanded women's rights and opportunities, and other Reconstruction-era developments.

Hilary Green
University of Alabama

ACKNOWLEDGMENTS

We are dedicating this book to Nathan and Elizabeth Busch, the founding codirectors of Christopher Newport University's Center for American Studies. The center is a wonderful place to exchange ideas with scholars and friends who are interested in America's history and form of government. The center's generous funding to hire Lydia as a junior fellow made this project possible.

J. Matthew Gallman and Michael T. Bernath both gave the manuscript a close and careful read and offered valuable suggestions for improvements, for which we are very grateful. Robert Colby and Phil Hamilton, of Christopher Newport University, also read portions of the manuscript and offered helpful comments. Ronald E. Butchart, of the University of Georgia, generously provided biographical information on eight teachers we had been unable to identify. Lynn Shollen, chair of the Department of Leadership and American Studies at Christopher Newport University, provided professional development funds that enabled Jonathan to travel to Philadelphia to photograph the Harriet M. Buss Collection at the University of Pennsylvania.

We are grateful to Elizabeth Varon for her support of this project and for including it in her wonderful series. Larry Treadwell, of the Shaw University Libraries; Phillip Cunningham and Lisa Moore, of the Amistad Research Center at Tulane University; John Pollack, of the Kislak Center for Special Collections, Rare Books and Manuscripts, at the University of Pennsylvania; and David Gibbs, of the Sterling Historical Society, all assisted us in our research. Nadine Zimmerli and Ellen Satrom, of the University of Virginia Press, showed wonderful support and enthusiasm for this project, for which we are grateful. Joanne Allen was a phenomenal copyeditor. Finally, Christopher Newport University's interlibrary-loan specialist, Jesse Spencer, tracked down a number of items for us that facilitated our research.

ACKNOWLEDGMENTS

INTRODUCTION

LOOKING BACK on their years in bondage, many elderly ex-slaves recalled the great lengths they had gone to to get an education. Such attempts came with substantial risk. Responding to questions he received from a Works Progress Administration (WPA) worker in the 1930s, Arnold Gragston said that his master "would near beat the daylights out of us" if slaves on his plantation learned to read and write. Eighty-two-year-old Sarah Benjamin stated in 1937, "Dey didn't larn us nothin' and iffen you did larn to write, you better keep it to yourself, 'cause some slaves got de thumb or finger cut off for larnin' to write." Some slaves, like Frederick Douglass, tricked white children into teaching them to read. Others taught one another in makeshift schools in the woods. As Mandy Jones, of Mississippi, described it, "Dey would dig pits, and kiver the spot wid bushes an' vines. . . . An' dey had pit schools in slave days too. Way out in de woods, dey *was* woods den, an' de slaves would slip out o' de Quarters at night, an go to dese pits, an some niggah dat had some learnin' would have a school." Slaves with an education were considered dangerous to Southern whites as they could breed discontent among the enslaved population. Nevertheless, by 1860 5–10 percent of slaves had learned how to read.[1]

Gaining an education continued to be a priority for African Americans during the Civil War and into the postwar years because they understood that education was a key to becoming full participants in the polity. As historian Ronald E. Butchart explains, education would "put as great a distance between themselves and bondage as possible." During and after the war, he continues, "African Americans acted on the possibilities of freedom with an overwhelming surge toward the schoolhouse door." One white New England teacher captured this dynamic when she wrote in her diary upon reaching South Carolina in 1865, "Their faces shone when we told them why we had come." Unfortunately, former Confederates understood the importance of education for ex-slaves as well. Some Southern planters tried to thwart the work of black schools because they believed that "learning will spoil the nigger for work." Moreover, many ex-Confederates hoped that keeping African Americans illiterate would prevent them from rising in society. In 1865, for example, a white North

Carolinian who was on trial for the murder of a black man tried to undermine the credibility of black witnesses by claiming that the testimony of "two ignorant collored witnesses" should not be given the same credence as that of "intelligent white witnesses."[2]

Fortunately, the Civil War created new opportunities for black Southerners to gain an education. The freedpeople themselves showed tremendous initiative, setting up what one white Northerner called "native schools . . . throughout the entire South." By 1866, at least five hundred of these institutions were in operation. Northern missionaries also played an important role in the education of freedmen and freedwomen. Within two weeks of the firing on Fort Sumter in April 1861, the *American Missionary,* the newspaper of the American Missionary Association (AMA), declared that the war would turn the South into "one of the grandest fields of missionary labor the world ever furnished." By June the AMA, a nondenominational Protestant organization that had been established by antislavery philanthropists in 1846, was planning to send teachers to Hampton, Virginia, near Fort Monroe. Others quickly followed suit. The following March, Gideonites from New England began instructing slaves in the Sea Islands of South Carolina. As Confederates lost control of more and more territory during the war, Union soldiers and Northern missionaries moved in to teach the formerly enslaved.[3]

Traditionally scholars viewed a teacher for freedmen as the "New England schoolma'am." In *The Souls of Black Folk,* W. E. B. Du Bois wrote, "Behind the mists of ruin and rapine waved the calico dresses of women who dared, and after the hoarse mouthings of the field guns rang the rhythm of the alphabet. Rich and poor they were, serious and curious . . . they came seeking a life work in planting New England schoolhouses among the white and black of the South. They did their work well."[4] Throughout the twentieth century, however, the reputation of the "Yankee schoolmarm" saw a decline. Historians of the Dunning School loathed the "'messianic' invasion of the South" by these intolerant and often corrupt radicals. One denigrated them as "horsefaced, bespectacled, and spare of frame." More recent scholars have criticized these Northern white teachers from the opposite perspective, arguing that they were not racially enlightened enough. James D. Anderson, for example, writes that "most" Northern missionaries and teachers "were bent on treating the freedmen almost wholly as objects."[5]

Recent scholarship has shown that the stereotypical white, young, female, wealthy "New England schoolma'am" was actually not the typical teacher of freedmen in the South. Most Northern teachers were from the middle and western states; no more than one-fifth of the teachers came from New England. Moreover, one in six Northern teachers was black. In fact, African Americans (including both Northern- and Southern-born) made up more than a third of the teachers at freedmen's schools, and roughly half of the teachers were Southern whites, including some ex-Confederate soldiers and former slave owners who needed income in the postwar South. Few of the Northern women came from wealthy backgrounds; nor were they generally young. Most were middle class, while some came from "genteel poverty." They were highly religious, and many prioritized spreading their denominational beliefs about Christianity. According to Ronald E. Butchart, "Remarkably few of the northern white teachers can be demonstrated to have been abolitionists before the war began." Over time, the number of white Northern teachers dwindled. By 1870, white Southerners outnumbered white Northerners in classrooms for black students. Many of the Northern teachers worked with missionary societies, while most of the Southern teachers did not. Funding their work could be a struggle for teachers who were unaffiliated with a larger, established organization.[6]

By the end of the Civil War, federal authorities realized that many Southern refugees needed federal assistance to survive. In 1865, Congress established the Bureau of Refugees, Freedmen and Abandoned Lands (the Freedmen's Bureau) to assist both white and black refugees in the South. The Freedmen's Bureau may have been short lived, but it played a substantial role in creating the nation's system of historically black colleges and universities (HBCUs). By 1869 the bureau had established nearly three thousand schools in the South (this number did not include private schools operated by Northern missionary societies). In that year, for the first time, a majority of the teachers in the South were black.[7] "The greatest success of the Freedmen's Bureau lay in the planting of the free school among Negroes, and the idea of free elementary education among all classes in the South," wrote W. E. B. Du Bois. By 1870, 150,000 black children were in school. "The opposition to Negro education in the South was at first bitter, and showed itself in ashes, insult, and blood; for the South believed an educated Negro to be a dangerous Negro," wrote Du Bois. "Nevertheless, men strive to know. Perhaps some inkling of this paradox, even in the unquiet days of the Bureau, helped the bayonets allay an opposition to human training which still to-day lies smouldering in the South, but not flaming. Fisk, Atlanta, Howard, and Hampton were founded in these days, and nearly $6,000,000 was expended for educational work, $750,000 of which the freedmen themselves gave of their poverty."[8]

*

One of the thousands of white teachers who traveled to the South was Harriet M. Buss. Born in Sterling, Massachusetts, in 1826 to Silas (1799–1871) and Sally Moore (1801–1887), Harriet grew up on a 181-acre farm, which in 1850 was valued at three thousand dollars. There the Busses raised rye, Indian corn, and oats and had one horse, seven cows, two oxen, three pigs, and three "other cattle." In one of her earliest surviving letters written away from home, Harriet said she longed to be "seated within the precincts of my own rural home."[9] In addition to being a farmer, Silas also worked as a chair maker, and his headstone calls him "Captain."[10]

Little is known about Harriet's early childhood, although many years later she recalled that she "always thought teaching was my life-work; I longed for it, I aimed and planned for it as soon as I knew what a school was."[11] In 1845, when she was about nineteen years old, she was listed as a member of the Teachers' Institute at Fitchburg, Massachusetts, where she learned from such luminaries as Horace Mann.[12] In 1847, she began attending the Charlestown Female Seminary, an institution "pleasantly located within one mile of Boston, in a healthy situation." According to the school's *Catalogue*, girls "whose character and habits give promise of usefulness" were given tuition assistance, "without regard to religious sentiments." Students studied the sciences, English, French, Latin, and other subjects of the liberal arts.[13] There appears to have been a strong sense of intimacy between the students and faculty at the seminary. After one of her beloved teachers, Martha Whiting, died, Harriet wrote a poem reflecting on the kindness of her deceased mentor: "From term to term they meet and part— / A classic band—in that same hall / Where she, with smile and friendly word, / So long was wont to welcome all."[14]

During her time at Charlestown, Harriet sent several letters to her parents. This early correspondence reveals aspects of her character that persisted throughout her adult life. She was a very hard worker. On one scrap of paper, probably written in 1850, she told her parents that she typically stayed awake past 11:00 p.m. and was often up before 4:00 a.m. Working hard, for her, was a way to prosper and gain independence. And doing well in school would enable her to make something of herself and

Charlestown Female Seminary, ca. 1840s. (Courtesy of the Boston Public Library)

leave a legacy. "I shall study my lifetime; something or nothing is yet my motto, I will have no halfway ground," she wrote in March 1850. "If life and health are continued, the *world* shall know that I live in it, and in the *future ages* it shall know that I have lived in it, for I will leave mine impress deeply traced upon it."[15] Ten years later she would write, "I like to make something of a stir in the world once in a while, and I intend to do it as often as it seems convenient."[16]

One common theme throughout her correspondence was food. "It seems as if I should never eat meat and pie enough," she wrote in March 1850. "I shall want ever so much beef-steak, ham, eggs, tongue, and mince and pumpkin pie, but no bread and butter." A year later, her obsession with food continued to be an important, if comical, part of her correspondence. "I think I will wend my way directly to the cupboard, for I feel very much like attacking a large mince pie, a nice loaf of cake, and whatever else I might find that is good to eat," she wrote her parents. "I shall next search for Apples, a dozen certainly, and a great slice of new cheese, then I will finish with a dish of nuts." In this particular letter she described seeing a building burn down. Then it was right back to her favorite subject: "I have had a great piece of cake up in Carrie Ayres' room tonight, and now I wish I had a pie from home, a large one too." A few months later she wrote, "O dear! I am so hungry, I do wish I had something to eat! If I could get to the cupboard at home, how busy I would be with a great pie. I shall keep something to eat next term; I must have luncheons."[17] Harriet's enthusiasm for tasty fare continued into the war years and will provide fodder to scholars of foodways in the American South.

In late 1850 Harriet was made an assistant teacher at Charlestown Female Seminary. Now that she had teaching responsibilities, the other teachers put pressure on her to go to bed before 10:00 p.m. In fact, she was paid three dollars per week, but the governess of the school offered to raise her wages "if I would not sit up late, she is so afraid I shall undermine my constitution." She enjoyed teaching her classes in geography, arithmetic, and the Bible, and she believed that her students "seem happy with me." But as a teacher she found that she could not find as much time for herself. "I cannot secrete myself if I try," she wrote. "Sometimes I steal away to be alone but some one will generally find me; I know not how, or why it is that I seem to draw so many friends around me, but it certainly makes it very pleasant for me."[18]

By December 1851, Harriet wanted to find a school where she would receive "a liberal compensation," for she wished to "rebel against being fettered by my scant means." She also longed "to control an Institution of high standing, one that I can constantly be raising higher; I must have the management of schools where I am, to do myself justice, and such management as I wish, I am determined to have (Providence permitting)." In 1852 she was invited to open a female seminary in New Mexico Territory, but being an only child, she did not wish to abandon her parents. In February 1852 she submitted her resignation to the seminary, in part because she could no longer stand the meals that were served at her boardinghouse and she wanted to earn enough money "to buy such food as is palatable." She trusted that God would lead her to the correct next place.[19]

By 1854, Buss was teaching at a school in Westport (presumably Massachusetts but possibly Connecticut). The school was small, with about thirty students, and she worried that her income would not be sufficient. She wanted to be at a school where she could support herself, start saving money, be pleasantly situated, and do good for those around her. In 1855 she was recruited to be the lead teacher at the new Marysville High School for Young Ladies in Ohio. An article in the local paper stated that she "furnishes testimonials of a high order" and that she was prepared to offer courses in English, Latin, French, and pencil drawing.[20] By 1857, however, she was back in Massachusetts at the Ladies Collegiate Institute in Worcester, where she was listed in the *Catalogue* as both a student and a teacher of mathematics and French. She appears to have spent one term there.[21]

About 1858 or 1859, Buss decided to move west, settling in Freedom, LaSalle County, Illinois. Life on the frontier was difficult. "A teacher who loves ease and wishes to be as genteel and as aristocratic as possible will stay East," she wrote her parents, "but one who teaches to bless the world, to make it better, and help save his country from ruin, must be willing to work in hard fields, and far from home too, perhaps." She relished the opportunity to be in charge of an institution. "I would like to have a colony of my own selection settled somewhere, all near each other, and then I would live right in the midst, and regulate them all around, just as an *old maid* ought to regulate society, keeping everybody else in exact order," she wrote. She believed she was "progressing finely in the art of managing such youngsters."[22]

Throughout the 1850s Harriet wrestled with the meaning of her singleness. As her twenty-sixth birthday approached in early 1852, she wrote her parents, "I shall soon have to stand in the Old Maid's ranks, shall I not?"[23] Eight years later, in 1860, when "the fifth of my Illinois scholars . . . entered the matrimonial state," she mused, "Am I not a good teacher to prepare pupils for married life?" But she did not wish to be married herself, for she did not want to be bound by the will of a husband. "Better at fitting others than preparing myself; well I don't want to obey one of creation's *lords*. Never could I be told to go or stay, do this or that, and surely never could I ask. I submit to no human being as my master or dictator."[24] Indeed, Harriet's life and letters speak to many important issues in women's history and the history of feminism in the United States. She was highly independent and ambitious, and unlike most nineteenth-century American women, she was geographically mobile from the 1850s until the end of her life. Her letters trace that trajectory—what Ronald E. Butchart describes as her "feminist determination to blaze her own path in life."[25]

As the Civil War approached, Harriet wrote with increasing fervor about national politics. She was incensed by the foolishness and incompetence of the men running the nation and believed that women were more capable of solving the nation's problems. "How they so act at Congress, what contemptible and unprincipled men we have there!" she wrote in January 1860. "Surely slavery is showing its cloven foot now, as it never did before; and yet we have northern men ready to fall down and worship the demon, some of them calling themselves Christians too. I do hope the [presidential] campaign of this year will thoroughly revolutionize our government."[26] (Curiously, she wrote nothing about Illinois's most prominent antislavery politician, Abraham Lincoln, during her time in the Midwest.) In February, Harriet went to hear four political lectures by the abolitionist Ichabod Codding. She was infuriated by what she learned about the Democratic Party's alleged plot to spread slavery into the western territories through the *Dred Scott* decision (1857) and by Senator Stephen A. Douglas's proposed "sedition law" in January 1860 to silence opposition to slavery. Her reaction is worth quoting in full:

> I never heard better political lectures, or sounder arguments advanced, they were unanswerable. Popular Sovereignty, and the Dredd Scott Decision were shown up in their true light, Douglass too was well dissected. Mr. Codding knows him from his boyhood, and I think he said he had stumped it considerable with him.
>
> Have you read the *Little Dodger's* last speech in Congress? What great things he will do! Enact a law, and shut up in prison all the leaders of agitation upon the slavery question! wont he have a fine time showing them all to their cells? How dignified the most contemptible of public men, the brandy-faced Steven A. Douglass would look opening a cell door for William H. Seward to enter.
>
> Let him go down South and shut up the agitators there if he can, but I think he would find more than he bargained for if he undertook it North.
>
> Even if he could stop the men's tongues, he would find another job after that, he must silence the women's too, and that is more than he can do. Why we would shut him up in a cell so dark and deep he would never get out again.
>
> Stop this agitation! he might as well attempt to stop the hurricane in its fury, or the ocean in its rage.
>
> When he immures in a prison cell William H. Seward and the rest of our bold men who dare condemn the foulest wrong that the sun ever looked upon; it will be time for the women to act boldly and decisively; and I for one shall be ready, if I have life and health when that day comes.
>
> If I were a man wouldn't I like to be in Congress? Wouldn't I be a Statesman?[27]

Although she did not write frequently about national politics in her wartime correspondence, her sentiments here reveal how deeply the subject could move her. Her political discourse also underscores the boldness of her personality. She would not be content in a life of quietude or domesticity. She would need to find a way to make her mark. And if the world of nineteenth-century American politics circumscribed her ability to be "political," she would influence it in other ways, teaching and training future leaders, white and black.[28]

Illinois winters could be harsh, and in March 1860 Harriet mused about moving to California and settling in a village "on the shore of the Pacific" where she "could look forth on the broad ocean." Instead, she moved back to Massachusetts (she may have been ousted from her position in Illinois in favor of a younger teacher).[29] But she hated New England weather. "Oh I do so dread coming home again to spend another long, dreary wretched winter," she wrote in September 1861. "I shrink from it, and I can't help it. I know of no way in turn, of no one in the world to whom I can look for any aid or sympathy." She began to feel depressed by her prospects and wanted to find meaning in life:

> I think disappointing me last year in regard to a good situation has laid me on the shelf for the rest of my life, and if so, I earnestly hope that the remainder of life will be short, and that I may soon be laid away under the sods of the valley. It may be wrong, but I can not help the earnest wish that I had never lived beyond my infancy. Life before me now all looks so dark, so desolate, and such black clouds seem resting over my path that I would fain stop and go no farther, for I can scarcely see one bright spot in all life's future. Who is ready to help me forward amid difficulties, who cares whether I succeed in any thing or not, who feels any interest in my welfare, whether I meet with merited success or suffer the grossest injustice, in fact who cares what becomes of me? Very few indeed I imagine. I think it is a cold, harsh, unsympathizing world, and I feel as if I had been stricken down right in the midst of sustaining myself, and accomplishing something of usefulness—pulled back when I was in a good way of going forward.[30]

Soon, however, Harriet was presented with a life-changing opportunity to be useful: teaching former slaves in the South. About a year after the war commenced, she expressed the desire to find "a field where I would like to be engaged fitting as large a class as possible for thorough and efficient Christian teachers of their own race." In the autumn of 1862, she hoped to obtain an appointment teaching black refugees in Washington, DC, but no opportunity availed itself. In the spring of 1863, she found a situation in South Carolina.[31] Some acquaintances doubted her ability to work with freedmen. After describing her as "a lady of the highest education and piety" in a letter of recommendation, Congregationalist minister Horace Dutton wrote, "She has had a long experience in teaching and has fitted young men for College. Her only lack is that she does not vigorously enough control those scholars who are not disposed to study. On this account I think she would do best in a normal sch [school], where pupils are anxious to learn & where she will probably be associated with others."[32] Nevertheless, Harriet quickly got her footing. Shortly after arriving in South Carolina in 1863, she found herself teaching upwards of eighty former slaves each day, on her own. And she loved the challenge, writing that she wished the people of the North would "wake up . . . to a true realization of the greatness and importance of this work among the colored people."[33] Over the ensuing decade, she spent considerable time teaching freedpeople in three different regions: the Sea Islands of South Carolina (1863–64), Norfolk, Virginia (1868–69), and Raleigh, North Carolina (1869–71).[34] This work fulfilled her desire to find meaning in life and to make her mark on the world. It also helped her grow as an individual. By 1869 she felt as though she "had been thoroughly transformed into another person." Or as Ronald E. Butchart describes her efforts among the freedpeople, "She was as much engaged in her own emancipation project as in the freed people's emancipation project."[35]

In deciding to travel south, Harriet was motivated by her antislavery politics, her Baptist evangelicalism, and her desire to train freedmen to become responsible American citizens. Much of her mission, as she saw it, was to combat the evils she perceived in Roman Catholicism. She fervently believed that Jesuit priests wanted to lead the freedpeople into heathenism and coerce them to vote for Democrats. "I know what mighty efforts are being made to introduce many religious errors among them, what exertions are being put forth to control them here and in political matters by superstition and here I see an imminent danger to them and to our country," she wrote in a letter of application to the AMA in 1868. "They need to be taught everything, but moral and Christian instruction should be the basis of all teaching; without these other teaching for them seems to be worse than none." She continued: "They need too to be most carefully taught the principles of a Republican Government, how to guard their rights as citizens intelligently, and how to improve their privileges acceptably to God. What a host of rightly-trained and able ones of their own race we now need to send among them, throughout the entire south!"[36] For Harriet, spreading evangelical Christianity would "help save my country from the curse of their [Catholics'] influence."[37] (Curiously, Harriet said very little about her actual theological beliefs; nor did she speak negatively about the Unitarians she encountered in North Carolina.)

In many ways, Harriet Buss represents the stereotypical "New England schoolma'am." She was a white, educated, middle-class woman who traveled from Massachusetts to the South to teach former slaves. Several times in her letters she even referred to herself as "their school ma'am," and on one occasion she speculated that when "the Virginia chivalry" saw her on the street, they thought, "Ugh! see the yankee schoolmarm and her niggers."[38] (This was the only time in her correspondence that she used this pejorative term, likely signifying that she heard it in the South but did not typically use it herself.) She spent more time in the South than was typical for Northern teachers, however, and her perspectives evolved as a result of her experiences. When she initially traveled to South Carolina in 1863, she went to teach and elevate former slaves. She called herself a "pioneer" and wrote about her black students in ways that suggest how culturally removed she felt from them. "You would be amused if you could come into my school, you would see darkey traits manifested to your satisfaction," she wrote her parents in 1863; "it would try your wits a little to discipline them, I fancy."[39]

Over time, however, Harriet came to see herself as having a shared mission with her students, and she believed the most important thing she could do was train up the next generation of black teachers. "The longer I am engaged in this work," she wrote to the AMA in 1869, "the more do I find to convince me that the great masses of this people are to be reached and elevated by the efforts of well-trained theologians and teachers of their own race." The schools created by Northerners would thus become "centres radiating a clear light; and exerting a powerful influence over vast areas." A year later, she echoed this sentiment in a letter to her parents: "They will disseminate far and wide among their people the light we bear to them." Indeed, Harriet's later correspondence reveals her genuine desire to empower her students to think well, to learn self-control, and to improve their own life circumstances. She compared her pupils in Raleigh quite favorably with her former white students in the North, and she hoped that education would enable former slaves to become "leaders among them"—a phrase she used in an 1868 letter of application to the AMA as well as in a private letter to her parents in 1870.[40]

Because of their geographical and chronological reach, Harriet's letters are unlike any other modern edition of private correspondence by a teacher of freedpeople.[41] Indeed, her long and varied experiences in the South were uncommon for a woman during the Civil War and Reconstruction. In each place she worked, she taught in a different type of school and engaged with different types of students. In South Carolina, she worked with rural, isolated, multigenerational ex-slaves who were caught up in the immediate friction and abrasion of the war. Initially, she was taken aback by the disposition of her black students. In early 1863 she described how she "must be very stern" to keep "the mischievous darkey children" in line, explaining that "they can not be managed as we manage our white children north." It was "up-hill work," she wrote, but she enjoyed it, especially since she knew they were eager to learn.[42] Her most famous pupils were Robert Smalls and his children. In Virginia, by contrast, she taught more "advanced" students in an urban high school, where most of her students were under sixteen years old.[43] The Norfolk letters describe race relations in the urban South as well as the dynamics that existed among a close-knit group of white teachers. Finally, in North Carolina she taught young African American men who were preparing for a life in Christian ministry. These letters give an on-the-ground view of the founding of Shaw University, an HBCU in Raleigh. Despite the pressures of being surrounded by hostile ex-Confederates, she found her work in Raleigh less emotionally taxing than her teaching of white students in the North. Her students were polite, respectful, interested in learning, and highly intelligent—and she gave them real responsibilities in church services and classrooms. "A School like ours does not wear upon the nervous system, like one composed of restless, ungovernable spirits, where the stern work of disciplining all the time is like holding with your utmost strength, a wild, headstrong, and hard-bitted colt," she wrote.[44] Indeed, her letters reveal that she grew to have genuine, deep affection for her students and lived in community with black men and women.

Harriet Buss's correspondence offers a broad view of the Civil War era and a social history of teachers and teaching, which are rarely captured in a single collection. Her personality and sense of self emerge in her writing, particularly when she quotes what her students had to say about her. She was very proud of her work among the freedpeople, her good health, and her stamina. Whereas most Northern teachers in the South grew fatigued and lasted only a short time, she would return again and again (in fact, she returned to Raleigh later in life, as described in the epilogue). Her letters also reveal a great deal about how she thought about herself as a single woman in a male-dominated society. She wanted control over her life (she wanted a "voice" in where she would go), and she wanted control of her classroom.[45] At various times she compared herself to a soldier, a military leader, and a queen. She made it clear that she would not be "domineered over" by anyone but that she would work with men who showed her respect and gave her autonomy. Ultimately, her letters reveal how one woman "who teaches to bless the world, to make it better, and help save [her] country from ruin," was "willing to work in hard fields, and far from home too," as she had written in 1854.

NOTE ON METHOD

THIS BOOK consists of unabridged letters written by Harriet Buss throughout her time in the South during the Civil War and Reconstruction. We omitted all of her prewar letters, as well as most of the postwar letters that she wrote while back home in Massachusetts, although we quote liberally from the omitted letters throughout the text.

We have kept our transcriptions as close to the originals as possible. Fortunately, Harriet's penmanship is quite legible. In a few instances we inserted words in brackets where we believe she inadvertently omitted words; we silently added punctuation in a few places; and we silently omitted duplicate words as well as crossed-out letters and words in the few places where they appeared. Harriet often used commas in place of periods. We retained those commas but silently omitted superfluous commas (including punctuation at the end of date and address lines). For the sake of clarity, we silently corrected her spelling in six instances; when we believe she mistakenly wrote the wrong word, we inserted our guess for the word she intended in brackets with a question mark. We retained her excessive and inconsistent use of hyphens. As a consequence, some words appear in variant ways, even within a single paragraph.

We identified as many of the people in the letters as we could. Many of the footnotes are based on detailed searches in Ancestry.com, NewsBank, Fold3, newspapers.com, and Google Books, which provide access to a great many historical and genealogical resources, including US census records, city directories, and obituaries.

ABBREVIATIONS

AMA Collection	American Missionary Association Collection, Amistad Research Center, Tulane University, New Orleans, Louisiana.
CMSR	Compiled Military Service Record, National Archives and Records Administration, Washington, DC.
HB	Harriet M. Buss
UPenn	Harriet Buss Papers, Kislak Center for Special Collections, University of Pennsylvania, Philadelphia.

MY WORK AMONG THE FREEDMEN

1

Beaufort, South Carolina, 1863

When the Union military gained control of the Sea Islands of South Carolina in November 1861, white planters fled the area, abandoning their houses, other property, and some ten thousand slaves. Military authorities began putting the "hordes of negroes" to work in "contraband camps," and former slaves grew cotton on abandoned plantations in a federal program known as the Port Royal Experiment. Abolitionists and other antislavery activists began flocking to South Carolina in March 1862 as teachers, missionaries, and medical professionals to care for the needs of the freedpeople. By the end of the year, more than twenty-two hundred black children were attending school on St. Helena, Ladies, Port Royal, Hilton Head, and Paris Islands. Children often studied or learned their lessons between their chores and fieldwork. Adults attended classes in the evenings. The Gideonites who taught the freedpeople sought to instill "all four of the essential rights of religion, education, self-defense, and self-government."*

The Northern teachers who traveled to South Carolina were pleased to discover that their students were ready and eager to learn. William Francis Allen, a Massachusetts teacher who arrived in South Carolina in 1863, found slavery's "barbarities so much greater than I supposed," but he found victims of the slave system "much, very much, less degraded than I expected." In fact, during his time in South Carolina Allen was impressed by how "rapidly" the "slave population has been turned into a free peasantry." In her award-winning study of the Port Royal Experiment, historian Willie Lee Rose sums up the experiences of these teachers, writing, "Conceived originally as a means of gaining the confidence

*Willie Lee Rose, *Rehearsal for Reconstruction: The Port Royal Experiment* (New York: Bobbs-Merrill, 1964), 229–37.

of the colored people, teaching became an exciting goal in its own right, and the readiness and eagerness of the Negroes to learn to read was the subject of endless comment."[*]

Under the auspices of the National Freedmen's Relief Association, Harriet Buss headed south for Beaufort, South Carolina, in March 1863 aboard the *Arago*, a wooden-hulled side-wheel steamer with brig rigging that had been built in 1855.[†] She later recalled, "This work among the Freedmen was one in which my interest was awakened as soon as an effort was made to teach them."[‡]

Steamer Arago
Monday, March 23[d], 1863

Dear Parents,

I suppose by this time you would like to hear something from the south. Charleston is not taken yet, and I hardly think we shall capture her today, for here we are at four o'clock in the afternoon, fast on a sandbar, and have been for the last five or six hours.[§] We are a few miles north of Charleston; all seem to be in good spirits; two gun-boats have come to help us off, and I believe two more are coming; we expect to go on our way in a few hours. I rather think we have had a very favorable voyage so far. There are nearly twenty ladies on board; two other teachers bound for the Port Royal mission beside myself; and five or six lady nurses. The lady who occupies the same stateroom with myself is a Mrs. Russell[¶] from New Bedford, a lady of fifty or so who has had charge in hospitals near Washington almost ever since the war began; she is now going to Port Royal for hospital duties. Mr. Leigh,[**] the secretary of the Freed-

[*] Hester, *Yankee Scholar in Coastal South Carolina*, 110; Rose, *Rehearsal for Reconstruction*, 230.

[†] Butchart, *Schooling the Freed People*, 116.

[‡] HB to E. P. Stone, January 15, 1868, AMA Collection.

[§] Charleston did not fall to Union forces until February 1865. In the ensuing letters, HB mentions several of the Union's failed attempts to capture the coastal city in the spring and summer of 1863.

[¶] Several women from New Bedford, Massachusetts, with the surname Russell and aged approximately fifty are listed in the US census for 1860.

[**] Rev. Charles C. Leigh (1812–1895) was a Methodist Episcopal clergyman who assisted in the formation of the National Freedmen's Relief Association at the Cooper Institute in New York in 1862. He received an endorsement from President Lincoln, who on February 27, 1865, wrote: "I heartily commend Mr. Leigh's object, and bid him Godspeed in it." Leigh wrote to William Seward that

man's Society is on board, also his wife and son, a lad of eleven years.* Mr. Pierce† of the Boston Educational Commission is on board, going to Port Royal. A large number of us have been sea-sick, several quite sick. Our chambermaid is one of the kindest I have ever seen on a steamer; she comes round with a smiling face, cheering every one, and waiting upon us all very pleasantly. She has been at sea twenty-nine years. I began to be sea-sick in less than three hours after we left New York harbor, several were sick sooner than I was. We sailed last Friday morning not far from ten o'clock. I clambered into my berth about four in the afternoon and was not out of it more than two hours till yesterday morning. I did not mean to give up, but I had to submit. I knew my system had been out of order for some time; it may do me good. I have been satisfied for some time that my head and stomach were very much out of order; had I been perfectly well, I don't believe I would have been seasick, however, I was not near as sick as several others; and I have got finely over it; I believe all the rest of our party have been sick. Don't picture us now in any of the disgusting plights you sometimes hear about, for we have every thing neat, comfortable and convenient. Every berth is furnished with a covered quart tin vomiting-cup, and you can hang it right on the side of the berth, close at hand. I think land has not been in sight since we left New York, till this morning. One of the gun-boats hailed us this morning, and met us to receive papers and so forth.

Wednesday, March 25th

Safe at the Mission-House at Beaufort, S.C.‡ Our party arrived here last evening. There are several teachers who are not permanently lo-

---

"true Americanism must oppose tyranny, and every tendency towards slavery in every form in which it can be presented. It can no more love or tolerate slavery in the Negro than in the white, under the Southern planter than under the Pope." See Walter Stahr, *Seward: Lincoln's Indispensable Man* (New York: Simon & Schuster, 2012), 152.

*Leigh and his wife, Josephine, had a son named Newell in 1852.

†Edward L. Pierce (1829–1897), a Boston attorney, was sent by Secretary Salmon Chase to work among the freedmen in Port Royal. Pierce had served under Union general Benjamin F. Butler at Fort Monroe and exhibited enthusiasm for the ex-slaves' transition into free society. Pierce helped form the Boston Educational Commission, which spearheaded activity in the Port Royal Experiment.

‡The William Elliot House, at 1103 Bay Street, Beaufort, South Carolina, came to be known as the Mission House during the war. It still stands today.

The *Arago*, June 28, 1864. (Courtesy of the National Archives and Records Administration)

cated yet, so I can not say where my field will be. The Arago remained aground Monday till about eight o'clock in the evening, when at high tide we moved off and came on our way; we reached the landing at Hilton Head sometime yesterday morning. There is a grand gathering of troops at Hilton Head, and the harbor is filled with our fleet. We changed boats at the landing and came up to Port Royal Island in a smaller boat, passing right through the fleet, and having an opportunity of seeing several of our monitors* close at hand. I was informed that they were to move today for the contemplated attack upon Charleston. I suppose we brought down material to aid in that attack; I understood the last night that we were on the Arago that she was laden with munitions of war for that attack. I knew there was the utmost care with regard to lights on the boat,

*For a list of ironclad vessels that participated in the Union assault upon Charleston, see Stephen R. Wise, *Gate of Hell: Campaign for Charleston Harbor, 1863* (Columbia: University of South Carolina Press, 1994), 250–51 (table 28).

Mission House, Beaufort, South Carolina. (Courtesy of the Library of Congress)

no matches were allowed anywhere, and all lights were protected as in close lanterns. The Arago is a very large vessel and said to be a very fine and firm boat; she was unusually heavily laden on our way down. A party of gentlemen and ladies from New York came down on her to witness the bombardment of Charleston but I think they will be obliged to return without seeing that feat.

The Mission House at Beaufort is one of the rank secesh* stands, and the very chamber in which I slept last night is said to be the place in which some of the first secesh plans were concocted; it was probably the parlor of the house. It contains five large windows, and I should say it was twenty feet square. General Saxton† occupies the next house; and Dr. Peck's family‡ are but a little way from here. The grass is green, the trees

* Secesh was a slang term used by many Northerners to refer to Confederates.

† Union general Rufus Saxton (1824–1908) served as military governor of the Department of the South, where he oversaw the recruitment of black soldiers for the Union Army.

‡ Solomon Peck (1800–1874), a white minister from Boston, set up a school for freedmen in Beaufort, South Carolina, in January 1862, and became the first

General Rufus Saxton. (Courtesy of the Library of Congress)

are leaved out and many of them are covered with blossoms; I find quite an agreeable change in the climate. Next time I write, I presume I can tell you where I am to be established. Our getting on a bar coming down was nothing unusual, the steamer got aground the last time she came down, and the trip was not as pleasant for the teachers who came down then as it has been for us. I think I have seen considerable that is new since I came

pastor of Tabernacle Baptist Church in Beaufort. His wife, Elizabeth Reeve Hooker Peck (1803–1881), and daughters, Elizabeth (1840–1931) and Sarah (1842–1897), are mentioned below.

Solomon Peck. (From Ira B. Peck, *A Genealogical History of the Descendants of Joseph Peck* [Boston: Alfred Mudge & Son, 1868])

from home. We are to have a wedding in this place tomorrow evening; a colored officer is to be married. The colored regiment have recently made a raid into Florida and captured Jacksonville;* a colored guard brought up some prisoners yesterday morning and marched them to Gen. Hunter's head-quarters at Hilton Head.† Among the prisoners were a son-in-law and nephew of Gen. Floyd.‡

*The Second South Carolina Volunteers (later designated the Thirty-fourth US Colored Infantry) participated in an expedition to Jacksonville, Florida, from March 6 to March 10, 1863, and then occupied the city until the end of the month.

†Union general David Hunter (1802–1886) commanded the Department of the South. In March 1862 he issued an order freeing the slaves, which Lincoln promptly repudiated.

‡Newspapers reported that a Lieutenant Driscoll, a son-in-law of Confederate general John B. Floyd, was captured at Jacksonville; however, Floyd had no children, so HB was probably correct in reporting that it was a nephew. Floyd had previously served as governor of Virginia (1849–52) and US secretary of war (1857–60).

Gen. Saxton was married two or three weeks ago to one of the teachers.*

Good by for this time with lots of love from Hattie.

Beaufort, March 31st 1863
Tuesday Evening

Dear Parents,

Being settled in my South Carolina home, or at least established for the present, I have concluded to despatch a note home. My Post-Office address is Beaufort, S.C. I am employed in a school in this city; there are about eighty colored children in the school, and they are of all shades, from the jet African to almost as light complexion as ours. My home is in the Mission house, a short walk from the school-house; our family will consist of twelve or fourteen members, besides four servants; five or six of us are lady teachers, and two are middle-aged ladies, one of whom presides over the housekeeping department. Three or four of us teachers are to occupy the large chamber of which I wrote in my letter last week; we have some pleasant ladies here, and we think we shall enjoy ourselves together very much. Dr. Peck's family reside about as far from our home as from our house to Mr. Harris' lane,† perhaps not quite as far, and Gen. Saxton's residence is the next house to us, but little farther distant than our shop from the house. Cavalry, Artillery and Infantry are stationed at various points on this (Port Royal) Island; we see them every day.

Wednesday, April 1st

Port Royal Island is about twelve miles in length and from three to eight in width; Beaufort is a city on the eastern side of it, and in this city were the residences of some of the most aristocratic families of South Carolina; northerners occupy them now; the secesh people left the island soon after the capture of Hilton Head, and our troops have held this and

*Rufus Saxton married Matilda Thompson (1840–1915), of Philadelphia, on March 11, 1863. The *Milwaukee Sentinel*, May 12, 1863, described her as "one of the best looking and most enthusiastic of the contraband school-teachers at Hilton Head," saying, "Young women entering upon this avocation have to run such risks."

†Possibly Foster Harris (1802–1875), who resided in Sterling, Massachusetts.

the neighboring islands ever since. There are now four colored schools in the city, and nearly three hundred pupils in the four schools. The schools are all within a quarter of a mile of the Mission House. We only teach from three to four hours in a day, five days in the week. Two afternoons in the week we have a sewing-school and teach the girls to sew, one or two afternoons in the week we go round visiting the negro families in our districts.

I have an assistant teacher in my school, who will remain a few weeks longer, when she leaves I intend to have one of the young ladies who was before the Committee at the same time with myself, if I can persuade the gentlemen who have the oversight of the schools to place her with me. My present Assistant is a girl of seventeen and has been in the school three or four months; the Principal has left the school since I came down, and this made just such an opening for me as I was desiring. I am not sorry I came. There is a great work here to be done.

Pop, pop, pop go the guns of the Infantry from their encampment about half a mile from here; almost every day we hear the practice of Artillery not far distant, and we see Cavalry parades frequently. I see more here in one day that looks like war than all I had seen before since the war begun. Charleston is about thirty miles from here in a right line, and we expect to hear the bombardment from there when it comes, and it will probably begin ere this week closes.

There are five or six hospitals fitted up in this city, and many of the wounded from Charleston will probably be brought here; should the carnage be great, and these hospitals be filled with wounded, I presume the northern ladies here would nearly all enter that department; we teachers hold ourselves in readiness for the work, and I should think there might be fifty ladies right at hand for the duties, beside the regular nurses. The hospitals in this department are under the superintendence of Mrs. Gen. Lander.* I have seen her twice; she thought of taking one or two ladies with her and going out on the hospital ship to the bombardment of Charleston, I don't know whether she will go or not. I should think her

*Jean Margaret Davenport Lander (1829–1903) was a British actress who moved to the United States in the 1850s. She married Brigadier General Frederick W. Lander (1821–1862) in 1860. After the death of her husband, Lander devoted herself to the aid of Union soldiers and was engaged by the federal government to serve in Southern hospitals, with a headquarters in Hilton Head, South Carolina.

nerves would carry her through almost anything. I wish I could see that whole affair, it will be a grand scene, as well as a terrible one. I dreamed a few nights ago of sailing right down through between the two forces during the conflict; I went the entire length of the opposing armies and back again, and the red hot shells were flying like rockets back and forth over my head, the contest was raging with all its power, but I felt not a particle of fear.* In a clear day you can see ten or fifteen miles on the water, and boats could lie at a safe distance from all the shot and shell near Charleston and witness the whole conflict; but I think none are to be allowed near except those in some way employed by Government. The hospital ships will be at a safe station.

We have no chance to get lonesome at our place, for company is constantly calling. Rev. Mr. French (a Methodist Minister) at the head of the Mission House, is a prominent man, and an active one for the Government.† Last evening Mrs. Lander, Gen. Saxton and wife, Chaplain Moore‡ (a great, tall, stout Methodist Minister, who was with Montgomery§ in Kansas, and is to be Chaplain of his regiment now), Col.

*On the dreams women had about combat, see Jonathan W. White, *Midnight in America: Darkness, Sleep, and Dreams during the Civil War* (Chapel Hill: University of North Carolina Press, 2017), 74–80.

†Mansfield French (1810–1876) was a strong advocate for reconciling the Northern and Southern wings of the Methodist Church at the end of the Civil War. Born in Vermont, he held posts in Ohio and New York before the war. At the close of the war he resettled in New York.

‡Homer H. Moore (1820–1913), an ordained minister in the Methodist Episcopal Church, became chaplain of the Second South Carolina Volunteers in January 1863. Born in Ohio, Moore moved to Kansas in 1857 because he wanted to see it become a free state. In 1861 he became chaplain of the Third Kansas Regiment. James Montgomery wrote that Moore sought to create a school for soldiers in the Second South Carolina so they could attain "all the privileges & duties of social and civil life." See Moore, CMSR; and Horace Ladd Moore, *Andrew Moore of Poquonock and Windsor, Conn., and his Descendants* (Lawrence, KS: Journal Publishing, 1903), 137–39.

§James Montgomery (1814–1871) had been a Jayhawker in Kansas, where he engaged in bloody fighting with proslavery settlers in the 1850s. After serving as an officer in two Kansas regiments early in the war, he moved to South Carolina, where he recruited the Second South Carolina Volunteers and then served as the regiment's colonel. In the coastal region he used guerrilla tactics similar to those he had used in Kansas.

Mann* and Lieutenant Dunbar spent an hour or two here, these with our present family of fourteen made quite a circle in the parlor. We have more or less company every day.

Our house is three stories in height; it has a wide hall right through it, and four good sized rooms on each floor, in each room is a deep fireplace, almost as deep as ours in the kitchen was years ago. Wood is plenty and we burn it freely. Our chamber is very large, I should say there was nearly as much room in it as in our parlor and my room too; it would make four pretty sized bed-rooms.

It seems quite a change from snow a foot and a half deep to roses and various other flowers in full bloom, orange trees and peach trees and creeping blackberries in blossom, and other things to correspond. For the last few days it has been cold, but warmer weather will soon come. I am blest with an excellent appetite; they tell me here that I begin to grow fat; I feel new life and new vigor in my whole system already.

I think the climate will agree with me finely.

One of the most formidable gun-boats we have is to lie by this island for its protection during the attack upon Charleston.† I wish you could just look in to my school-room some day; you would be amused to watch the mischievous darkey children. I must be very stern with them to keep them in tune; they can not be managed as we manage our white children north. I must wear my dignity constantly, and be decided every moment.

You would like to hear them sing, they are nearly all singers. Robert Small's little girl‡ is in my school; you recollect he run that boat right out of Charleston harbor to our navy last year. I suppose he will pilot some of our fleet in the attack.

How I should like to take some of the Sterling people round here a day or two.

* Possibly Col. Orrin L. Mann (1833–1908) of the Thirty-ninth Illinois Volunteers. It is unclear who Lieutenant Dunbar was.

† For a list of gunboats stationed in the Port Royal Sound in July 1863, see Wise, *Gate of Hell*, 230–31 (table 10).

‡ Elizabeth "Lizzy" Lydia Smalls (1858–1959) was four years old when she escaped from slavery in South Carolina with her father, Robert Smalls, aboard the *Planter* in 1862. On Robert's efforts to educate his children, see Cate Lineberry, *Be Free or Die: The Amazing Story of Robert Smalls' Escape from Slavery to Union Hero* (New York: St. Martin's, 2017), 224–26 (which does not mention HB's school).

Colonel James Montgomery. (Courtesy of the Kansas State Historical Society)

Write as often as you can and tell the rest of my friends to write. Did I write that I went out to Elizabethport and had a pleasant visit at Mrs. Marsh's? He has been dead more than a year, did you know it? Mrs. Marsh and Rebecca live together.

Enclosed is a little flower or two, which I have pressed.*

Thursday Evening

I have met Col. Montgomery (Jim Montgomery of Kansas notoriety) this afternoon, and I told him he was one of the last men I should think of being afraid of. He is of medium height, rather slender, very mild and unassuming in his manners, pleasant looking, and has an unusually pleasant, gentle voice. I never saw a person so entirely different from the picture I had formed in my own mind. He says he could go anywhere

*These flowers are still in the collection.

during the Kansas difficulties for the descriptions given of him in the papers were so different from himself.

I expected to meet a great, tall, stout westerner with coarse, bushy black hair, and a black, wicked looking eye, a fierce, terrifying countenance and a voice at whose sound one would tremble; instead of meeting the mild, gentlemanly and agreeable man that Col. James Montgomery is. His hair is a dark brown, soft and wavy, his eyes are grey, and there is a little expression in his countenance like Gen. Fremont.*

Friday, April 3d

Col. Montgomery has dined with us today, it is quite interesting to listen to his account of his adventures, and of his creeping upon the rebels in their camps asleep, sliding all their arms out of their possession, and then waking them up to find themselves his prisoners. He is to remain on this island, Col. of one of the South Carolina Regiments, (negroes) for the present.† He has just returned with his regiment from Florida, where they sent the rebels skedaddling. Two or three other regiments and three gunboats are to guard this island during the attack on Charleston.

Monday, April 6th

We expect to hear the guns from Charleston very soon, perhaps tomorrow. The fleet have gone to their places, and the land troops have gone too. Several of us at the house want to go up and witness the engagement; perhaps Mr. French will obtain a boat and take some of us along.

When I was at Dr. Brown's in Jersey City, Mrs. Brown gave me an account of the mode of preparing tea in Assam.‡ She will not use green tea because she considers it poisonous. She says in Assam the tea plant was nearly stripped of leaves at a certain time, after the picking, the leaves are sorted over, and the oldest, coarsest leaves are saved for the poorest kind of black tea, the next oldest for the next kind, and so on; the little round buds not opened at all hardly make the gunpowder tea. After the sorting, the leaves are wilted in the sun a few hours, then put away, the next day, perhaps, they are heated over the fire a while, and so for several days they

*John C. Frémont (1813–1890) had been a famous explorer in California in the 1840s. He had been the Republican candidate for president in 1856 and became a Union general during the Civil War.

†Montgomery served as colonel of the Second South Carolina Infantry (Colored).

‡Assam tea is a type of black tea named after the region of India where it is produced.

are dried by the fire a while each day; during this process they are rolled once or twice as we roll with a rolling-pin, and at last they are rolled with the hand. The different kinds of black tea are wilted by the fire on iron articles, and the green teas on copper, and sometimes she says some poisonous substance is sprinkled in or rubbed over the copper vessels to give the teas a lively green. No tea will be green when dry unless there be something poisonous with it.

Wednesday, Apr. 8th

The Charleston affair is begun, we have heard the guns a few times this morning, and I believe some of our household heard them a few times yesterday afternoon or last evening. I wish I could be there within seeing distance, it seems sometimes as if I could not stay away; if there was an opportunity to go up and witness the contest, I certainly would go.

You would be amused if you could come into my school, you would see darkey traits manifested to your satisfaction; it would try your wits a little to discipline them, I fancy. However I find I can train them without much trouble, and I like the work, if it is up-hill work; I enjoy myself very much both at home here and in school. Miss Wakeman,* one of the ladies from New York, and I have called on a few of the negro families today. Robert Small's wife was one of the women on whom we called, she is quite a genteel, pretty-appearing negress, not a full black, but pretty near it.† Another woman we called upon was about sixty, I should think, an Aunt Sukey, her little cottage and everything I saw in it was just as neat as wax.

Sunday afternoon I went down to Col. Higginson's‡ camp and heard a sermon preached to his regiment of South Carolina Volunteers (negroes) by Mr. Leigh from New York. I was very much interested in their appear-

*Mary S. Wakeman (b. 1837), from Manhattanville, New York, taught in the South for eight years, including the years 1862 to 1867 in Beaufort, followed by two years in Mitchellville, South Carolina, and one in Greenville, North Carolina.

†Hannah Jones Smalls (1825–1883) was born into slavery in South Carolina and escaped with her husband, Robert, and children aboard the *Planter* in 1862. She insisted on making the attempt, telling Robert: "It is a risk, dear, but you and I, and our little ones must be free. I will go, for where you die, I will die." See Lineberry, *Be Free or Die,* 13.

‡Thomas Wentworth Higginson (1823–1911) was a Unitarian minister and abolitionist who became colonel of the First South Carolina Volunteers, the first regiment of freed slaves mustered into government service.

ance, they went through the various military evolutions well; no one need tell me that the negro can not be a soldier.

The Arago has come down again from New York, she brought me one letter. I hope the next time she comes she will bring me a letter from home. Two more lady teachers came down on her, and are at the Mission House now, and I presume she will bring more down next time.

I think this letter will be long enough for one. If you read any reports in the papers, or hear any rumors that Port Royal has been attacked or is going to be, don't you be alarmed. We find timid people ready to get up a scare any time. You can not rely upon newspaper stories very much. The truth is often very different from what you read in the papers. Good by with love from Hattie.

Beaufort, April 16th 1863
Thursday

Dear Parents,

I suppose by this time you have received my long letter which started north on the Arago last Saturday. We are safe in Beaufort yet, and have neither been killed nor captured by the rebels, and we do not expect to be either. A rumor from Hilton Head reached us last week that Beaufort had been attacked and captured, but we never knew anything about it, and I presume we should have known something about it if it had been so. I believe they get up rumors and stories of very large size down here, quite as readily as they do up north. We do not pretend to believe much that we hear.

The great attack upon Charleston has been made and has amounted to nothing;* what the next great movement will be, I am unable to say. I wish you could all take a look at us here in South Carolina. We are very pleasantly situated in the Mission House. Our housekeeper is an intelligent lady from New York, she is very efficient in her department, and keeps things in good order.

There are a great many things that we should like in addition to what we now have, which would tend much to our comfort, but we get along very well. If I were in Sterling, I think I could pick up a great many things for the comfort and convenience of teachers in this department, and things that the people there would freely give. You ought to see the flow-

*Using nine ironclad vessels, the Union's South Atlantic Blockading Squadron unsuccessfully tried to capture Charleston on April 7, 1863.

ers that adorn our table every day; the children bring them to school to us every day in abundance, roses of various kinds, orange blossoms and many other flowers. A few days ago one of the young ladies had one of the handsomest white roses I ever saw, it was perfectly beautiful.

Monday, Apr. 20th

Another movement on Charleston is the order now, and this time I hope it will prove successful. Gen. Hunter and President Lincoln's private Secretary, Col. Hay,* dined with us yesterday, they came up from Hilton Head in the morning, attended meeting in one of the churches, and in the afternoon went to the other church to hear the colored children sing Sabbath-school hymns. I was not particularly interested in or pleased with Gen. Hunter; but Col. Hay appeared very well indeed, he was intelligent and unassuming, I should not think him more than twenty. Gen. Hunter was well enough I suppose, only I did not happen to take a fancy to him.

The weather here now is comfortable summer weather, we have a fine breeze from the water every afternoon. The Mission House stands on the shore, there is just the width of a broad street between us and the water at high tide. The channel for boats between this city and Hilton Head is right in front of us a few rods out, and the landing-place is not more than twenty or thirty rods from us. Our large chamber, twenty-five feet by twenty-two, is in the front of the house, it has five large windows, three of which open out on a broad veranda about ten feet wide extending along the entire front of the house; the wall below one window is arranged to open, so we walk right out when we choose. You may well judge that our room is a very pleasant one, commanding as it does a fine prospect of the water.

Creeping blackberries are nearly ripe, and I should think there would be bushels of them, for I have seen blossoms upon blossoms in all directions, whole fields covered with them; I am told they are very large and sweet. We have a cow at the Mission House now, and we have good milk for our tea and coffee.

I like Dr. Peck's family very much; his wife is a very kind, agreeable

*One of Lincoln's private secretaries, John Hay (1838–1905), traveled to South Carolina in April 1863 to carry dispatches to Admiral Francis Du Pont. During his more than two months in South Carolina, Georgia, and Florida, he also cared for his sick younger brother, Lt. Charles Hay, who was serving as an aide-de-camp to General Hunter.

woman; she has always been a Congregationalist, but a week ago yesterday her husband baptized her and thirty-five colored candidates and welcomed them to the church. Yesterday morning, I think there was no white lady at the Baptist church but Mrs. Peck and myself. There is a large congregation of colored people, and some of the soldiers come there. The Doctor's two daughters are fine girls, they have one of the schools in this place.

Apr. 21st

We have company in our schools very often, the shoulder-strap gentlemen* call in and stay awhile; I suppose they want to see whether the negro can learn or not. One was in my school quite a long time this morning and expressed himself very favorably in regard to its appearance, he said he had seen schools north with no better order than mine here had.

Apr. 23d

I hope the next time the Arago comes down she will bring me a letter from home. Is there any news in that part of the world since I left it? So far I am glad I came. If teachers waited for the full consent of their friends, I think there would be very few in the field; now I believe there are about sixty teachers in this department. Most of those with whom I am associated came against the wishes of their friends.

Write soon and often. Good by, with love from Hattie.

Beaufort, May 22d 1863

Dear Parents,

I hope when the Arago comes again she will bring me a letter from home. I suppose you are now having such weather as we had here soon after my arrival. We are having pleasant summer weather, creeping blackberries are ripe, and there are quantities of them. We consumed ten quarts on our table yesterday. Wild plums are getting ripe, the oleanders are in

*Historian J. Matthew Gallman explains that "shoulder-strap" gentlemen were officers who "were soldiers, but in name only. These were the war's new breed on confidence men, now operating under the guise of the Union cause rather than the banner of individualism." Such officers, the *Philadelphia Inquirer* reported, "sport their tinseled uniforms and blazing shoulder-straps on promenade; sleeping at the 'best hotels,' and enjoying costly liquors and wines, while their men have been neglected." See J. Matthew Gallman, *Defining Duty in the Civil War: Personal Choice, Popular Culture, and the Union Home Front* (Chapel Hill: University of North Carolina Press, 2015), 19, 70, 82–87.

full bloom and some yards are very handsome. The far-famed magnolia trees too are in blossom.

I have been out this afternoon having a boat-ride, Gen. Saxton's father,* another one of the teachers and I were the passengers, and five darkies managed the boat. Mrs. Russell, the lady who occupied the same stateroom with me on the passage down, was up here day before yesterday from Hilton Head; she came and took dinner with me. I am going down there some day to spend the day, and perhaps stay all night. I have a new Assistant in my school now, the daughter of Rev. E. Porter Dyer† of Lynn, Mass. He has written for the Home Monthly,‡ you have frequently seen his name.

Monday, May 25th

I suppose you at home are about finishing planting, and perhaps beginning to make cheese. We are having July weather every day the first part of the day, but about noon or a little before we have a fine sea-breeze, and it continues for some hours. Beaufort is the most healthy part of the island, and the street on which our house stands is considered the most healthy street. I am inclined to think I can spend the summer here and enjoy very good health; thus far I have borne the change of climate quite as well as any of the teachers. One of the ladies who came down when I expected to come has been sick; she was taken sick about two weeks after I came and was out of school five weeks. I consider her very imprudent, and I would not be surprised if she should get down again and be obliged to go home. Mrs. Hayward of Charlestown§ went back north two weeks after I came; her health failed and I took her school soon after I arrived here. I presume we shall all come north by the first of September to spend that month and the next in a cooler region. I am informed that September and October are the two most unhealthy months in the year.

*Jonathan Ashley Saxton (1795–1883) was a Unitarian minister and abolitionist. For an account of his life, see William S. McFeely, *Yankee Stepfather: General O. O. Howard and the Freedmen* (1968; reprint, New York: Norton, 1994), 50–52.

† Sarah Elizabeth Dyer (1845–1882), daughter of Rev. Ebenezer Porter Dyer (1813–1882), was a graduate of Mount Holyoke College and later served as a missionary to China.

‡ See, e.g., Dyer's poems "Song for the New Year" and "Earthly Things Wax Old" in *Home Monthly* 7 (July 1863): 85–87.

§ Likely Caroline Elizabeth Hayward (1827–1872), of Charlestown, Massachusetts.

The climate seems to agree with me. This is truly a sandy country, and the sand is fine like ashes; it is pretty to walk in, where it is several inches deep. Fleas are numerous, and they bite well; one of the young ladies can always catch them, but I never can. Mosquitoes are beginning to come, we must all sleep under nets pretty soon to be out of their way; they have not troubled me much yet. The Arago came in again Saturday, but not a single letter did she bring to me; I think it very strange.

Dr. Peck's wife and one daughter expect to return to Roxbury soon, the Dr. and his other daughter will probably remain here till August; I think the family will come back again the last of October or the first of November.

I am in there frequently, and I like all the family very much, the more I see of them the better I like them.

Does Aunt Esther[*] stay at our house most of the time? What is Mrs. Harris[†] doing? Have you seen Mrs. Kidder[‡] since I came away?

Has Mr. Carpenter[§] left Sterling? Where has he gone, and who has come to take his place?

I don't feel in any more danger from the rebels here than I should at home; I hope they will be subdued sometime. Have you any intelligence of any from Sterling or vicinity being killed or wounded in any of the recent battles? You are to have Vallandingham[¶] for a citizen of Massachusetts; I think Fort Warren[**] will be a very good place for him, but the gallows would be a better one. Stonewall Jackson[††] is really dead, this is

[*] Esther Kendall (ca. 1799–1868) lived in Sterling. She never married, and it is unclear whether she was related to the Busses. Her death is described in HB's letter of December 6, 1868.

[†] Likely Mary Richardson Harris (1803–1872), wife of Foster Harris.

[‡] Probably Martha W. Kidder (ca. 1806–1900), a housekeeper in Sterling, who was married to Jedediah Kidder, a farmer who is mentioned below.

[§] Likely Rev. William Carpenter (1822–1901), a Baptist minister.

[¶] The antiwar Democrat Clement L. Vallandigham (1820–1871) was arrested by the military on May 5, 1863, for "disloyal speech" in Ohio. A military commission sentenced him to hard labor for the duration of the war, but Lincoln commuted the sentence to banishment to the Confederacy. He was never sent to Fort Warren.

[**] Fort Warren, on Georges Island in Boston harbor, held many political prisoners during and after the war, including many members of the Maryland legislature, as well as former Confederate vice president Alexander H. Stephens.

[††] Confederate general Thomas Jonathan "Stonewall" Jackson (1824–1863) was mortally wounded by his own men at the battle of Chancellorsville on

certainly good news for us. When you meet any copperheads* round town, tell them I wish they could try a slave's quarters down this way a little while, I think they would learn a few good lessons in such a position, if they were not utterly incorrigible. I have become much interested in my scholars, and I intend they shall yet show to the world that colored children can learn something.

Are the Sterling people doing much for the soldiers now? I thought I should get a letter from home by this steamer, but I have been disappointed; I hope a letter will come soon.

Good night, with love to all from Hattie.

(Ps. Take good care of all my cats; I have scarcely seen a decent looking puss in secesh land.

Beaufort, June 11th 1863

Dear Parents,

I received a letter from home a few days ago, and I suppose a mail will go north in two or three days, so it is best to have a letter prepared to make the journey. Are there any strawberries on the farm this year? I suppose there is nobody to pick them now. What is the prospect for blueberries? We are beginning to have sultry days, but we get a nice sea-breeze every day.

I suppose you will read in the papers an account of Col. Montgomery's raid over on the main some days ago.† He took five or six companies and went about thirty miles from here; they destroyed a large amount of property, killed some rebels, and brought away between seven and eight hundred contrabands of all ages and sizes. I saw them all the day after their arrival in Beaufort, and such a sight I never saw before. You can scarcely imagine what a medley array of clothing, or rather rags in place

---

May 2, 1863. After Jackson's left arm was amputated, Confederate general Robert E. Lee remarked, "He has lost his left arm but I my right." Jackson's death on May 10 was a major blow to the Confederacy.

* *Copperhead* was an epithet that Republicans used for Democrats during the Civil War.

† On June 1–2, 1863, Colonel Montgomery's troops participated in the Combahee River Raid in the South Carolina Low Country, destroying property owned by Confederates and freeing more than 750 slaves. Harriet Tubman, the Second South Carolina Infantry, and a detachment of white soldiers from the Third Rhode Island Heavy Artillery participated in this military operation.

of clothing they presented. They were almost wild with the idea of being free. Had they been brought from heathendom, they could scarcely have looked much worse. I believe there were nearly one hundred and fifty men that Col. Montgomery took right into his regiment for soldiers. There were lots of children of all sizes. When the regiment, or rather part of it went over, a colored woman by the name of Harriet Tubbs* went with them; she was sent down into this department more than a year ago by Gov. Andrew.† She was once a slave in Virginia but years ago she escaped to Canada, then she came back again to get away some of her friends, and so she kept traveling back and forth till she had been over the ground nine times each way, making about eighteen thousand miles she journeyed on foot, and she helped away her own kindred and one hundred and fifty beside. When she got over on the main a few days ago she went to burning buildings, and she helped bring away contrabands. She brought over two pigs in a bag for roasters, one for Gen. Hunter and the other for Gen. Saxton. A large number of the planters' mansion-houses with all their nice furniture were burned down by our troops; not one of our forces was injured.

Last Saturday several of us went out in a boat to a plantation several miles from here having a Massachusetts man and his family on it. Next week Saturday we are all to go and spend the day, and the fatted calf is going to be killed for us. We are in sight of the main at their house. Our schools are favored with a great many visitors, one of the reporters of the New York Tribune was in mine the other day.

We do not have any expenses out for provisions, our housekeeper sets a very good table. Dr. Peck's wife and younger daughter are going home on this trip of the Arago; he and his elder daughter will stay till August, I think; I presume I shall not come home till September.

The Fifty-Fourth Massachusetts Regiment (colored) arrived in Beaufort one day last week, they were a fine-looking set of men, and very soldierly in their bearing. They have gone down to Montgomery's rendezvous on St. Simon's Island, some eighty miles below here, he moved his quarters from this island some days ago.

Stonewall Jackson is really dead and buried; I hope our army is progressing in some quarters. Rumor says Gen. Hunter is to be superseded

*Harriet Tubman (ca. 1822–1913) was enslaved in Maryland, not Virginia. During the Civil War, she assisted the Union army as a spy in South Carolina.

†Massachusetts governor John A. Andrew (1818–1867), a staunch advocate for African American rights, sponsored Tubman's trip to South Carolina.

in this department, I hope he is; I have no very high opinion of him in the position he now occupies.

You ask if our scholars learn; yes, quite as well as I expected they would. I have Robert Small (the one who ran that steamer Planter out of Charleston last year) for a private scholar now; he comes to the house every afternoon. He will soon learn to read and write. I am very well, but my humor has been badly broken out ever since I came to South Carolina. I am far from being sorry I came to this part of the world.

With much love to all friends, good night from Hattie.

Beaufort, June 22^{d} 1863
Monday Eve

Dear Parents,

Your letter and one other from the north arrived today. I should like the pies and various other articles very much, and think it quite likely that I would have no trouble in finding a plenty who would help me dispose of them. I presume you have read or will soon read in the papers an account of the capture of the rebel ram Fingal* a few days ago. That was a sad joke for the rebel women. It seems they contributed their jewelry and silver plate for the construction of the formidable ram, and the very first time she tries to come out the yankees catch her. Word was received at Hilton Head some days ago that this rebel craft was about ready to venture out from Savannah, and so the Monitor, Weehawken, Capt. Rogers,† just went down to be ready for her. The Captain ran the Weehawken up into a creek, into a nice place where it was well hidden and then he waited for the foe. By and by down came the fast steamer Fingal, wholly unaware of the presence of a Monitor in this quarter of the south, the first intimations she had of the fact were given by a shot from the Weehawken which struck her pilot-house and killed both pilots; she was soon obliged to

*The *Fingal*, a British-made merchant steamship, was purchased in 1861 by James Bulloch, a foreign agent for the Confederacy in Great Britain, and used as a blockade runner to ferry supplies to troops in Savannah, Georgia. After the Union forces closed the exits from Savannah, the *Fingal* was converted to a casemate ironclad. She was renamed the CSS *Atlanta* and made two attacks on Union warships in 1863. After her capture in June 1863, the USS *Atlanta* was stationed on the James River to support Grant's operations in Virginia.

†John Rogers (1812–1884) was the commanding officer of the USS *Weehawken*. His capture of the CSS *Atlanta* in 1863 later earned him promotion to commodore.

surrender, and her crew of one hundred and sixty were taken prisoners. She was provisioned for six months and started to do great things; Col. Montgomery's command on St. Simon's island were to be annihilated, then Hilton Head was to be visited, and destructive work was to be made in our fleet; the women came along on other steamers to see her sink and destroy our ships; I fancy they went back rather crest-fallen. This new prize lies at Hilton Head, I went down there Friday afternoon to see it; it is an ugly looking craft, and will probably prove very valuable to us. I think she is considered worth between two and three millions.

Tuesday Evening, June 23[d]

Robert Small informed me today that half a dozen colored people had escaped from Savannah and arrived at Hilton Head last evening; they reported the women as having returned to Savannah sadly mourning for the loss of their ram, and also that some of the public buildings were dressed in mourning. Robert thinks these southern women are worse than the men, he says if he had his way, he wouldn't leave one of them alive to tell the tale; he says too that one of the greatest reasons of their being so opposed to having the colored people free, they are afraid the

Robert Smalls. (Courtesy of the Library of Congress)

colored men will marry their daughters, but he thinks if the colored men were all like him there wouldn't be much danger, the southern women would never get married if they waited for such as he. Robert is learning well; he is under Government pay all the time as a pilot, he receives fifty dollars a month. His little girl is in my school, and she is as pretty a child as any white child I ever had in school, she is well-dressed, and always looks neat and clean; I should really like to bring her home with me. Her father and mother dress well and look well, they are real negroes, or pretty near it, but Lizzy is quite light, though she resembles her father and mother very much. I don't believe there is a person in Sterling who would not say she was a pretty-looking and pretty behaved little girl.

Appearances now indicate another attempt on Charleston soon. I should like to celebrate the fourth of July in that city. You ask how much my scholars learn, &c. They do not learn rapidly like white children of the same age, but they learn as fast as I expected they would. I have one hundred and eighteen names on my list now, and I average between seventy and eighty a day. You can judge whether we are kept busy or not. Miss Dyer and I are obliged to be diligent to get round. The government requires some tact and some patience; I fancy you would think so if you were to try it a little while. It is like holding a wild, strong-headed colt, with stout bit and close rein every minute. I think I now have my school brought down into pretty good discipline for darkey children from heathendom; I use the rod sometimes to a good effect. I have a real black boy in my school, about seven years old, I should think, whose name is Abraham Lincoln.*

I hope you will keep Mrs. Houghton some time. I am very well; think it quite likely I may be at home three months from now. Love to all friends. Good by, with lots of love from Hattie.

New York Harbor
July 17th 1863

Dear Parents,

I presume you will be a little surprised to learn that I have reached the north again some five or six weeks earlier than I anticipated coming. I should probably reach home sometime the last of next week; but I expect to go to the *city* of *brotherly love* first. I am going home to Phil-

*This former slave was probably named Abraham Lincoln before he knew anything of the president, but he may have changed his name in honor of Lincoln during the Civil War.

adelphia with Captain Thompson[*] of the 2^{d} South Carolina regt. (Col. Montgomery's).

Captain T. is a little slender, delicate youth of twenty-one, he has been in the war ever since it began, has been through some of its hardest battles. He was well acquainted with Mrs. Crowell in St. Louis. Now he is quite out of health; if not in consumption, I fear he is tending towards it; I sometimes think he may never see another winter. He is now going home on a furlough for the benefit of his health; he stopped at our Mission House in Beaufort several days before he started home and was under my special charge. For several days he was urging me to come on home with him, but I thought I could not leave my school. The last of last week the weather came on so very warm, and I began to feel it so much, people were getting sick in Beaufort and the prospect seemed to be for quite a sickly season, that I finally concluded it might be best for me to come north now and not wait to get sick first; so I have come with Captain Thompson and am going to his home for a few days. He informs me that Senator Sumner[†] stopped at his father's a while after being assaulted by Brooks.[‡] Mrs. General Saxton is Captain T.'s only sister. The Captain will take some trips for his health while north, and among others he proposes going to the White Mountains. If he makes this trip to New-England he will come to Sterling and take me along with him. He may possibly come home with me, but probably he will not come till some two weeks after I get home. If I can help prolong the life of a young and interesting soldier who has served his country as he has done, I think I ought to do it.

Dr. Peck and daughter are coming north next week. I presume I may go back south in September or October. We have had a pleasant passage north on the steamer Fulton. The young lady who went down from New York on the boat with me has returned with me. We left Hilton Head

[*] Thomas N. Thompson (ca. 1841–1897) served as captain of Co. D of the Second South Carolina Volunteers (Thirty-fourth US Colored Troops). The remarks on his military service record for July and August 1863 state, "Left Regt sick June 30, 1863. Not been heard from since. Reported absent without leave." He was discharged on May 28, 1864. His sister was Matilda Thompson Saxton.

[†] Charles Sumner (1811–1874), of Massachusetts, was a Radical Republican in the US Senate.

[‡] On May 22, 1856, Representative Preston Brooks (1819–1857), of South Carolina, viciously attacked Sumner with a cane on the floor of the US Senate after Sumner's "Crime Against Kansas Speech."

Wednesday morning about ten o'clock, and here we are near New York at ten o'clock Friday evening. I don't know whether I shall find Charlie in New York or not; he left a month ago in a regiment for Harrisburgh; they were to be gone thirty days.

If Captain T. comes to Sterling you will be very much interested in his account of scenes through which he has passed. He has been through a great many hardships and seen much of the world for one so young and slender.

I suppose haying is progressing towards an end. I hope there are lots of berries. I'll tell the rest of the news when I get home. Good night, with love from Hattie.

Saturday Morning, July 18th

Here we are whirling along on the way to Philadelphia, we expect to get there at two o'clock this afternoon. We found New York City under martial law; a large battery from the [Army of the] Potomac were stationed on Broadway.* Capt. Thompson was afraid to have me walk from the Astor House up to 303 Broadway, Charlie's place of business,† this morning. I sent up a note by a waiter boy and learned that he has not reached home yet. Capt. T. was obliged to use great precaution to get his servant, (an intelligent negro) along through the city with him. Great times these days of riot in our northern cities! I feel just like fighting some myself.

Good bye; the cars tilt too much for nice penmanship.

Love from *Hattie.*

*From July 13 to July 16, 1863, New York City erupted in violence against the draft—the most deadly riots in American history. Irish rioters directed their fury against black civilians, whom they blamed for their economic hardships during the war. More than 100 people were killed and 2,000 wounded. Eventually Union soldiers were brought in to quell the violence.

† Several businesses were located at 303 Broadway, including a photography studio and a fancygoods store.

2

Hilton Head, South Carolina, 1863–1864

AFTER A BRIEF respite in the North, Harriet returned to South Carolina in November 1863. This time she went to Hilton Head Island, where in the spring of 1864 the National Freedmen's Relief Association made her principal of her school.* She remained in Hilton Head through the summer of 1864, although her last surviving letter is from January 1864. Her new home would be at Coggins Point Plantation, also known as Joe Pope Plantation, which was located on Port Royal Sound, Hilton Head Island, in Beaufort County. The house had been built by "Squire" William Pope Jr. about 1806. It was taken over by Joseph J. Pope Jr. in 1852. In 1861 the Union Army occupied the plantation, making the main house the chief quartermaster's office and the telegraph station.†

Hilton Head, Nov. 21
Saturday Evening

Dear Parents,

You see my letter has a new date. I have made a move today and come to a new field. An urgent call was sent to Beaufort this week for help on a plantation on Hilton Head Island; the call was laid before me, and it seemed best for me to come, so here I am. Now we are starting new on a plantation, and we have very little to do with in the way of housekeeping. I am going to write to our Relief Society and see if the ladies don't want

* Butchart, *Schooling the Freed People*, 116.

† Richard Dwight Porcher and Sarah Fick, *The Story of Sea Island Cotton* (Charleston, SC: Wyrick, 2005), 414–16.

Joe Pope Plantation. (Courtesy of the Library of Congress)

to make up a box of cooking utensils, &c. &c. and send to me through the care of the New York Association. I should like that old bake-kettle we used when I was a little girl, and one of our tin bakers, the largest I guess; and every thing I could have in the line of pots, kettles, spiders,* tin or earthen ware, knives and forks, &c for housekeeping. I want something for dishtowels, dishcloths, holders, dusting-cloths, some wings too; and I want a lot of garden seeds. I want some more bedding too, for on every plantation we need a spare bed. Can't you and the Sterling ladies make up two boxes of articles to send me; one a box of kettles, pots, spiders, gridiron, flatirons, baker, shovel and tongs &c. &c.; the other some tin ware, crockery, garden seeds and bedding; I think I have two or three plates or more in the parlor cupboard, I should like those. Some tin pails with lids would be very nice to keep things in, and a table-cloth or two for company would be very acceptable.

A superintendent and teachers on a plantation need almost everything when they start for housekeeping here now, for this department is nearly exhausted, and the government agents are calling in and selling nearly every thing that was left by the secesh people. It seems to me a good quantity of things that we need very much might be picked up in Ster-

*A spider is a long-handled skimmer used to remove food from a hot liquid.

ling, among articles that are laid aside entirely or seldom used, in many houses.

I can assure those who are interested in this work among the contrabands, that in this way of helping make the teachers comfortable they will be helping the cause; and if they send any thing more to me than we need, it shall go to some other plantation where it is needed.

I wish I could wake up all the northern people to a true realization of the greatness and importance of this work among the colored people, the longer I am here, and the more I see of the people, the more I feel it, and the more I want to do.

Sabbath Evening, Nov. 22^d^

Would you like to look in and see me tonight? You would find me in a large, comfortable front room of the house on the Joe Pope Plantation, Hilton Head Island; I have a nice fire in a deep old-fashioned fireplace, and am feeling very well contented, though I am five miles from the steamer's landing of this island, and I do not suppose there is another white woman within four miles of me. I am a pioneer now, that is certain, there has never been a school on this plantation before. You should have seen the children come together from the cabins near, yesterday, when the carriage drove up to the great house; they wanted to see the white lady, their school-mistress. Today about noon I had a Sabbath School exercise in one of the chambers of the house, a large chamber which is to be fitted up for the school-room, forty children came and two women; there were no seats in the room, they all sat on the floor; it was an interesting scene, you would have said so if you could have looked in. After a little talk with them and opening exercises, I had them repeat the Lord's prayer together after me, they all knelt of their own accord while repeating it, then I read to them the 2^d^ chapter of Matthew, talked with them about it, asked them questions &c. &c. when I had finished it. I thought I had kept them long enough, and was going to dismiss them, but they were not ready to go home, they wanted me to read and talk to them some more, so I went through the 3^d^ chapter. Tonight Rev. Mr. Martindale* had a meeting in his room, about forty children and adults came, most of them adults.

*Cyrus S. Martindale (1817–1878), born in Hartford, Connecticut, was educated in Massachusetts and settled in Ohio in 1834. From 1846 to 1863 he worked with the American Bible Society. In 1863 he was ordained in the Presbyterian Church and traveled to the South under the direction of the US Christian Commission. He appears to have worked briefly for the Freedmen's Bureau in

Tuesday Evening Nov. 24th

Today I have commenced school, nearly forty children came, a motley group you would have said, if you could have seen them. There is quite a class of grown people on this plantation who want to learn to read, and last night seven colored young men from the lighthouse between one and two miles from here, came up, they want to come evenings and learn to read, of course I shall teach them. There will be enough to do here to keep two teachers well employed all of the time, and I intend to have another lady with me as soon as I can make the arrangements.

Rev. Mr. Martindale, the superintendent of this and four other plantations is a Presbyterian Minister from Cleveland, Ohio, he is a man not far from fifty, has been a city missionary or home missionary several years. He came down on the Arago with us, was sent by the New York Society; Dr. Peck's family and I were all well pleased with his appearance on board the steamer, and we formed a high opinion of him; he has two sons in the army;* he certainly appears to be an excellent man, and he tries to do everything he can to render me comfortable and to make it pleasant for me; I think he is one of those few men that are just what they seem to be. The oversight of five plantations and preaching to the colored people every Sunday will keep him well employed. I consulted Dr. Peck's family before coming here, and they thought it advisable for me to come.

I shall have my hands full for a few weeks, for I can tell you I am a pioneer in good earnest. I have to oversee the cooking and all the household arrangements, and it taxes my wits more than they were ever taxed before to know how to cook the articles we have with the few conveniences we have for cooking, and the very few cooking utensils and dishes. To cook by an open fireplace with no crane, and a good deal of pitch-pine wood that smokes every thing all up is a new school for me; and with all the rest, the red ants are in troops all over the house, I guess. We have no butter, and there is no cow on the plantation; butter here is fifty cents a pound and miserable at that; eggs are sixty cents a dozen. Don't think I

Georgia in late 1865. Following the war Martindale returned to Ohio and remained there until 1874, when he moved to Kansas to direct the operations of the American Bible Society in that state, which he did until blindness forced his retirement about a year before his death. See *Topeka State Journal,* April 18, 1878.

*Martindale had four sons live to adulthood. These were likely Henry and Charles. See *Scranton (KS) Gazette,* December 25, 1896.

am discouraged or wish myself back north, for I do not; I would not leave this field willingly unless duty called me elsewhere. I calculate to laugh at dilemmas that try my wits, and march through all difficulties like a brave soldier. I must make some bread tomorrow morning, and I don't know how to make it, nor what to make it in. I wish I had three large tin pans. I can't sift the flour, I have some preparation for yeast, must mix with water I suppose; and first I suppose I must try out some pork and use a little of the lard for shortening, I must put the dough in something and bake it somehow.

Our cook and servant is a colored man,[*] he does very well as far as he knows how, but he does not know how to make bread and pastry. He is neater, I think, than a great many of them, and he is real clever, he is willing to be told and shown; he wants me to show him my way because he wants to learn and he wants to suit me. I shall be housecleaning and clearing up rubbish outside for some time; I can only do a little in a day. I began yesterday, did some, have done a little more today, and intend to do more tomorrow.

Thursday is Thanksgiving,[†] I am invited out to spend that day, received my invitation yesterday morning. I am to go to a plantation about five miles from here, and they want me to come early so as to have as long a visit as possible. I believe they are Massachusetts people, have been here some time, one of the ladies visited my school in Beaufort last spring. (Beaufort, by the way has more teachers and other people there now than can well be accommodated. Dr. Peck's people have no house yet, they are staying almost anyhow, they may get settled comfortably after a while.) Well, I am to go to Thanksgiving in a cart with a mule, and I expect to have a fine time.

I set two boys at work yesterday morning to improve the yard front, and I shall find considerable work in that line for them; I have had two or three out on the roof sweeping off the old rags, leaves, dirt and rubbish. I have made a general war on spiders' webs and other drapery of similar character. The house itself is very comfortable for a southern house, it fronts the south, or nearly so, has a broad verandah in front; there are two large front rooms with a hall between; I guess my room is fifteen feet by eighteen. Back of these rooms are two smaller ones; one of these

[*] According to the 1870 census, Carolinus Gilum (Ancestry.com renders his name as Gilun) was a sixty-year-old farmer; his wife, Dido, was a fifty-six-year-old housekeeper; and they had a daughter, Hannah.

[†] Abraham Lincoln established Thanksgiving as a national holiday in 1863.

we use for a kitchen, in the other an old colored man and his wife live; up stairs there is one small chamber, and the large one which I use for a school-room, and where we shall have meetings. The plantation is a fine one, one of the charming ones I think; several orange trees grow near the house, but their fruit is gone now. When I get through the cleaning and clearing-up process, then if I can have a few home comforts and conveniences added, and have one or two lady teachers of my own choice with me, I shall feel quite at home.

Wednesday Evening Nov. 24th [25th]

If I could get into the old house at home, I would find a lot of old things we don't use, which would come in play here. If I had an old yarn coverlet pretty well worn, I would cut it up for pieces to lay down by the wash stand and beside the bed, and if I had two old sheets, I would cut one in two crossway for tablecloths, and keep the other for a larger table. If I could get to my old straw bonnets, I would cut them all up for table-mats. I want my other silver spoon; are there any old pewter spoons in the house? If there are, I want those, my German silver spoon too. Any articles to be used on a table, if only just decent, no matter how odd, how old-fashioned, cheap or variegated, would be worth ever so much here. Any articles of tin or earthen for general housekeeping or cooking would be almost invaluable. I should like a couple of wooden dippers like the one I brought, also some spices.

This plantation is rather a noted one I find, a popular one to visit, and we shall be liable to have considerable company, unless we lack in enlightened civility and courtesy; if I stay here I must get fixed up some. I know there are plenty of old cast off or laid aside things in Sterling to help make several people on plantations comfortable, and many Sterling ladies would gladly send them for this purpose, if they only knew how valuable these cheap, odd, abandoned things would be to us. I know Mrs. Harris, Mrs. Kidder, Mrs. Phelps, and several other ladies would be glad to be represented in my home among the wronged colored people. It cost me a dollar extra to get my luggage to New York, that was all, no charges from there. Things sent to me through the Freedmen's Association will not cost any thing beyond New York. New things bought here cost about twice as much as they do north. Can you spare some butter? If so, can you get a small box like your salt-box and fill it and send it in the middle of a box of things? Mr. Martindale desires me to say if you will send some he will pay for it. Whatever boxes are sent, let them be strong and well secured; my box started a little before it arrived. I send a list of things I want, or would like, if any one has them thus to dispose of; and the way to direct. Good night with love from *Hattie.*

Shovel & Tongs, Dust Pan
Bake Kettle & Lid.
Large Baker.
Iron ware of any kind for cooking.
Tin or earthen ware of any kind.
Knives & Forks of any kind. No matter if all odd ones.
Spoons.
Bread Knife.
Little Knife
Meat Knife
Table Crockery
Bedding
Pillow Ticks
Large Bed Tick
Pillows.
Sheets.
Pillow Cases.
Blankets.
Quilts
Spreads
Table Cloths.
Dish towels
Dish Cloths.
Holders.
Wash rags
Table mats
Dusting cloths. Wings &c. &c.

Garden Seeds
Strawberry Peas.
June Peas.
Peas.
Early Beans
Large White Beans.
Cucumbers.
Pumpkin Seeds
Hubbard Squash
Turnip Beet.
Long Red Beet.
Turnip
Carrot.
Cabbage.
Parsnip.
Sweet corn.
Dippers
Butter
Spices

Get Carrie McCollom* to write to Mr. Leigh a few days before the box or boxes are sent, tell him about them, when they are coming, and give a general idea of the contents, something of a list.

For bedding, very cheap calico or Patch Spreads, Old home-made blankets, yarn coverlets, gentlemen's shawls, worn and laid by; double blanket shawls faded and put away, answer a good purpose.

*Caroline McCollom (1837–1907) was the daughter of a farmer in Sterling. She married Addison Bailey (mentioned below) in November 1867.

Direct like this in large letters, with Mr. Kilburn's* brush and paint for marking.

Rev. C. C. Leigh
National Freedmen's Relief Association.
No. 1. Mercer Street.
New York City.
To be forwarded to the Port Royal Mission.
H.M.B.

[On a separate scrap of paper]

The weather here has been warm and pleasant nearly all the time since I arrived in this department. I have picked roses from the bushes near the house since I came out to this plantation; I think I saw some in bloom today (Wednesday, Nov. 24th [25th]). I made something for bread today, mixed it and kneaded it in a tin can the shape and size of a two quart tin pail. The red ants!!! I set some beans and rice in a new place last night where I had washed the day before, and had seen none, I thought they would be safe one night certainly in that place, this morning there was an army in each dish, and it took me towards an hour to get them blown away or otherwise disposed of. Send me a few walnuts for their benefit.†

Are you all well at home? Has Aunt Esther been up to our house since I left? Did she get the basket I left with Mr. Currier?‡

Is George Houghton at our house yet? I want to hear from home.

Write soon; love to all friends from Hattie.

[P.S.] An old quilt, blanket, coverlet, comfort or something to put between the sheet and bed-tick would be worth considerable.

Joe Pope Plantation
Hilton Head Island
Sabbath Evening, Nov. 29th 1863

Dear Parents,

Would you like to walk into my room this evening? You would find me in the southeast room of this plantation-house, sitting before a nice

* Possibly Levi Kilburn (1804–1891), a farmer in Sterling.

† Walnuts can serve as an ant repellant.

‡ Likely Isaac H. Currier (1814–1881), the depot master in Sterling, Massachusetts.

fire, having a good sprinkling of fat pine burning with the other wood. I don't think of being lonely, the novelty of my position and the many duties connected with it afford me little time or inclination for loneliness or depression of spirits. I had a perfect dread of being located permanently on a plantation till I tried it, but I like it much; in many respects it is much pleasanter than being in Beaufort. I am getting my hand well broken into housekeeping down here with a soldier's rations, and when I get my house all cleaned and arranged, the grounds around it cleared of all rubbish, get some comforts and conveniences from the north, and a teacher of my choice with me, as I hope to have soon, I shall feel quite contented. We had a thunder-shower last evening, and this has been a rainy day. At my Sabbath School today I had eighteen or twenty; those in the cabins near the house came; the negro quarters of this plantation are [a] quarter of a mile perhaps, from the house, it was too rainy to come from there. At a meeting in the school-room this afternoon a little before five o'clock there were about thirty adults. Two or three women brought babies, and dirty as they are, these little dark-hued infants look cunning. The school-room is a large chamber over my room. I wish you could come into school and meeting, there is much to interest one whose heart is in this work; you should hear and see them sing and shake hands at the close of a meeting; they keep time to their music by swaying from side to side and frequently courtesying [curtsying].

Friday Evening, Dec. 4th

I am baking pies this evening, you should look in and see me manage, you might learn something; I am sure you would see some new manoeuvering. I bake down on the hearth before the fire. I have two nice looking apple-pies baked, another one is nearly done, and two blueberry-pies are doing well. I made some ginger bread last evening that got badly burned, but I cut the scorched part off and the rest is real good. Tomorrow morning I am going to make a loaf of cheap cake and put some of my currants and blueberries in for fruit.

I get along finely, have plenty of sweet potatoes all the time, and these I like very much; the colored people are glad to exchange them for some of our salt-meat or flour, or something of our rations. This week I have had some as nice beef-steak cooked three or four times as you ever ate. We draw so much fresh-meat every month, and we draw a month's rations at once, where there are three or four in family, and you only draw for one at a time, it keeps things along very well through the month. I came down here a week ago last Saturday, and we had no butter in the house till this week Tuesday, but for all that we had something good to eat all the time. Mr. Martindale paid thirty-five cents a pound for the butter and it looks and tastes good. My box of fruit, &c. comes into good service.

I have finished cleaning my room today; this morning I washed the bed-stead, a large, old high-post article, and since four o'clock I have scrubbed the floor. There are four windows in it of good size, these I have washed, washed all the paint in the room, and every article in it, inside and outside. There is the greater part of an old sideboard in it, this is my cupboard and dish-closet, *for all our dishes;* I have expelled the red ants from it by setting it just out from the wall and having each leg stand in a little tin can of water. There is a small plain pine board wardrobe in my room, also a small cupboard, these have had thorough ablutions; three apologies for chairs and a small table are in it, also an old wash stand, all have seen soap and water since they came under my rule. I have had a good cool closet or pantry under the hall-stairs; I have had this white-washed and cleaned, here I keep our meat and potatoes, flour &c., under lock and key. I lock my own room always when I go up to school. A great many soldiers and others come to this plantation; soldiers come and get the colored man in the house to cook them a meal. I think he sets them a very decent table. Today I set our servant's wife, Dido, to washing, I told her how to do, and showed her, and I think she tried to do just as I told her, she has washed very well. I hope to get a letter from home tomorrow. Good night with love from Hattie.

Joe Pope Plantation
Hilton Head Island
Saturday Evening, Dec. 5th 1863

Dear Parents,

I sent away a letter this morning to go home by the next steamer, but I'll begin another for the next time. Did I write you how I went to Thanksgiving in a cart drawn by a mule? I went to our next neighbor's four or five miles from here and had a very pleasant time; for supper they had oysters, roast beef, stewed chicken, roast turkey, sweet potatoes, rice pudding and pumpkin pie. I reached this place the Saturday afternoon before Thanksgiving, and the next Monday morning I received my invitation. I am baking cake this evening, have two small loaves nearly done. The pies I made last night are real good. Today I have made a soup, the first one I ever made in my life, and if I did make it, it was good; I made it in an old bake-kettle with a lid to it, and it relished as well as any soup

I ever ate. I put in rice and some of my Indian meal. Mr. Martindale pronounced it first rate, and my cook and servant Carolinus wanted I should show him how to make one like it.

Carolinus is a good servant for a colored one in this department; he appears to be perfectly honest and he is very clever, he has given me five eggs since I have been here, eggs are sixty cents a dozen; the other day he brought me a large quantity of peanuts all nicely roasted and out of the shell, once or twice he has brought over some of his own sweet potatoes to cook for us, and he wants to bring some more tomorrow.

Sabbath Evening, Dec. 6th

It does not seem much like December north. I picked off roses and buds today from a large bush a little way from the house; I have them in water with some orange leaves and a crocus; they all made a very neat little bouquet. Come in my room tonight and I will give you a cup of orange leaf tea, I made some a little while ago and it is very good. The colored people told me about making it, I picked off about a dozen leaves and steeped them as you would any tea. Several orange trees grow front of the house. I have some fresh fish for breakfast; Isaac, the colored man in one corner of the house gave me a couple tonight already cooked, they look nice. I guess they are good. My people here call me Missus, the lady, the white lady, and the schoolmistress. I had quite an interesting Sabbath school today up in the schoolroom, several grown people came before I was through.

Monday Evening, Dec. 7th

I have had company today, Mrs. Russell and another lady from the hospital, a Miss Kendall* from Plymouth, Mass. They came this afternoon just as I was beginning about my dinner and supper (I have both in one meal, about four o'clock) and I persuaded them to stay. I gave them broiled beef-steak, broiled salt pork, sweet potatoes, Irish potatoes, bread, butter, cheese, apple-sauce, raspberry-sauce, blueberry-pie and some of my cake with home-prepared fruit in it, also a good cup of tea. I think I set a very good table now, and I never cooked better than I do here. My currants and blueberries were nice in my cake, and my pies were just as nice as they are when made of fresh blueberries, if anything, a little better. I shall have stewed beans for supper tomorrow, they are soaking now. I tried out the fat from some of my fresh beef, for shortening, and

*Julia P. Kendall (1823–1874) served as a nurse in a Union hospital in Washington, DC, in 1862.

I saved it all from my soup; I tried out a piece of pork too for lard, and I save what I fry or broil out from my salt pork. My blueberries for pies I soaked several hours before I baked them.

I rather expect a man here from Beaufort tomorrow to stay all night. I received a letter from Thomas (Capt. Thompson) a few days ago, he is on Morris Island, improved in health. He was quite sick while he was north, had a severe hemorrhage from the lungs; he wrote to me twice but received no letter from me; and I received none from him, I think it strange. I presume he will be down here to see me as soon as he can be allowed to leave the island for a day or so.

I have breakfast between eight and nine, dinner and supper about four. Mr. Martindale is generally away during the day among his other plantations; but when I come out of school, not far from one, I have a dish of coffee and hard bread. Tell Mrs. Harris, I guess she would laugh several times, if she could spend a day or two with me and see all my manoeuvering. I never dreamed that I could get along so smoothly on a plantation as I am doing, I like it much, but I have no idle time.

Friday Evening, Dec. 11th

The Arago came in again yesterday; I expected a letter from home this time, but none has arrived. Am I never to hear from home? It has been a very rainy day here, I like the weather here much better than the northern winter.

The gentleman from Beaufort came Tuesday evening and staid all night. Wednesday Rev. Dr. Barrows* visited my school. He is from Chelsea, Mass., is our new Superintendent, I liked his appearance very much, he seemed to me like just the right man in the right place. In regard to our work in this department, and every other theme upon which we conversed, my views perfectly harmonized with his. I am to have another teacher very soon. Today, Mr. Sanford took tea with us; he is the gentleman who invited me to his house to Thanksgiving.

I get along swimmingly through all difficulties; I am well, have an excellent appetite; food never tasted better, I never enjoyed my meals

*Lorenzo Dow Barrows (1817–1878) was a minister in the Methodist Episcopal Church. From 1863 to 1865 he served as superintendent of schools for the National Freedmen's Relief Association in coastal South Carolina. His wife, Minerva, and daughter, Ella, also taught there for one year. From 1871 to 1872, he moved to Atlanta under the auspices of the Methodist Episcopal Church's Freedmen's Aid Society to teach at Clark Theological Seminary, which is now Clark Atlanta University, an HBCU.

more than I do now. I wish you could come in and see how I live, come and stay a day or two and you will see some new things, get some new ideas.

I received letters today from Miss Esther Waite* and Mrs. Towers of New York. My box of fruit is worth a good deal to me; the cheese is first quality. Good night with lots of love from Hattie.

Joe Pope Plantation
Hilton Head Island
Sabbath Evening Dec 13th, 1863

Dear Parents,

I suppose my last letter for home will start from the Head tomorrow. This is the sixth letter written home since I left the last Wednesday in October, and I have not received one yet. Did you get Sumner's speech† that I sent home from New York?

I have picked roses today from bushes a little way from the house, they are very pretty; what kind of weather are you having? I fancy you do not find many flowers out of doors. I enjoy looking at the shrubbery and the trees all green as in summer. The Orange trees are rich looking trees, their leaves are such a good green and so smooth and glossy. The Live Oaks are majestic, they are not quite so graceful and handsome as a Weeping Elm, but they are next to it; there are some fifteen or more almost in a circle around this house, at a little distance from it, just far enough. This is one of the most comfortable southern houses I have seen. I think I am fortunate in my house and its surroundings. I wish you could look in and see me. When I get those supplies from Sterling which I have sent for, I shall be as cozy as you please. I received a very kind letter from Mr. Leigh two or three days ago; he said he would forward to me anything

* Esther K. Waite (1812–1872) of Sterling was a member of the Unitarian Church. Her death was the third in her family in a two-week period. See *Gloucester Telegraph*, December 11, 1872; and *Monthly Journal of the American Unitarian Association* (Boston), 6 (May 1865): 256.

† Senator Charles Sumner of Massachusetts delivered a speech entitled "Our Foreign Relations: Showing Present Perils from England and France, the Nature and Conditions of Intervention by Mediation, and also by Recognition, the Impossibility of any Recognition of a New Power with Slavery as a Cornerstone, and the Wrongful Concession of Ocean Belligerency" on September 10, 1863, at the Cooper Institute in New York. It was published as a pamphlet in 1863 by the Young Men's Republican Union in New York.

my friends might send to him in New York for me. I wrote to him a little more than two weeks ago to know if the Association would appropriate the sum they usually expend for a stove for the school-room, towards a small second-hand cooking-stove, as they would not need supply my school-room, for it has an open fire-place. He informed me that by the last steamer he had sent down several stoves, and he directed me to call on Dr. Barrows for one, and for anything else I might be in want of. I have written to Dr. Barrows and shall expect to have a stove this week sometime.

I had quite a large Sabbath-School today; I have plenty of work to do on this plantation, there are about twenty families to instruct; and help lift to a higher position.

Dec. 17th

Mrs. Russell and Miss Kendall have called to see me again today; they found me making cake. I was just greasing my dishes, and with dish and fat I met them at the door; I expect considerable company Saturday, and so I am cooking a little each day for them.

Saturday Evening, Dec. 19th

How I wish you could come in and see how I am situated. Miss Kendall staid with me all night Thursday night; I was all alone and was expecting to stay alone over night in the house, the superintendent had gone away on business, and the old colored man and his wife were both away, I invited one of the ladies to stay with me, and Miss Julia Kendall was very happy to stay, she wanted to see something of plantation-life. Mrs. Russell, you know, is the lady who roomed with me on the Arago last March. Miss Kendall is from Plymouth, Mass. I should think she was nearly my age, she is the old minister's daughter, Dr. James Kendall, her mother belonged to Templeton; she staid with me till after dinner yesterday. A superintendent from another plantation was here to dinner (or supper) yesterday, and just before it was ready, Mrs. Russell came out after Miss Kendall, she was going to take her right away without dinner, but I told her she could not, they should both stay to dinner, and they did. Mrs. Russell says if I am sick, send in at once to her, and I shall be taken care of.

Today two military gentlemen were here to dinner, one an Ohio Chaplain, an old acquaintance of Mr. Martindale's, the other a private; just as we were through dinner three other military gentlemen rode up; we invited them in, but they had taken dinner before coming; they sat and talked while I cleared away the table. I expected Mr. Sanford's family all here today, they made arrangements to come, but I presume something detained them. This is the family with whom I spent Thanksgiving, it consists of Mr. Sanford and wife and son, a little boy about ten or twelve, and Miss Carter,* teacher, a cousin of Mr. Sanford's. Miss Kendall thinks she would like to come out here and teach with me; she assisted me about my house and in my school. The superintendent of this place is to leave next week for another station.

There are many interesting and amusing things connected with this people; my servant Carolinus and his wife Dido both say they are going with me where I go. Dido has washed for me twice, she washed well; the last time I let her have a loaf of bread towards paying for it, (I pay her out of my rations) I asked her afterwards if she liked her bread, yes, she said she liked it well, she liked any thing that belonged to a yankee.

One day some weeks ago, Mr. Martindale heard an old man who lived in the cabin nearest the house whipping his grandchild very severely (a girl about eight or ten) [and] he checked him in his severity; "Why" said he "haint I ben a slave all my life, and haint I ben kicked about and knocked about and whipped this moren seventy years, and now I'se free can't I whip somebody?"

Old Isaac, the colored man in the house, sent in a nice smoked herring to me one night this week, I never tasted one before, but I liked it much. I have a very handsome tumbler of flowers on the table, roses and buds, and a white flower, I don't know the name, all picked a few days ago.

Sunday Evening, Dec. 20th

The steamer is in again, but not a single letter or paper do I get; I think it is a little too bad. Here it [is] almost eight weeks since I left home, and not one word have I heard in that time, I begin to feel very anxious; what does it mean? Why don't I get a letter? Are you all sick, or am I forgotten? Do let me hear from home soon. I am very well, and comfortably situated, and contented, and much interested in my work. Good night, with love from *Hattie*.

*Two single women named Carter were in South Carolina at this time. Anna Francis Carter (possibly born ca. 1842), from Wilmington, Massachusetts, taught in the Port Royal area from 1862 to 1864 and in Washington, DC, from 1864 to 1866. Harriet Carter (b. 1840), from Framingham, Massachusetts, taught in Port Royal in 1863 and 1864 and in Washington, DC, and Richmond, Virginia, from 1864 to 1870.

Joe Pope Plantation
Hilton Head Island
December 25th 1863

Dear Parents,

It is Christmas evening, and I'll write the beginning of a letter home tonight. Your letter was received today, and I was glad enough to get it; it relieved my mind considerable, for I had begun to feel very anxious. Only think, I left home eight weeks ago Wednesday evening, and this letter today is the first word I have heard from you. I am glad I am to be remembered by Sterling people, for I do very much need all they will be likely to send me; yet I am in no way suffering, for I have borrowed some things of the colored people, so I get along and live much better, much more comfortably than the poor soldiers do. A steamer will be in very soon and I shall look for my tokens from the north when it arrives; if it has not come in today, it probably will tomorrow or Sunday.

I wish you could come in and see how comfortable and cozy I look in my nice, large, tight and pleasant room, with my bright, warm fire throwing out genial heat and cheerful light. I am alone now, but I am not lonely; in truth I feel quite contented and happy here alone. I shall have plenty to do to keep me busy, and my evenings I can devote to study and writing, and this just suits me. If I am sick, I shall at once be cared for, you need not be worrying about me the least bit; I think my position much pleasanter, and much better in many respects than it would have been in Beaufort, and my expenses will be considerable less. My health is very good; I never felt better in my life than I do now; and I never enjoyed my food better, it does taste so good, and I eat a good quantity. I have disposed of nearly half a bushel of sweet potatoes in two weeks. I put my salt beef and pork on the table in good shape; I soak them before cooking and freshen them so they are good; sometimes I soak a piece of beef twenty four hours, and change the water two or three times; then I change it once while it is boiling. My cooking is not bad, sometimes I have baked a pie on hot bricks, turning the spider over it. I find necessity is the mother of invention. I have baked two loaves of bread, four of cake, four of gingerbread and eighteen pies since I came down here. My box of dried fruit is worth a great deal to me; my cheese has but one fault, it is so good it goes off too fast.

Saturday Evening, Dec. 26th

I have been washing today, I borrowed tubs &c. of old Isaac. I believe it does him good to do me a favor; this morning he called me into his room and gave me a nice herring and a piece of fine cabbage, I had them for my supper, the cabbage cut up in vinegar; there is enough of each left for tea tomorrow. This afternoon he brought me a little tub and gave me, it is in circumference about the size of our little mackerel tubs and a little more than half their depth; it will do me much good. In the midst of my washing I had company; first, Miss Julia Kendall from the hospital and Miss Ellen Lee* from Templeton rode up. Miss Kendall has been connected with hospitals for a long time; she was with the army of the Potomac quite a while, she is now thinking of leaving the hospital; she will leave, if she can not make such arrangements as she desires, and if she leaves, she is coming down here to teach with me till spring. Miss Lee is Col. Lee's daughter, Mrs. Bond's† granddaughter; she has just come south, is going with another lady to a plantation on Port Royal Island, a delightful locality, and one to which I might have gone if I had chosen; there are already two gentlemen and one lady on the plantation, but I believe they are all Parkerites,‡ and I did not wish to be placed with them. Just after Miss Kendall and Miss Lee came, Mr. Sanford and his wife rode up on horseback; they are the people where I went Thanksgiving. I was hindered from my washing an hour or a little more.

I send back one of the bills you let me have; I could not pass it here, it is not a greenback;§ and I do not need it; Dr. Barrows has twenty-eight dollars ready for me now when I call for it, and the fourth of January twenty more will be due me. I wish you could look in upon me now; I still have flowers in my room, picked out of doors, roses, and a pretty white flower. I picked most of them yesterday; and I have quite a collection of pretty shells. I feel thankful that I am so pleasantly and comfortably situated. Good night, with lots of love from *Hattie*.

*Ellen M. Lee (b. ca. 1833) was the daughter of Col. Artemus Lee (1793–1870), a merchant in Templeton, Massachusetts, who served several terms as a state senator and representative, as well as a Republican delegate to the state convention in 1868.

†Lucy Fiske Bond (1781–1861), mother of Lucy Bond Lee (1811–1897).

‡Parkerites were members of the 28th Congregational Society in Boston, a "free church" led by Theodore Parker, a prominent Transcendentalist and Unitarian preacher, lecturer, and social reformer.

§During the Civil War, the US government began printing paper money known as "greenbacks." These bills were deemed legal tender and were therefore a form of payment that had to be accepted in commerce. HB's parents had likely sent her a banknote from a local private bank, which would not have had value in faraway South Carolina.

Joe Pope Plantation
Hilton Head Island
Monday Evening, Jan. 4th 1864

Dear Parents,

I hear that the steamer is in again, so it is time we were preparing our letters for the north. My two barrels are safe in the Quartermaster's department at Hilton Head, and I shall probably get them tomorrow. I spent a little more than a week on this plantation alone, and I really enjoyed it very much. My people and scholars keep me well supplied with wood and water, and I live here so comfortably for winter-life in South Carolina that I feel very thankful. The superintendent here has gone to a plantation on another island to close up business there. As for the rebels, I have no more fears of them here than I have at home. I have considerable company at my plantation; yesterday six gentlemen were here a little while; they stop to have old Isaac get them a dinner or lunch, and they like to come into my part of the house. Two of the six came down on the Arago when I did; one was a correspondent of the Philadelphia Enquirer, the others were all military characters. All the gentlemen who have called upon me since I have been here have been very gentlemanly in their whole deportment. I am no longer alone; Miss Elizabeth Hill,* a member of the same graduating class at Charlestown with myself, and a Baptist lady is now with me. We shall get along here finely.

There was a New Year's celebration at Beaufort last Friday for the colored people, and they presented a sword to Gen. Saxton.† I went up to Beaufort and there I met Miss Hill; she had come down but a few days before; and Saturday morning she came to this island and out home

* Elizabeth R. Hill (1824–1867), of Scituate, Massachusetts, served as an AMA teacher in Hilton Head, where she died of malaria on November 28, 1867. In applying for the position, she wrote, "I have long been interested in the colored American race and should be very glad of the opportunity to do something as an educator." See Hill to Mrs. Tappan, September 12, 1865, AMA Collection.

† Honoring Saxton's service and the first anniversary of the Emancipation Proclamation, General Rufus Saxton was presented with a gilt Tiffany sword engraved with the words "To Brig. Genl. R. Saxton / MILITARY GOVERNOR. / as a testimonial of the gratitude of the Freedmen / of the Dept. of the South, for his sacrifices and / labors to secure their liberty, protection, and elevation / Beaufort. S.C. Jan. 1st. 1864." See Seth Isaacson, "A Tiffany & Co. Sword To Celebrate the First Anniversary of the Emancipation Proclamation," Rock Island Auction Company blog, November 27, 2019, https://www.rockislandauction.com/riac-blog/a-tiffany-co-sword-emancipation-proclamation.

with me, and is going to stay with me. Friday night another lady and I spent the night at the hospital with Mrs. Russell and Miss Kendall. Miss Kendall has made arrangements to go to Beaufort into the colored hospital, so she could not come out with me, as she intended to do if she left the hospital. I am anxious to get my barrels home, I want to pull them over and see what is inside. Miss Hill has a barrel with mine. I am very well, and I eat ever-so much. If you will come in, I will give you a piece of thimbleberry-pie, a piece of gingerbread and a piece of fruit-cake. I don't live without having something to eat. Old Isaac is as kind as ever; my people all seem happy to do something for me. Good night, with love from Hattie.

Joe Pope Plantation
Hilton Head Island
Monday Evening, Jan. 18th 1864

Dear Parents,

It is time to be preparing our letters for the next steamer, so I will begin another one home. I sent one last week, and wrote something about the Sterling ladies and you filling another barrel for us, if you wished to do so, I will name one or two things more I should very much like, some rye meal in a small bag, and a small light-gridiron with hollow bars and a trough to catch the gravy. I shall use that great old one principally to toast bread; I can't spare the pork-fat, I want to save it all for shortening and for gingerbread, and I want all my pork broiled, it is not as good fried in the spider. Mr. Martindale had a nice little gridiron, the bars were light and thin, they looked like tin. We live very comfortably and cozily. Old Isaac and Hannah are very kind to us; they are above the average negroes in this vicinity; Isaac was the coachman and Hannah was waiting-maid in the house. I showed Isaac one of my teaspoons sent to me by Mrs. Holbrook* the other day, and told him how I had some sent to me with many other things from the north, and asked him if he did not think my friends at home thought something of me. "Yes" he said, "well they ought to, if they didn't, I wouldn't spect em, now I spects you and them too." He wanted I should let him send a message when I wrote to them.

Yesterday three military gentlemen stopped here on their way to the farther end of the island, they had Isaac get a dinner for them; two of

*There were several Holbrook families in Worcester County, Massachusetts, at this time.

them came into our Sabbath school and staid till it was through, they appeared to be very much interested, three other gentlemen also, came in a few moments, and seemed interested. The two military gentlemen very politely invited us to dine with them and were quite anxious that we should, they wished to sit down at the table with ladies, but we had declined just such an invitation from gentlemen the last two Sabbaths before, and from principle we declined theirs. We learned however that they were coming back today, and Isaac was to get dinner for them again, so we thought we would today accept their yesterday's invitation.

We had the dinner in our kitchen, we have Isaac's large table there all the time. I put on the two little table-cloths you sent, they did nicely, the table is a large one, or rather a long one. I had some cold boiled beef, I cut up and put on, I made coffee, and found sugar and milk, Isaac found tea and I made it, I put on bread, gingerbread, a little loaf of fruit-cake, pie made of currants and high blackberries mixed, potatoes, apple-sauce and stewed cherries. I also had one of the Indian puddings I made Saturday warmed over, and had a sauce of white sugar, butter and nutmeg; cheese and butter too I put on; Isaac furnished a large dish of oysters, and a platter of ham and eggs, and a dish of beets cut up in vinegar, so we had quite a dinner, the gentlemen enjoyed their dinner very much, and they spoke particularly of the pudding and butter being nice. They also enjoyed sitting down by a cheerful fire in our room; one of them said it was a treat to come into a pleasant, comfortable looking room, with a clean floor, to sit down. They were all from New England, Captain Hudson[*] is a native of Connecticut, but he has spent much of his life in Massachusetts, Lieutenant Holt[†] is from Boston, and Orderly Willis is from Easton, Mass.; these were the three gentlemen who dined with us. Captain Hudson was wounded in the attack upon Fort Wagner, and is still some lame.

You see that what conveniences you and the Sterling ladies send us may do some good to the soldiers, too. Old Isaac is known all about as a cook, and this is a half way place on the island, a pleasant plantation, and a stopping-place for meals. Now when the weather is cold or stormy, politeness demands that we should invite the soldiers to a seat by our fire, as old Isaac has but one small room, and we have two large ones

[*] Capt. Edward P. Hudson (b. ca. 1833), of the Sixth Connecticut Infantry, was wounded at Charleston on July 18, 1863. According to his CMSR, he was born in New York. He resigned on February 19, 1864.

[†] Possibly Lt. Charles V. Holt of the First Massachusetts Cavalry. It is not clear who Orderly Willis was.

down stairs, beside our kitchen, we have one small chamber too, beside our school-room. Yesterday the three gentlemen paid Isaac two dollars for their dinner, today they paid him the same, and after they were gone, he insisted upon handing half to me. Miss Hill and I are going to get us some nice syrup with the dollar; the ladies sent me a tin can that will hold a gallon, they also sent a quart can, in that we get our kerosene. We are getting gourds and fixing them for dippers, and other purposes.

[The end of this letter is missing.]

3

Massachusetts, 1864–1868

BUSS'S LAST surviving letter from South Carolina was mailed in January 1864. By August of that year she was suffering the "painful experience" of significant health issues. As she later explained, "From the malarial districts of South Carolina, with health completely undermined, I barely escaped with life in August 1864; I was laid aside from active life for a year, and it was nearly another two years before I recovered my usual strength and vigor."* She returned home to Massachusetts to recuperate. By May 1866 she was teaching in a small school in South Gardner, located near the center of the state in Worcester County. It was an idyllic spot. "I find this town is the height of land between the Connecticut and the Merrimac; from a hill just above where I board, the water runs both ways," she wrote to her parents. Her school numbered just over thirty pupils, but she hoped that it would grow.†

Harriet found it "a very hard school," and she appears to have had behavior issues among her students. "I never saw just such acting scholars in school among civilized children," she wrote. But, she added, "I have them pretty well trooped down now, they are doing better every day." Fortunately she had the support of the school committee as well as of "many of the parents." When she expelled one student, a member of the school committee told the other students that "the Committee would sustain me in sending him out and any others who could not obey." She wrote: "The weeks slide away very fast; the Saturdays come round often, but they are quite welcome, my school has been so hard that the resting days seemed none too frequent; yet I am always ready for Monday morning's

* HB to E. P. Stone, January 15, 1868, AMA Collection.

† HB to parents, May 16, 1866, UPenn.

work again."[*] A week later, she added, "My school improves; if I could have it long enough, I think I should make quite a respectable school of it in time."[†]

In March 1867 Buss moved to a school in Wareham, a town on Buzzard's Bay, in eastern Massachusetts. School opened on March 6 with twenty-eight students, and by the afternoon there were thirty-two. This "considerably exceeded our expectations for the first day," she wrote with evident pride. "I think I have a prospect of a very pleasant school. I am to have some three or four French and Latin Scholars, a few of the pupils (perhaps eight) are as low-price as $.25 cents per week. We hear of several others who are coming to school." Managing the classroom could be exhausting for her. "I hope I shall soon get rested and feel like something or somebody, for I have been so tired, so nervous, so cross and irritable for the last six or eight months that I could scarcely endure myself."[‡] In a week she was up to thirty-eight students, and she hoped the number would rise above forty. "There seems to be quite a feeling of interest in the school and quite a desire to have it continued through the year," she wrote. She taught lessons in arithmetic, geography, grammar, math, algebra, reading, spelling, French, Latin, writing, and bookkeeping—"enough to keep one busy, but I like it, for I am reviewing branches that I wished to keep fresh in mind, and I have no care out of school, nothing to do except school duties, beside taking care of my room."[§] As the weeks passed, the school continued to grow. "My school flourishes and prospers," she told her parents. "I think in time I can have a good school here."[¶] As in South Gardner, she had to maintain strict discipline. "I am getting my scholars ruled down into much better habits than some of them had at first; but the discipline has been rather hard, or rather it has required a firm and decided hand."[**]

Harriet occasionally took note of national politics in her correspondence. Following a parade in Boston in June 1867 when President Andrew Johnson came to the city for the dedication of a new Masonic temple, she wrote, "I should have gone to see the display if I had been near, but I

[*] HB to parents, June 14, 1866, UPenn.
[†] HB to parents, June 21, 1866, UPenn.
[‡] HB to parents, March 7, 1867, UPenn.
[§] HB to parents, March 14, 1867, UPenn.
[¶] HB to parents, March 28, 1867, UPenn.
[**] HB to parents, April 23, 1867, UPenn.

would not have shaken hands with Andy Johnson if I could. I hope this summer's Congress will put him where he belongs."[*] (By 1867 Johnson, a conservative War Democrat from Tennessee, had broken with the Republican Party over Reconstruction policy. In 1868, Republicans in the House of Representatives would impeach him.) A few months later she wrote, "Nothing but earnest and decided radicalism in the right channel will ever restore and preserve our Government."[†] Harriet also recorded her reaction to the Civil War monument that was unveiled in Sterling in June 1867. "The Soldier's Monument was dedicated last week I suppose," she wrote to her parents. "I neither like the monument nor its location." The granite obelisk, which cost about twenty-two hundred dollars and contained the names of twenty-six men who had died in the war, was erected in the town common across Main Street from the Town Hall. "If I were rich as Croesus, I would have the memory of the Sterling soldiers preserved by a monument with military emblems and it should stand in a more suitable place."[‡]

Being near the ocean was restorative for Harriet. "I am beginning to feel quite well, better than I have before for the last eight months," she wrote in March 1867. "I expect the sea air is in part the restoring agent."[§] By the fall she felt even better. In October she wrote her parents: "My school is very pleasant this term, I have thirty-nine names on my list. I believe I still continue to improve in health and strength. If I stay here long enough, I may be a giantess in power yet."[¶]

By January 1868 Buss appeared ready to return to the South. On January 15 she wrote to E. P. Stone, of the American Missionary Association, informing him that "the good people" of Wareham were raising funds "to send me among the Freedmen for a year." Buss thought it "advisable" to inform Stone "what I feel able and willing to undertake, in the strength of the Lord, provided your Association should decide to give

[*] HB to parents, June 27, 1867, UPenn; *New England Farmer* (Boston), June 29, 1867.

[†] HB to parents, October 10, 1867, UPenn.

[‡] HB to parents, June 27, 1867, UPenn; *Fall River (MA) Daily Evening News,* June 20, 1867. Part of the dedication ceremony included the singing of "an original hymn by Mrs. E. Waite," as well as a procession of about fifty veterans from Sterling. Croesus was the king of Lydia from 560 to 547 BC.

[§] HB to parents, March 14, 1867, UPenn.

[¶] HB to parents, October 4, 1867, UPenn.

me an appointment." She was not willing to go "very far south" because of the health troubles she had experienced in South Carolina in 1864. Nevertheless, she explained, "I have never abandoned the hope of again laboring among this people; nor have I ever lost my very strong desire to be located at Washington specially employed in training for influential teachers and leaders among them as great a number as possible of those who give promise of usefulness and faithfulness."* A few days later she added, "I am willing and anxious to enter the work again. My term in this place is drawing to a close, and if I am not sent among the Freedmen, I shall probably continue teaching here."†

On January 17 the AMA informed Buss that they might send her to Virginia (Norfolk or Fort Monroe, in Hampton) or Maryland. On January 31 she replied that she "would be very willing to go to either of those places [in Virginia], as I find by experience that seaboard towns are to me far the most favorable to health and strength." In this same letter, Buss also replied that she would be willing to go to Maryland "unless the locality were an extremely unhealthy one from malaria or other causes." She also stated her desire to train future teachers in a normal school.‡

Wareham, Jan. 15th/68

Dear Parents,

I received your letter yesterday. I am glad of the improvements made at home. Why didn't you have a few more things to attend to at once? I call this a cold, stormy winter; I do want to get away from snow and cold weather, they make me shiver and curl so. I would like to migrate with the birds; a warmer clime and sunnier skies for me when the freezing breath and leaden clouds of the north come sweeping down. I have suffered severely from the cold this winter, notwithstanding I have such comfortable quarters. Cold weather and I are not in sympathy, and I fear we never shall be again. I don't desire to spend another winter north. I call this a severe winter so far; my feet, hands, and back are cold a large portion of the time. If I could have a house thoroughly warmed all over, and be wrapped in furs from head to foot when I went out, I might endure our winters better.

* HB to E. P. Stone, January 15, 1868, AMA Collection.

† HB to Mr. Thayer, January 23, 1868, AMA Collection.

‡ HB to C. L. Woodworth, January 31, 1868, AMA Collection.

Monday, Jan. 20th

Mr. Dutton,* the minister who is preaching here for the Congregationalists, says he saw Mr. Gerry† in Boston the first of last week and told him the people here were going to send me among the Freedmen; so I presume Mr. Gerry has borne the intelligence to Sterling. I do not feel that it is certain yet that I shall go, I shall not go out unless I can have a voice in the matter where I will go, and that will be not much farther south than Washington. The way has seemed to open in a most unexpected manner, and I was really taken by surprise. Two weeks ago yesterday, Rev. E. P. Stone,‡ Agt. of the Missionary Union preached here in the morning and also in the evening, presenting the claims of the Freedmen and urging the people here to do something towards supporting a teacher among them. At noon I was speaking with a gentleman about the sermon, the subject, and my own experience among them, and mentioned that I only left the work because my health failed; I also spoke with his wife about Mr. Stone's statements that the call for teachers was great and the number of applicants ready to go was much greater than their funds would allow them to send, and I remarked to her that this was true, that the lack of funds in the Associations was the reason of my not being returned to the field after I recovered my health. She said she thought this was too bad, if any one was willing to go there ought to be the means furnished. Well, she spoke at home of what I said, and her home is where the Minister boards. In the evening, Mr. Stone presented the subject more forcibly than in the morning, told us one of the greatest dangers now was

* Horace Dutton (1840–1920) attended Andover Theological Seminary during the Civil War and then took pastorates in various communities in Massachusetts, including in Wareham at this time.

† Elbridge Gerry Pratt (1837–1891) graduated from Middlebury College in 1862 and from Andover Theological Seminary in 1866. He lived in Sterling from 1866 to 1868. He was ordained in 1868 and moved to Oregon for a few years before returning to New England. (In 1856 he dropped his surname and simply went by Elbridge Gerry.)

‡ Rev. Edward P. Stone (1830–1920) served as chaplain of the Sixth Vermont Infantry from 1861 to 1863. After the war he worked as an agent of the AMA until 1869. One reporter called him "a pleasing and eloquent speaker, and his experience as a chaplain in the army, and as a resident in the south for some time before the war, help to fit him for his work." *Berkshire County Eagle* (Pittsfield, MA), August 16, 1866; *Christian Mirror* (Portland, ME), September 28, 1869.

from Roman Catholics who were making very great exertions among the Freedmen; that Jesuits were going among them by hundreds, to teach them, and as they gained an influence over them they would control their votes;* he was very earnest in urging that protestant teachers be first furnished in sufficient numbers to occupy the ground in advance of these designing Jesuits. He told the people how other churches smaller than their own were supporting a teacher, related many instances of self denial that had come to his knowledge, where individuals had given up cigars, tobacco, tea, coffee, or something else, that the sum thus saved might be given to this object; and he asked the people here to think of the matter and do something. After he sat down, the gentleman I had been talking with at noon rose and said there was a lady in the house who had been engaged in this work and was ready to go again, and he would promise forty dollars; he was willing to give up tea and coffee for a year and he thought his family would join him in it.

Soon after he sat down Mr. Dutton rose, called the lady's name, made what complimentary remarks he saw fit and said he would give one hundred dollars, so the ball was fairly set in motion; quite a number raised their hands, promising to do something.

I saw Mr. Stone that evening and told him I should not be willing to go very far south. Mr. Dutton has since informed me that Mr. Stone proposed to him to send me to a Normal School; this I should like, for I should be fitting them for teachers, and I imagine I should teach them pretty thoroughly the principles of a Republican Government. The contributions are being collected here with the understanding that I am to be sent; for Mr. Stone told them that if they contributed a sufficient sum they should have in the field a teacher of their choice, with whom they would be in correspondence, who would write to them every month. I do not know how much they have collected; I heard a day or two ago of one man who promised ten dollars, and if Miss Buss was the one sent another ten. Mr. Dutton told me last week I should go if I was willing, for he would make up the deficiency if there was not enough collected. I believe Mr. D. was a classmate of Mr. Gerry's at Andover, but he is a man of very different stamp from Mr. G.; he seems to be wholly lacking in self-conceit, in fact to forget all about self and just go to work doing with his might what his hand finds to do. He has been preach-

*Roman Catholics tended to support the Democratic Party in the mid-nineteenth century.

ing here a few months, and will preach a few longer I suppose. He is to be ordained tomorrow, as a Minister at large, as Mr. Labbaree[*] was ordained at Sterling.

He belongs in Boston, is from a wealthy family, I learn, and has ample means of his own. I have been told he purposed being a Missionary. He has been among the Freedmen, this probably accounts for his interest and liberality in this line. Mr. Gerry seemed quite surprised at the idea of my going; perhaps it did not suit his notions that an Orthodox society should send out such an unyielding Baptist as I am, but that is their own affair, they know what I am; Mr. Dutton has once attacked my Baptist views, I defended my position, and he finally said, "Well we won't quarrel about these matters," so he gave up the attack and has never renewed it since.

I wrote to the Office in Boston last week, stating what I felt able to do, and that I would prefer to go to Washington, also that I could not go much farther south than that. I received a reply Friday; the Association have no schools in Washington, as those are supported by the city; but it was thought possible there might be a field for me at Norfolk or Fortress Munroe.[†] I would go to either of these places, I should have a good sea-breeze at either.

I do not feel that any thing is certain yet. I would not be surprised if I taught here right along. But I am certainly ready to take the field against Jesuitism, and help save my country from the curse of their influence.

Hattie M. Buss.

Wareham, Jan. 23[d] 1868
Thursday Eve

Dear Parents,

I mailed a long letter home Tuesday, I suppose you have received it ere this. Have you had a real driving storm this week? We have, it began storming here Monday afternoon, stormed all that night, the next day and the next night; sometimes it snowed, sometimes rained, and I think

[*]John Codman Labaree (1835–1924) was born in Tennessee and taught school in Pennsylvania in the 1850s before graduating from Andover Theological Seminary in 1861. In 1863 he was ordained in the Congregational Church, and over the ensuing decades he served as a minister in several towns in Massachusetts, including Sterling from 1861 to 1865.

[†] Fort Monroe, located on the Chesapeake Bay in Hampton Roads, Virginia, remained a Union military stronghold throughout the Civil War.

it hailed some; the storm finally ended in snow and wind. Tuesday was a very unfavorable day for Ordination; I intended to have gone in the afternoon but the storm prevented. I fancied you might be having a severe and drifting snow-storm. Today, for a change, a south rain has commenced, and it is pouring this evening.

Monday Eve. Jan. 27

I have received a letter from New York today informing me of the death of Sarah Low. So one after another of our early friends, in the tedious life-journey, gives out by the way, and lies down to slumber in the grave!

Wednesday Evening

Raining again fast. There has not been a pleasant day this week; it has snowed some every day since Sunday; now it has been raining for some hours. I have been out to a Sewing Circle this afternoon and evening, had a fine time.

Friday Evening

The last day of January; winter will soon be gone. I have just finished reading a book giving an account of Speaker Colfax[*] and his party's travels across the continent. It is very interesting.

I learn from Boston today that the Missionary Union will send me to a good place in Maryland, if I am willing to go. I presume I shall go to that state.

I shall probably come home the first of [the] week after next.

Good night, with love from Hattie.

[On February 21, Buss learned that the AMA would not likely have a post for her until the fall. "I am truly disappointed," she wrote, "for I had left the position in which I had been teaching for nearly a year with the idea that I should at once enter a new field. . . . Had I understood before I left Wareham that I could not go out this spring, I should probably have made arrangements to teach there until autumn. It is probably too late now."[†] Buss remained in Sterling with her parents until October, when she began her journey to Norfolk, Virginia.]

[*] Schuyler Colfax (1823–1885), of Indiana, served as Speaker of the US House of Representatives (1863–69) and vice president of the United States under Ulysses S. Grant (1869–73). HB likely read a campaign biography.

[†] HB to C. L. Woodworth, February 21, 1868, AMA Collection.

Steamer Providence*
Tuesday Morn, 5 o'clock
[October 13, 1868]

Dear Parents,

I will just send a line back from New-York City, and by the time you receive it, I shall probably be in Norfolk. We are nearing the city, shall reach it in about an hour. So far I have come straight along with no adventures, although a new route from Worcester.

Yesterday afternoon I was much interested and amused by two dogs in the cars. A young couple in the car to Worcester had a baby and a puppy, and I hardly knew which was the prettier. The lady said both were born the same day, and they were ten weeks old; the baby was very bright-eyed, white, plump and well-behaved; the puppy was white as milk, except his head, his hair was soft as silk, and glossy as satin, he had as handsome a face as I ever saw belonging to one of his race, both sides marked just alike; his ears and part of his face were of a color between a yellow and a mouse color; the people were going on to Michigan.

Between Worcester and Uxbridge a gentleman and lady seated opposite to me had a handsome black and white dog, a real Rat Terrier, with silky, curly hair several inches long; the lady just said rats to it, and it started up, and looked all round earnestly for them; she told it to dance and it stood up straight on its hind feet and danced very gracefully quite a while; I don't know much about dancing-steps, but I should think it danced as well as people and kept its fore-feet moving very prettily. So much for the dogs.

As I stepped into the Junction Depot in Worcester yesterday, a lady at once met me and said "Is n't this Miss Buss?" I answered in the affirmative, then she said "Don't you remember me?" I replied, "I recognize your countenance but do not recall your name." "Don't you remember Sarah Bliss at Charlestown?" she said.† She was one of the Charlestown scholars, from North Brookfield, I think; her home is now in Illinois, a short distance from Chicago; she had been East a few weeks, visiting; her

*The *Providence,* constructed in 1866 by the Merchants Steamship Company along with the *Bristol,* was regarded as one of the largest, most lavish steamships of its time. Described by the *New York Herald* on May 5, 1875, as one of "the finest specimens of marine architecture," the *Providence* carried passengers such as President Ulysses S. Grant in 1869.

†Sarah Bliss Howe (1833–1916) married Jabez Howe (1833–1920) on February 9, 1858.

husband and three pretty children were with her, her husband is a Mr. Howe, a nephew of Mr. Jabez Howe of Boston. Edward Hildreth* from Sterling had once been their minister in Illinois, but I think she said his health had failed, and he had given up preaching.

Good bye with love from Hattie.

A splendid morning!

I am safe at the pier in New York.

A gentleman from the Missionary Rooms has met me on the boat.

*Edward Hildreth (1833–1907) was born in Sterling, Massachusetts. He graduated from the Chicago Theological Seminary in 1861 and served as a pastor in Illinois and Minnesota. According to his obituary, "a throat difficulty" brought his ministry to a close, and he spent the remainder of his life in business, eventually moving to California.

4

Norfolk, Virginia, 1868–1869

In Norfolk, Harriet taught at the Coan School, an institution for African Americans that had been established in April 1863 by William L. Coan, a missionary with the AMA who later served as the superintendent of "colored schools" in the city of Norfolk. The school had originally opened in a Baptist church when Norfolk was occupied by the Union army, but it soon outgrew that location and with army approval moved into a building that had been "erected for the children of the [white] aristocracy of Norfolk." In 1864 Coan had 564 students enrolled in his primary school, which met during the day, and 681 students enrolled in evening classes. Their ages ranged from four to sixty-one.

Coan wanted his school system to serve as a model for other, smaller schools. His curriculum included geography, history, and arithmetic. He also expected his teachers to be racially egalitarian. When, in 1864, a white teacher expressed her unwillingness to live with African American teachers, Coan issued the following statement:

1. There should be no discrimination in employment and remuneration of service on account of color.
2. Persons, including the superintendent, with color prejudice should be dismissed.
3. No low seat should be assigned to people because of color when boarding together.
4. Social relationships between males and females of different colors should be discouraged.
5. Separate boarding is preferable.

Coan School, Norfolk, Virginia. (From *Harper's Weekly,* October 3, 1868)

According to one scholar, "Norfolk was a showplace for Negro education."*

Harriet taught in the Coan School's high school, which met at the US Dispensary. In her first monthly report back to the AMA, in November 1868, she reported that she had twenty male students and twenty-eight female students, thirteen of whom were "over" sixteen years old. Thirty of her students attended her morning class, and twenty-three attended in the afternoon; only five attended both. She also taught twenty students in night school and twenty in her normal class (meaning that they were in training to become teachers). In her first monthly report, she listed all forty-eight students as "advanced" and indicated that twenty-four were learning to write. In response to a question on the monthly report form asking how many of her students had been free before the war, she wrote, "Probably None."

* *Boston Recorder,* February 17, 1870; John McClure, "The Freedmen's Bureau School in Lexington versus 'General Lee's Boys,'" in *Virginia's Civil War,* ed. Peter Wallenstein and Bertram Wyatt-Brown (Charlottesville: University of Virginia Press, 2005), 189–200; Norfolk city directory for 1866; Sing-Nan Fen, "Notes on the Education of Negroes at Norfolk and Portsmouth, Virginia, during the Civil War," *Phylon* 28 (1967): 197–207; Cassandra L. Newby, "'The World Was All Before Them': A Study of the Black Community in Norfolk, Virginia, 1861–1884" (PhD diss, College of William and Mary, 1992), 110–11, 206–7; DeBoer, *His Truth Is Marching On,* 16–17.

Harriet's class size held steady until April 1869, when her class shrunk to only thirty-two students. By the summer of 1869 it had gone down again to only twenty-six students, only four of whom were older than sixteen. Most were at work in the fields picking strawberries and peas. Throughout the school year very few of her students were "always Punctual." In some months she reported no punctual students, in others only one.

In addition to teaching during the week at the Coan School, Harriet taught 134 students in the Sabbath School at Catharine Street Baptist Church, which was pastored by Rev. Thomas Henson. The Sabbath School grew considerably during her time in Norfolk; by the spring of 1869 it had 150 students and 11 teachers. In February 1869 Harriet informed the AMA that she was also teaching in a white Sabbath School at the Union Methodist Church. These were her only white students in Norfolk—she never listed any white students in her classes at the Coan School.*

Norfolk, Va.
October 15th 1868
Thursday P.M.

Dear Parents,

I just wish you could look in upon me here in my comfortable, cozy establishment. I don't think you would feel that you need to worry any more about my being south. I consider myself as safe here as if I were at home.

I had a safe, comfortable and quick trip here; on the steamer Providence, Monday-night. I lay down in the Ladies' Cabin quite early, (before nine o'clock) but I did not sleep at all during the night, there was a woman in the cabin with two children, and one of them was crying and fussing nearly the whole night, and the woman herself made about as much noise as the child. When people travel with their children, the children will almost invariably show out what kind of family-government they have at home. When I take my children with me travelling, I think they will be perfect models of correct home-discipline.

I gave the Messenger from the Missionary rooms a letter to mail for you Tuesday morning. I presume you have received it ere this. The gentleman had my baggage checked through to Norfolk, he went over [on] the Ferry with me from New York to Jersey City, and saw me on board the cars for Baltimore. The train left Jersey City a little before nine o'clock in

*See HB's monthly school reports in AMA Collection.

the morning and reached Baltimore not far from four in the afternoon; I at once entered an omnibus and rode down to the steamboat landing, went on board a steamer of the Bay-Line, and about five was started on my way down Chesapeake Bay.

I suppose the cars run through the meanest part of Baltimore, but it seemed to me it was the dirtiest, dingiest city I was ever in, and the accommodations for transporting passengers to the steamer were stinted, only one omnibus, that an old dingy-looking thing, and it was more than full, the horses, a span of large, strong-looking animals, could scarcely start with it. I was surprized at one thing in Baltimore, a large Union Flag hung suspended across a street near which the cars passed, and on it

"Grant and Colfax
Should govern
What Union and Loyalty preserved."

I was surprized that such a flag should be allowed to remain undisturbed in the rowdy-looking part of the city.*

The weather was delightful all the way from home here; I should have enjoyed being out on deck the first few hours of our trip down the Chesapeake, had I not been so sleepy, but it was with difficulty I could keep awake on the cars Tuesday, so I took a stateroom on the steamer and retired about six o'clock, rose at five Wednesday morning rested and refreshed with a good night's sleep. At six, or a little after, soon after the steamer landed at Portsmouth, Va. I went out from my stateroom to take observations and was soon met on the boat by a colored boy, looking for teachers; he had been sent over by Miss Gleason,† the Matron at our

* Baltimore, a southern city with pro-Confederate sympathies during the war, was notorious for political violence during nineteenth-century election seasons.

† Fannie Gleason (b. ca. 1833), of Glens Falls, New York, worked as a housekeeper for about seven years before moving to Norfolk, where she was matron of the teachers' home from 1864 to 1869. One earlier employer wrote that "her character is without blemish" and that she would work with "efficiency" as a housekeeper in the South. However, Gleason reportedly discriminated against African American teachers who worked for the AMA. Sarah Stanley, a black teacher, wrote that Gleason had threatened to resign from her position if black teachers were not removed from the teachers' home. In 1871 and 1872 Gleason spent time with the AMA in Atlanta and Charleston. See P. K. Belden to Mr. Jocelyn, June 30, 1863, AMA Collection; and Judith Weisaneenfeld, "'Who Is Sufficient for These Things?': Sara G. Stanley and the American Missionary Association, 1864–1868," *Church History* 60 (December 1991): 493–507.

Teachers' Home, to meet teachers and take charge of their baggage. She was expecting three teachers certainly, yesterday morning, and perhaps four, but I was the only one. I left the steamer at once and came over to the Norfolk side on a Ferry-boat. You would have laughed when I landed, I was at once surrounded by a troop of colored boys, and when I inquired the way to the *Teachers' Home*, they all wanted to go and show me the way, and carry my satchel and box, each one would go and carry them for twenty-five cents; I guess six or eight caught hold of them, and each one insisted upon having them to carry; a colored hack-man would carry me up for fifty cents, and to avoid the difficulty, I jumped into his hack and rode up, reaching the house a little before seven; I was in ample time for a good breakfast; I think I never saw nicer, whiter or lighter biscuit than we had, or drank a better cup of coffee.

Our home is a house in a brick block in the pleasantest part of the city; No. 5 Freemason Street is the locality; the street is a broad one, and one of the principal and best streets in the place; twelve or thirteen persons can be accommodated; there are only six of us here yet, two more are expected, and the remaining room may be occupied by boarders. The Missionary Association hire this house for us, paying $500. rent. My room that I have taken is a little cozy hall bedroom on the second-floor above the basement, the window looks out upon the street and the sun shines in nearly all day; a single iron bedstead, a tall-writing-desk, a small table, a wash-stand, a cane-seat chair and some swinging bookshelves are the furniture; it is lighted by gas; two large rooms on the same floor can be occupied by four others, and on the floor above two large rooms can be occupied by six persons; the floor below has two large rooms beside the hall, and stair-cases; the front-room is our parlor, the room back of it is occupied by Miss Gleason, the Matron, or Housekeeper. Beneath this floor is the basement part, all above ground, there are our kitchen, dining room, store room, &c.

The ladies here now are Miss Gleason who came down week before last, Miss Kildaire* a Scotch or Irish lady (a sort of Missionary, appears

*Mary Kildare, an immigrant from Newry, Ireland (possibly born in 1844), began teaching at the Lincoln School in Norfolk about December 1867. She wrote, "Seeing there were so few Teachers, I felt the necessity of becoming one myself." She remained in the Hampton Roads area until the autumn of 1869. Later she taught in Wilmington, North Carolina, and Beaufort, South Carolina. See Kildare to E. P. Smith, October 29, 1868, AMA Collection.

like an excellent woman) a Miss Ward[*] from Rochester, N.Y. who arrived last Saturday, a Miss Colburn[†] from Worcester, Mass. (Dr. Cutler's Church) who spent the Sabbath in New York City, left Monday morning, reaching here Tuesday morning, myself arriving yesterday morning, and a Mrs. Rogers[‡] arriving this morning. More particulars next time. Good bye, with love from Hattie.

[P.S.] We heard good Election news from Penn., Ohio and Indiana yesterday morning. Three Cheers! Hurrah! Hurrah!! Hurrah!![§]

[*] Anna F. Ward (1844–1879), of Rochester, New York, taught in Norfolk from 1867 to 1869.

[†] Mary K. Colburn, of Worcester, Massachusetts, worked as a teacher for freedmen in Savannah, Georgia, from 1865 to 1867. Colburn was a poor teacher in Massachusetts and also an orphan, and on her way to Georgia many of her belongings were stolen from her. After spending 1868 and 1869 at the Whipple School in Norfolk, she went to Newton, Georgia, where she taught for about a year. In late 1870 Colburn moved to the San Francisco area, where she taught in a Chinese mission school. In 1875 she became a missionary in China, where she appears to have spent the remainder of her life. She died in 1882. On her prewar background, see Mrs. Amos Dean to William Whiting, November 23, 1865, and William C. Capron to M. E. Strieby, September 27, 1864, both in AMA Collection.

[‡] Margaret Rodger (1833–1909), a 32-year-old widow and former teacher in Gouverneur, New York, wrote to the AMA in July 1865, "Having become interested in the freedmen more particularly since the arrival of my friend Miss Burnett from Va. I desire to become a teacher." She continued, "Since the death of my husband I have often felt that I would like to again engage in the work of teaching." She admitted that it had been "a number of years since I taught," but she assured the AMA that "I have not lost my interest in children and schools." She concluded, "I feel that these poor ignorant people need help and think I can not spend time more profitably than engaged teaching them." After arriving in Norfolk, she reported, "I teach the primary school. It seemed a formidable task at first to teach so many children the alphabet and the proprieties of the schoolroom but I never enjoyed teaching better in any school. . . . My class in night school is composed of women and girls. I am very much interested in them and only regret that I have not more time to spend with them." She remained in Norfolk until 1870. See Rodger to W. E. Strieby, July 25, 1865, and Rodger to George Whipple, November 30, 1865, both in AMA Collection.

[§] Republicans carried the elections for auditor general in Pennsylvania, secretary of state in Ohio, and governor of Indiana.

Norfolk, Va.
Oct. 15th 1868
Thursday Evening

Dear Parents,

I mailed a letter this afternoon for home, but I closed it long before I had finished, so I am going to commence where I left off and continue. When I came up from the boat yesterday morning, I rode by the Norfolk Market, and from the quantities of meats, poultry of all kinds, wild game, vegetables and fruits there displayed, I should judge we might easily obtain enough to eat. After breakfast four of us went out about the city, we went through the market, and I must say many things looked very tempting, particularly the sweet potatoes and other vegetables. Sweet potatoes are cheaper here than the other kind, I shall feast on them, they are nicer than any that I ever saw before. We went into the Freedmen's Bank, and Mr. Percy,* the Cashier said to us "Have you heard this morning the glorious news from the Elections north?" He told us the results in the three states Pennsylvania, Ohio and Indiana; he gave us several numbers of the little paper, one of which I sent home today; I also sent one to Miss Esther Waite.

This afternoon Miss Gleason and I have been out on the street; we went to the Post Office and then to a News-room for a yesterday's paper. Miss Colburn wished me to get a New York Tribune for her, I could find none, for they had all been sold; the man offered me a New York Herald and a New York World, the World I wouldn't have, the Herald I opened and looked over it to see if it had run up the Flag for Grant and Colfax, I heard a statement weeks ago that it had done so, but I could not find their names in the paper; finally, I called for a New York Times and obtained one.†

*Henry C. Percy (1840–1898) was an AMA missionary and cashier of the Freedmen's Bank in Norfolk. One acquaintance described him as "a young man of irreproachable character and true worth" and added, "With good literary qualifications he has a good Christian character, a very pleasing manner, and, above all, *a desire to do good*." See *Virginian-Pilot* (Norfolk), January 5, 1899; and testimonial from Charles Northend, September 19, 1864, AMA Collection.

†Horace Greeley's *New York Tribune* and Henry J. Raymond's *New York Times* were two of the most important Republican newspapers in the mid-nineteenth century. The *New York World*, edited by Manton Marble, was one of the most important Democratic newspapers in the country. James Gordon Bennett's *New York Herald* was an independent paper. On October 3 the *Herald* declared, "As in the war, the cool head, the solid good sense and remarkable

This evening we have read in it an account of the outrage in Baltimore Monday evening, the attack upon the train from Washington to Philadelphia, in which were a number of Republicans going on to vote the next day; you will probably read the account before you receive this letter.* Now I saw nothing, heard not a lisp of this the next afternoon when I passed through Baltimore, there was nothing that indicated such a riot but a few hours before; as I have written today, what I saw of the city looked mean and rough, but every one with whom I came in contact was polite to me, and I was surprized to see a Grant and Colfax Flag floating in the part of the city through which we passed. I think I never traveled when I heard less political conversation than during this trip south; Miss Gleason says it is much more quiet here than north, there are no demonstrations, is no excitement manifested. There is a good sprinkling of northern Republicans here in Norfolk.

As for Baltimore, it is almost a pity certain parts of it were not laid in ashes at the commencement of the war, and the roughs therein pierced with bullets.†

Saturday Evening, Oct. 17th

I suppose we shall commence our work in school next Monday. The school-houses were not in readiness for teaching this week. I have had a

---

practical mind of General Grant placed him alongside the greatest military geniuses of modern or ancient times, so in his civil administration of the affairs of the Union we expect the same solid qualities will prove him equal to the highest order of statesmanship. In a word, we expect in General Grant a first rate President, and from him, domestic and foreign, a first rate policy."

*On Monday, October 12, 1868, a train traveling from Washington, DC, to Philadelphia stopped at an Annapolis station, where an informal "vote" was conducted by a newspaper boy in order to determine which passengers would vote for Seymour or Grant in the upcoming presidential election. When the train reached Baltimore, the purpose of this vote became evident, as the passengers voting for Seymour exited the car, leaving primarily Republicans on board. A "villainous and cutthroat-looking" mob stormed the car, physically assaulting the passengers who remained. According to the report in the *New York Times* on October 14, 1868, "One passenger was pulled bodily out of the side window, and kicked and beaten by the mob till they could pummel him no more."

†On April 19, 1861, citizens of Baltimore rioted when Union troops passed through the city, leading to the deaths of twelve civilians and four soldiers. According to one report, Lincoln said, "*I will lay Baltimore in ashes.*" See Jonathan W. White, *Abraham Lincoln and Treason in the Civil War: The Trials of John Merryman* (Baton Rouge: Louisiana State University Press, 2011), 1, 14, 18–19.

fine opportunity to get rested, and to look about. If I could have occupied part of the time doing some things at home I should have been better satisfied.

Do tell Mrs. Lord[*] and Mrs. Rockwood that I intended to call upon them before I left, but I had not the time. And Abby Bailey I intended to see again and pay her more for her work.

Will you give them (Abbie and Lizzie)[†] their papers up on my bureau? Lizzie spoke of sending the Watchman[‡] to me; whoever sends anything to me should direct to P.O. Box 272 Norfolk, Va.; that box is for our household.

Yesterday three of us went over to the Portsmouth side and visited the Navy Hospital at Portsmouth. I think we were there two hours; an elderly sailor escorted us about the building, garden, and cemetery.

The building is quite large, in the form of a hollow square, and four stories high. We went to the top and out on the roof; the prospect there—from it—is very fine. In the garden we picked ripe figs from the trees, and ate them; there were bushels of green figs upon the trees that will not have time to ripen this year. Roses and other flowers were in bloom; the sailor cut off one of the most beautiful roses I ever saw and gave it to me; it was very fragrant. I picked up three *mock-oranges* and brought home, I should like to hand them in to you, they are quite a curiosity.

There has been a Mercantile Convention in Norfolk this week, I believe it commenced Wednesday, and it continued through yesterday; last night they had a sort of torch-light procession, and representations of different trades, but it was not much like a torch-light procession north.[§] It is said two thousand visitors have been in Norfolk this week; it would have been better for some to be in other places than where they were; we would see them drunk in the streets when we were out, and sometimes the police would be escorting some away.

A great many of the white men I see on the street are contemptible-

[*] Harriet H. Lord (1834–1908) was the wife of Friend D. Lord (1822–1883), a physician in Sterling.

[†] Sisters Abigail Bailey (1820–1897) and Elizabeth R. Bailey (1815–1896) lived in Sterling, Massachusetts. Their brother, Addison, is mentioned below.

[‡] The *Christian Watchman*, of Boston, was the organ of the Massachusetts Baptist Missionary Society.

[§] Torchlight parades became popular in the North during the presidential election of 1860, when Wide Awakes marched by the thousands through the streets of Northern cities and towns.

looking; they have red, bloated faces as if they drank freely, and I suppose they do. If there is any one thing that I do perfectly hate and detest, it is every thing that can intoxicate; I would annihilate the whole list, if it were in my power. I never see a sign of liquors or wines for sale, that I do not want to drag it down, and send every drop to the bottom of the ocean. They are the cause of nine tenths, perhaps of ninety-nine one hundredths of the misery, poverty, suffering and crime in the civilized world, I honestly believe. The longer I live, and the more I see of the world, the more fully convinced am I that the use of any thing which can intoxicate is wrong, is wicked; and the more decided am I that the only safe ground is its utter banishment; I want nothing to do with it in sickness or in health; I want no physician ordering any thing of this kind for me; when I get so low that nothing but an intoxicating stimulant will prolong my life, then let me die, rather than commit the sin of lengthening out my days by the use of satan's most efficient agent in the world, the very fire of hell, which burns out the brains of men, and converts into perfect demons those who might aspire to a standing with glorious angels.

Wednesday, Oct. 21st

One week have I been in Norfolk, and I do think we are going to have a very pleasant family-circle. We all seem to enjoy ourselves very much together; I am becoming quite interested in every member, there are six of us. Miss Colburn from Worcester is a pleasant lady, she was left an orphan when quite young; I think her mother died when she was but three years old. She engaged in this work when I left it; she has taught the Freedmen in Savannah four years. If we have additions to our circle so that she has any one to room with her, I am going in with her. She arrived here the morning before I did; she spent the Sabbath in New York, and left the city Monday morning; she learned at the rooms on John Street that I was expected the next morning, and wanted to wait till I arrived, so that we could come on together; but some of the Board thought she had better come right along. After she arrived here, and learned the arrangement of the house, then she planned to have me room with her, and she tells me she was a little disappointed that I did not come right in with her.

Miss Gleason who has charge of the house, takes good care of us; she looks out for our comfort and happiness, sets a good table for us, gives us good food and well cooked, she knows how to do it herself.* I just feast

*Early on in her time as matron of the teachers' home, Gleason wrote to George Whipple, of the AMA, to resign from her position as housekeeper. She

on sweet potatoes. Our house is a home; we teachers have no more care than if we were teaching and boarding north, our work is done for us, washing and ironing too, and we have our strength and energy to devote to our teaching and mission-work. I certainly think my winter here will be much easier for me than to be north teaching one of the public schools in Lancaster.

Tell Miss Esther Waite, if she wishes to spend the winter in a milder climate than New England, she had better come to Norfolk. There is a very large, nice hotel just completed and opened here; it is built of brick, and on the outside looks equal to the new first class hotels in Boston or New York.*

Miss Kildare, one of our family, is from the northern part of Ireland; she is a Presbyterian lady of refinement and education. Her wardrobe indicates wealth and good taste, and I should judge her family to be of the highest circle in Ireland. She is here to do missionary work particularly; she says she thinks the Roman Catholics are putting forth great efforts among the colored people here, they often cross her path as she visits daily from house to house. This week she has gone into school with the rest of us; we have opened five schools; she goes to the same building with me and wants to learn from me how to manage a school.

I hope I shall hear from home soon, I want to know how you do. Remember if you are sick, or anything happens, to telegraph at once for me to *The Teachers' Home*, No. 5 Freemason Street, Norfolk, Virginia.

Mother, I shall soon write to the church at home and to the Baptist Sabbath School in Clinton to know if they do not want to send me a box of their Library books that have been laid by for our colored Sabbath schools here; if you should have a lot of squash stewed and dried that you could put in, and would like to do so for our Home it would be very acceptable. Good bye for this time, with much love from Hattie M. B.

---

asked instead for permission to teach in a primary school or to open an industrial school because, as she saw it, "It seems necessary that the fingers of these people should be taught as well as the intellect." Nevertheless, Gleason remained in domestic work, and by the time HB arrived in Norfolk she seems to have taken pride in her work as matron. See Fannie Gleason to George Whipple, February 25, March 8, 31, 1864, AMA Collection.

*The Atlantic Hotel in Norfolk opened in the late 1850s but burned on January 8, 1867. Construction on the new Atlantic Hotel began in August 1867, and the building opened in downtown Norfolk on October 8, 1868.

[On a separate scrap of paper]

Tell Caroline,* when you see her, that I did intend to visit there before I came away, but was ordered off in such a hurry. I could not see any one.

Norfolk, Virginia
Nov. 1st 1868
Sabbath Evening

Dear Parents,

I suppose my last letter home reached you yesterday. I wonder if it has rained in Massachusetts today as it has down here in Virginia; if so, I think my letters to the Sabbath Schools would not have many hearers. It began to rain here last night some time in the night, and has rained pouringly the greater part of the day; a little before night it cleared away and is now a pleasant evening. We have none of us been out to meeting or Sabbath School today. Generally, I expect to attend to three classes in Sunday School. Yesterday afternoon three of us went over the ferry to the Portsmouth side and called on three teachers over there, all Baptists and living very pleasantly together. You see if I am in the southern country, there are several other northern people down here, too.

Roses are in bloom here yet, and very beautiful many of them are. I hope this week will settle *Seymourites, Blairites,* and all their rebel train down in quiet obscurity, for the next four years, at least.† When I read the accounts of the rebel outrages in Louisiana, Mississippi, Alabama, Georgia, and other southern localities, I feel as if I would like to be *Commander-in-Chief* of the Military for a time.‡

Thursday, Nov. 5th

Election is over, and so far as we can learn, our Republican Party have gained a grand victory; Grant and Colfax are triumphantly elected to

* Probably Caroline McCollom Bailey, mentioned above.

† In 1868 the Democratic Party ran the former New York governor Horatio Seymour for president and Francis Preston Blair Jr., of Missouri, for vice president.

‡ For a complete analysis of the reports HB was describing here, see William A. Blair, *The Record of Murders and Outrages: Racial Violence and the Fight over Truth at the Dawn of Reconstruction* (Chapel Hill: University of North Carolina Press, 2021).

take their places at the head of the Nation the 4th of next March.* There is to be a grand mass meeting of Republicans in Norfolk today to rejoice over the victory and attend to other matters. News reached here Tuesday afternoon sufficient to assure us of our triumph; and some of our ladies who were down street the latter part of Tuesday afternoon saw a bulletin out giving notice of this meeting in honor of the Election of Grant and Colfax. A Grant and Colfax Flag was waving down street yesterday morning. Several Seymour and Blair Flags have been out in different parts of the city, but a gentleman who called last evening and spent part of the evening (Mr. Haskell† from Maine, the Superintendent of our Missionary Schools here last year) said, part of them had come down, part were at half-mast and a few were still up.

Gov. Wells‡ of Virginia and several other speakers are to address the masses at the Court House in Norfolk today; we lady teachers shall not go to the meeting as we would North because the crowd will probably be a rough one. The different Societies of colored people are to come out in procession; I do not imagine that our schools will amount to much today, I think we shall dismiss for the day, for our pupils will all have caught the spirit of triumph and rejoicing, and the task of keeping them in order will be about as easy as it would to discipline so many monkeys.

Afternoon

I went to school this morning with the intention of dismissing my school at once, but found so many scholars present I concluded to stay

*In the presidential election on November 3, 1868, Grant defeated Seymour, taking 214 electoral votes to Seymour's 80. He would be inaugurated on March 4, 1869.

†Joseph C. Haskell (1836–1896) was a teacher in Auburn, Maine, before going to Norfolk in 1865 to teach freedpeople. According to the supervisor of schools in Auburn, Haskell "has proved himself a superior teacher & thorough disciplinarian." After about three years in Virginia he returned to Auburn, where he became a bookseller. On July 7, 1896, he committed suicide by hanging himself in his stable. See *Boston Globe*, July 8, 1896; and testimonial of J. L. Nammett, December 9, 1863, AMA Collection.

‡Henry H. Wells (1823–1900) served as an officer in the Twenty-sixth Michigan Infantry during the Civil War. A Radical Republican, he served as provisional governor of Virginia from 1868 to 1869.

till noon; they were much more orderly than I expected. After school was dismissed, some of them were singing "Seymour's falling."

The procession have just passed our *Home*, they have marched through the principal streets of Norfolk, there were but few white men in it, but a mass of colored people, with Flags and Banners; one had a picture of Grant on it, with this motto, "I will occupy the White House this time."

It must be rather cutting to the aristocratic pride of Norfolk to witness such scenes as these today. I think the Norfolk people are remarkably quiet, Mr. Haskell spoke of it last evening, how quiet they were. Old Virginia has no part in this Election, she is under martial law; she must feel rather humiliated.*

Another teacher from the State of New York arrived yesterday, we now have six schools opened, and we expect one more teacher yet. Mine is the highest school, another teacher has the next highest, in the same building with myself, two other teachers go together to each of the other two buildings in which schools are held, there being in each of those a Primary Department, and a Department next above the Primary.

I think I am very highly favored in the field to which I am sent by the Association. Norfolk is such a healthy place, *our Home* is such a pleasant one, such a good one, too; and our Matron, Miss Gleason is such an excellent person for her place. She takes good care of us, spares herself no effort to render us comfortable and happy, and the teachers who have been here some time tell me how good she is to them if they are sick. Beside, I have just the school which I would have chosen to all others here, if I had taken my choice. Miss Gleason has been here four or five years, the family has always been much larger than it is now, last year there were twelve, and that was a smaller number than ever before; she says there has been no death in the family, and never a case of severe sickness. I do not think there is any other locality where I could be in this work, that I would prefer to this where I now am, unless it were Washington, D.C., or St. Augustine, Florida.

I hope I shall hear from home soon. I intend to write to Miss Esther Waite soon. Remember me to all friends.

*Virginia was not restored to the Union until January 26, 1870, and consequently was not allowed to participate in the presidential election. Texas and Mississippi were also excluded.

I feast on sweet potatoes, I wish I could send a barrel home. Our family disposed of a barrel in less than two weeks.

Good bye, with love from Hattie.

Norfolk, Virginia
Nov. 7th 1868
Saturday Evening

Dear Parents,

I suppose you received another letter from me this morning. Shouldn't you judge from my letters that we were having a nice time down here in Old Virginia, the Old Dominion? Well we are; I don't think a family of seven or eight people could be collected from various places, who would form a pleasanter circle than ours, or work any more harmoniously. A Miss Chappel* from New York State, a Baptist lady, has been added to our number this week; she appears like quite an intelligent lady, was at Wilmington, N.C. last year. Miss Gleason, our Matron, I think is quite a nurse and almost a physician in sickness. She has been giving a sweat to one of our ladies tonight (Miss Kildare from Ireland, who has been suffering with a severe cold for several days) and I have just been in there laughing at her. Our Matron is a Methodist, two of our teachers are Presbyterians, two are Congregationalists, and two are Baptists.

I have finally moved into the room with Miss Colburn from Worcester; she did not like to be alone, and wished me to room with her. We went into a furniture and carpet store this afternoon to get a little remnant of carpeting so as to put a strip down in our room. As we went in, we saw a very pleasant young man, and I thought at first he did not appear like a southerner; in the course of conversation, he told us where some of

*Clara C. Chappell (1833–1880) was the daughter of a laborer and a housekeeper in Brockport, New York. The 1860 census listed her occupation as teacher. In a recommendation to the AMA, Rev. P. I. Williams, of Marion, New York, referred to Chappell as a woman possessing "tact, energy, and perseverance and who accomplishes anything she undertakes." See recommendation from P. I. Williams, July 20, 1867, AMA Collection. Chappell reported that "Mrs. Rodgers was in the Primary School at the Dispensary with a colored girl to assist her until other help should come. This morning I began teaching with her. I am not accustomed to Primary scholars but hope after a while to bring them to order." See Chappell to E. P. Smith, November 5, 1868, AMA Collection.

his carpets were manufactured, not far from Philadelphia, and I inquired if he had any of the Bigelow's[*] manufacture from Clinton, he had not, but began to inquire if I was acquainted in Clinton, I told him my home was in Sterling, the next town to Clinton; then he spoke of Maj. Pratt[†] and Capt. Beman,[‡] and I learned that he was from Westminster, and was out in the 53[d] Regiment; I don't know his name.[§]

Sabbath Evening, Nov. 8th

A mild and pleasant day this has been, almost summer-like. Are you having cold weather and snow-storms up north? I read about them in the papers, or hear them spoken of from time to time. The weather here most of the time since I came has been like September. For the first time since I came, I have this evening been into a southern meeting-house belonging to the white people. There is a large Baptist meeting-house next door but one to us. Miss Chappel and I have been in there this evening. I have no comments to make, may go again sometime.

Wednesday Evening, Nov. 11

Another teacher from Saratoga, N.Y. arrived yesterday morning; we now number eight in family. Am I never to hear from home? If a box of books, or other articles is sent for my distribution, it should be directed to me before being sent to New York.

Thursday Morn.

Another teacher has arrived this morning, one who was here last year; she is from the State of New York. We now number seven New Yorkers, and two from the Old Bay State.

I do hope I may hear from home soon.

Good bye, with love from *Hattie*.

[*] Horatio N. Bigalow (1816–1868), of Clinton, Massachusetts, was listed as a manufacturer in several state and federal censuses.

[†] James A. Pratt (1827–1870), of Sterling, Massachusetts, was a major in Company K of the Fifty-third Massachusetts Militia Infantry. He enlisted in October 1862.

[‡] Samuel B. Beaman was captain of Company B, Fifty-third Massachusetts Militia Infantry. He was thirty-one when he enlisted in October 1862.

[§] Probably Jerome S. Ames, who enlisted as a private in the Fifty-third Massachusetts Militia in 1863, when he was twenty-two. The 1869 Norfolk city directory listed him as working at the "furniture and carpet house" of S. A. Stevens, another Massachusetts native.

Norfolk, Va.
Nov. 14th 1868
Saturday Evening

Dear Parents,

Your letter and one from Aunt Nancy were received yesterday morning. I was glad to hear from home at last, and very glad to hear that you were both better than when I left. My letter this week has not reached you today; by mistake it did not go to the Post Office till yesterday, when I intended it should be mailed Thursday; I presume it will reach Sterling Monday morning.

Aunt Nancy writes that she and Mary were sorry enough to have their visit at Sterling cut short. I have received a letter from Mrs. Bodfish* of Wareham this week. I shall soon send the Wareham people a long letter.

I said in my last letter that seven of our family were New Yorkers; I forgot that one was from Ireland. We number one from Ireland, six from New York and two from Massachusetts. We ate a barrel of sweet potatoes in eight days, don't you believe we eat to live? I wish I could send you a barrel; I would if I was sure they would go directly through; we get such nice ones here and they cost less than the other kind. One of our teachers sent *two* barrels, I think, somewhere in New York.

Tuesday Evening, Nov. 17th

It is raining here finely tonight, has rained nearly all day, but the weather continues very mild. I think the climate here will suit me nicely; the salt-water breeze keeps me vigorous, makes me feel very well and strong.

The last teacher who came, Miss Chase† from somewhere in New York, says her father was sun-struck one day last summer, and the stroke

*Susan G. Bodfish (1831–1902), of Wareham, was the wife of the merchant Parker N. Bodfish.

†Helen L. Chase (ca. 1842–1928), of Parma, New York, was listed in the 1860 census as a domestic and the daughter of a farmer. In 1865 her occupation in the state census was given as schoolteacher. She worked as an AMA teacher in Norfolk from 1868 to 1869. In 1874 she requested a new position with the AMA, writing, "I would like again to enter the work if I can be located in a healthy place & not have too great labor to perform. My health is not good but I think I could do justice to four or five hours teaching per day." She added, "Should like to go to Raleigh, N.C. if you have schools there." See Chase to George Whipple, August 22, 1874, AMA Collection.

came very near proving fatal; his nervous system does not fully recover from it.

Yesterday morning a rush of visitors took me quite by surprise; two gentlemen, three ladies and a little girl came in and stopped about an hour. Rev. Mr. Crane* Pastor of the Seamens' Bethel here (supported I suppose by some Society north) his wife, his brother from New York, two ladies and a little girl, were the parties. Both gentlemen addressed the school, and I thought they complimented both scholars and teacher all they would bear. The gentleman from New York seemed perfectly delighted; he handed me a five-dollar bill as a prize to be presented at the end of the school-year, by me in accordance with my judgment, to the scholar who in all respects has stood the highest during the year. I may present the money, purchase a nice book with it, or a silver medal, whichever I may deem the most advisable to present. If there be more than one equally deserving I may divide the sum.

Mr. Henson,† the Pastor of the colored church in whose Sabbath School I labor, is an educated man (almost white) from the north; he was once Pastor of a colored Baptist Church in Boston; his family are now in New Bedford, and he expects to come north soon to see them; he says he shall go to Wareham and Marion to see the people who send me. He has been in Sterling sometime when Mr. Lerned‡ has been our Minister.

Had I known before I came just how I was to be situated, I could have dried some squash, made some pic a lilly, fixed some citron for cake &c. &c. to bring with me, and we all should have enjoyed eating them.

Next week Thursday is Thanksgiving. Geese, ducks and hens run the streets here, and I propose that each one of us, a day or two before

*Rev. Elias N. Crane (1827–1895), a Princeton graduate and Presbyterian minister, served with the US Christian Commission throughout the Civil War and as pastor of the Seaman Friend's Society Chapel in Norfolk, Virginia, for eighteen years. See *Brooklyn Standard Union*, May 28, 1895.

†Rev. Thomas Henson (1811–1888) served as the pastor of First Independent Baptist Church in Boston from 1856 to 1858 and of Catharine Street Baptist Church, renamed the Banks Street Church, in Norfolk, Virginia, from 1862 to 1872. According to his obituary, "In his youth he was a slave at the South." See *Boston Journal*, June 26, 1888; and Michael Hucles, "Many Voices, Similar Concerns: Traditional Methods of African-American Political Activity in Norfolk, Virginia, 1865–1875," *Virginia Magazine of History and Biography* 100 (October 1992): 550.

‡John H. Lerned was the pastor of the Baptist church in Sterling. He considered HB "a beloved Member of the Baptist Church" in Sterling. See Lerned to "To whom it may concern," January 9, 1868, AMA Collection.

Thanksgiving, catch some kind of a fowl and bring home; Miss Gleason seems to think she may venture to engage to cook them when we bring them. I don't believe there is a pleasanter or happier Mission-family in the South than ours; if you could see us all in the parlor sometimes and witness some of our performances, you would not think we felt very bad down here among the southrons. Good night with much love from Hattie.

[Undated scrap, ca. November 14, 1868]

Will the Sterling people fill a box to send to Norfolk for my distribution? Our Home has to be provided with bedding of all kinds, and just now the Matron says we are getting short of sheets and pillow-cases. The Home sheets that I have seen since I have been here are pretty well patched and torn. Miss Colburn and I are using our own sheets, *we* have a plenty. If any one in Sterling wants to donate any thing of the kind to *this Mission Teachers' Home* in Norfolk, they would not come amiss.

[The following letter is on AMA stationery.]

Norfolk, Va.
Nov. 23[d] 1868
Monday Evening

Dear Parents,

Thanksgiving week is really here. I suppose the turkey and plum-pudding will be forthcoming at home that day. Can't you manage to slide a plate of each down here to Norfolk, some way? I imagine we shall have a good Thanksgiving, too, I don't know what it will be, but our Matron will do something to make us remember the day.

We do not have any southern society at all, but we are vain enough to believe our own is the best to be found, and we are quite contented therewith. I don't think many livelier circles than ours are to be found, especially when we nine are all together. We have the acquaintance of the few northerners in Norfolk, and our time is so well occupied that we scarcely miss general society.

I suppose nearly all the people in this city know where we live, and recognize our group, or its individual members when we traverse the streets; and I presume they feel vastly above us; but I could most decidedly inform them that I feel as far above the whole of them as they can possibly feel above any of us.

I do enjoy being down here, and thereby escaping our long, cold, dreary

New-England winter. How well and strong I am! and what fine weather we have had most of the time since I left home! Roses are yet in bloom here in some yards. Is it very cold up north? I hear of cold weather and snow-storms, or read of them, at various points in higher latitude than Old Virginia.

Is Miss Esther Waite in Sterling yet? I think I shall write to her this week. I believe, so far as climate is concerned, she would enjoy wintering in Norfolk. How are they at Mrs. Jones Wilder's?* What will the family do now? What news in Sterling? I hope father has sold the old horse, and will not have him to bother with this winter.

Aunt Nancy hoped she should receive a letter from you soon. She wrote that she met Cassius Darling a short time before, and he appeared very well; she says he does not follow in the political footsteps of his illustrious father, for he is a true Republican.†

I wish you could see us all here in our Home, and see our schools, hear them sing with all their might. I am training my school into different order from what they were inclined to have when I first went into it. Some of my pupils' pranks would amuse you, I think. I teach eight or nine hours a day; some of the other teachers think I must have something in my composition beside flesh and blood, I can teach so many hours and not get tired; but why, it is mere play to me, when I have nothing else to do.

This letter will probably reach you Thanksgiving morning. If I had wings, I would come too, for a little while, but I think I should soon be ready to start back to a warmer region. Good night, with much love from Hattie.

Norfolk, Virginia
Nov. 26th 1868
Thanksgiving Day
1 o'clock P.M.

Dear Parents,

I suppose my this week's letter has reached you and been read this morning.

*Arethusa Wilder (1796–1875), of Sterling, had lost her husband, Jones Wilder (1791–1868), on November 7.

†Possibly Cassius H. Darling (1845–1912), whose father, Joseph S. Darling (1802–1883), served as the constable of Fitchburg, Massachusetts, and as colonel of the Ninth Massachusetts Regiment before the Civil War. See *Fitchburg Sentinel*, March 14, 1883.

It is a lovely day here, warm and pleasant as a September day. It rained last night, and was rather damp early this morning, but cleared away all bright sometime before the hour for meeting. I have heard this morning one of the best Thanksgiving sermons I ever heard; I intend to ask Mr. Williams, the Minister, to let me copy it. The sermon was preached in the little neat, northern Methodist Church I have written about, as having been just completed here in Norfolk this last summer.*

We are to have dinner today at 3 o'clock, a regular Thanksgiving dinner, too. There are *nine* of us, and some *dozen* people, or more, have been invited to dine with us; Mr. Williams and wife and two children are here now, and since I have been writing this page, I have heard the door-bell ring once or twice, so I expect to see others when I go down into the parlor. I should like to look in at home just now, I hope you have some one to eat dinner with you. We are a lively circle here.

Evening

We have had a Thanksgiving in good earnest. Rev. Mr. Crane and wife, Rev. Mr. Williams and wife, Mr. Percy and wife, Mr. Howell and wife, a younger Mr. Howell,† Mr. Worcester,‡ Mr. Barbour§ and Mr. Haskell were here to dinner. We had three turkeys, and other things accordingly. Mr. Crane and wife were in my school a few days ago, and it was his brother who gave me the five-dollar bill for a prize for my best scholar. Mr. Percy was employed by the A. M. Association two or three years ago as Superintendent of the colored schools in Norfolk, and his wife was then one of the teachers. Mr. Howell belonged to New York in his boyhood, and his wife is a Baltimore lady. I think he has a store of some kind here in Norfolk, and his younger brother and Mr. Barbour are with him in business. Mr. Worcester is in some business here. Mr. Haskell is from Maine, was Superintendent of the schools last year, and a member of the

*According to the 1869 city directory, C. S. Williams was the pastor of the Northern Methodist Church, located on the north side of Charlotte Street between Granby and Brewer Streets in Norfolk.

†Murdoch Howell (1839–1927) was a lumber dealer who had been born in New York. His wife, Salome (1844–1921), was from Maryland.

‡Henry P. Worcester (1839–1882), a native of Maine who had been wounded twice while serving in the Union army, was a commission merchant with an office behind the custom house.

§John W. Barbour (1846–1920), a native of Rhode Island, was a lumber dealer.

Mission family. I expect all the neighborhood must have heard us tonight, for we were not very quiet; we sung several pieces, some national songs, among others "The Star Spangled Banner" and we sung it in earnest, I raised the window on the street, that others might have the benefit of our music. I asked Mr. Williams for a copy of his sermon, but it was not written out, only in parts.

Wednesday Evening, Dec. 2[d]

I forgot to say that I found myself seated at table Thanksgiving-day, between two Ministers, and supposed I must be very sedate, but I found they were as lively as any of the party. This climate does suit me so nicely; I teach about nine hours a day most of the time, and never think of being tired at all. It surprises all the other teachers, that I am never tired, and they will say sometimes, "Why Miss Buss, what are you made of?" I tell them, of flesh and blood, like the rest of the human family; well, they think I must have something else in my composition. I do like my school very much; my scholars are from ten to twenty years old; they will stay round me at night talking after they are dismissed, I don't know but they would stop all night, if I would remain; nearly a dozen of them lingered half an hour tonight; they are all shades, from the pure ebon of Africa, to almost white. I wish you could see them, I am proud of them. I teach in the morning from nine till one, usually; in the afternoon from two till five; my regular school hours are out at four, but I have something else every day till five; Mondays, it is a Bible class from four till five, of adults, Tuesdays and Fridays a Normal class of about twenty, that I am then instructing in the art of teaching, Wednesday afternoons I have History and Spelling exercises at this hour, and Thursdays I have a Bible-class of all of my scholars who wish to be in the class. Mondays, Tuesdays, Thursdays and Fridays we have a Night School from seven till nine. This is for men, women, and those young people who can not attend during the day. I think there are 175 in this, six of us teach in it; I need not go out in the evening, unless I please, but I choose to go; I have about twenty in my Night-class, the building where we teach is not far from our Home, six or seven of my scholars go and help us in this school, one of my large boys helps me in my class, and he seems very much interested; last night I wanted to go to a meeting of a Literary Association in Norfolk, and I left my class with him.

You have probably read in the papers an account of the recent shooting in Richmond of the Editor of a low southern paper; last evening at the meeting they had a *mock trial* of a young man (young Mr. Howell, one of our friends) *supposed* to have assassinated an imaginary Editor of an imaginary paper in Norfolk. I was very much interested and amused in the trial, some of the witnesses were quite shrewd. Mr. Haskell called for one of the other ladies and myself.* Good night, with much love from Hattie.

Mission Home
Norfolk, Va.
Sabbath Eve, Dec. 6th 1868

Dear Parents,

I received your letter this morning. It makes me sad to think of Aunt Esther's dying so alone, and lying in her house dead, a whole week, right in the village, with so many neighbors close at hand. It sounds almost barbarous; and yet no blame can be resting upon any one; she was so in the habit of going away at any time, day or night, and staying a few days.† And John Butterick‡ has gone, too! he has probably drank himself into his grave! What a fearful death to die!

How many changes will have taken place in Sterling during the few months that I may be away!

I am glad Miss Waite received my letter, I was almost afraid she would have left Sterling for the winter, ere my epistle arrived. I shall be glad to hear from her. I do think she would enjoy the climate of Norfolk; it seems to me very delightful. You had a cold rain-storm Thanksgiving day, did you not? I judged so from the papers. Did you have a north-east snow-

* Henry Rives Pollard (1833–1868), the editor of the Richmond paper *Southern Opinion*, was shot and killed on November 24, 1868, by James Grant as retribution for publishing an article reporting the scandalous elopement of his sister, Mary Grant, the daughter of William H. Grant, a wealthy Richmond tobacco manufacturer. Grant was tried for murder, pleaded not guilty, and was acquitted. *Richmond Daily Dispatch*, December 7, 1868.

† Esther Kendall's death was reported throughout New England and the Mid-Atlantic. The *Brooklyn Union* reported on November 18, 1868, that "the dead body of Miss Esther Kendall, of Sterling, Mass., was found on the floor of her sleeping-room yesterday, where it had apparently laid several days: Miss Kendall . . . lived alone in the house. Her death is a mystery."

‡ John Butterick (1812–1868), a farmer from Sterling, Massachusetts, died on November 10 from pneumonia. His wife, Elizabeth (1811–1894), is mentioned below.

storm Tuesday, the first day of winter? I suppose my last week's letter reached you yesterday morning.

Wednesday Evening, Dec. 8th

I saw ice here today for the first time. Yesterday, or the day before, I noticed buds and opened blossoms on some rose-bushes in yards I passed on my way to school.

I walk about as far to my school as from our house at home to the brick school-house; there is a good sidewalk all the way. I do like my school here very much, I have some nice scholars, and I think just as much of them as I do of my scholars north, when I teach there. Four of my boys, almost young men, are very good boys; one of them has been away to Hampton to the Normal-school* for a while, but since I have been here, he has come home, and he prefers staying in my school.

I do wish you could spend a day in my school-room, I know you would be very much interested, and so would many of my northern friends. I think you would enjoy wintering in Norfolk much better than up there in cold, bleak, snowy New-England. It seems so pleasant to be able to move about, and not feel half-frozen; I am glad I came here.

You do not say any thing in your letter about Thanksgiving; did you not have any one. If you received my letter last week, you learned that we had a Thanksgiving worth having; I enjoyed it very much.

Has Mrs. Charles Stuart paid the $1.12 she owes me for her boy's tuition last spring? When she does, you just hand the dollar to Mrs. Newhall for the muff I took of her.

We have lively times here at our house now and then; Miss Colburn is a steady one up on our floor, but the other three of us do not pretend to be always prim and sedate; Miss Gleason, our Matron has a large vein of mirth and mischief, and Miss Kildare, the lady from Ireland is not a particle behind where there is any fun; she is as tall as Mrs. William Richardson,† and as strong as a lion, proportionally; she just put me flat on the floor the other morning, but I imagine I can pay my debts, one way, if

*In April 1868, Union general Samuel Armstrong opened the Hampton Normal and Agricultural Institute to train young African Americans to become teachers and leaders in their communities. The school is now Hampton University.

†Rebecca Buss Richardson (1806–1881) married William B. Richardson in 1830. Her father, Benjamin Buss, was the brother of HB's paternal grandfather, Silas Buss (1764–1827).

not another. Miss Gleason is nearly as tall, and well-proportioned; sometimes she and Miss Kildare try their strength, but Miss Kildare generally gets the advantage. There is one other wide-awake teacher in the family, and I imagine all enjoy the lively times.

Good night, with love from Hattie

[P.S.] I have written to New York to Mr. Smith,* requesting that any thing sent to the Rooms for me might be forwarded at once.

I wish I could have my Album that is at Mrs. Wilson Morse's† sent to me in the box. I want it very much.

Mission Home
Norfolk, Va.
Dec. 12th 1868
Saturday Eve

Dear Parents,

I suppose another of my letters reached you this morning. What is the weather up in Old Massachusetts? Did you have a northeast snow-storm yesterday? We did down here; I think two or three inches of snow fell, and it was cold and is today for this place, but nothing like winter in New England. We are all comfortable, have stoves in our rooms, a boy to make our fires, and coal to burn.

I this morning received a letter from Miss E. K. Waite, a good long one too; I hope she will write to me again. Has father sold the old horse yet? I hope he has, so that he will not have him to bother about this cold weather. I suppose the poor pig will soon cease to be an animate animal, if he has not already, and then you will have extra work for a while.

*Edward P. Smith (1827–1876) worked with the US Christian Commission during the Civil War. Following the war, Smith was appointed the general field agent of the AMA. According to his obituary in the *New York Times*, August 16, 1876, he was in charge of the AMA's "work in the Southern States," and he was instrumental in the creation of schools for freedmen and women in the South, including Fisk University in Nashville. In 1873, President Grant appointed Smith the US commissioner for Indian affairs, and in 1875 he was selected to be president of Howard University, but he died before he could begin in that role. This letter from HB to Smith, December 7, 1868, is in the AMA Collection.

†Wilson (1818–1899) and Eliza (1813–1881) Morse lived in nearby Clinton, Massachusetts. He was a carpenter and appears to have owned a farm in Sterling.

How is Mrs. Harris this winter?

Time does get away so fast down here; it seems as if Monday morning was not more than fairly commenced ere Friday night came round. We do not have any southern society at all, but we have enough among ourselves, and the few northern people in the place, all we need or care for. The southerners let us entirely alone, I presume they know us all when they see us on the street, but I have not heard the first word or seen the first look or act of impudence towards us from them since I have been here. The down-stairs teacher at my school-house said she heard one boy say to another as she passed a couple a few days ago "There's a yankee teacher"; but little would she care for that.

Sabbath Evening

I have this evening attended meeting in the Presbyterian house in this city, listened to a very good sermon from quite an able preacher, but I do not feel at home in these meeting-houses of the white southerners, yet we were politely treated tonight.

The Rev. Calvin Fairbanks,* from Northampton, Mass. is now stopping with us a few days. He is a Methodist, was imprisoned in Kentucky thirteen years for helping slaves to freedom, gained his liberty again in 1864.

He says that in eight years he received 1,003 whippings, inflicted upon the bare body with a leather strap the thickness of a boot-sole, and each time from 225 to 240 lashes were given. He seems a little shattered, and I do not wonder.

Tuesday Evening, Dec. 14th

Tell Lizzie Bailey I received four papers from her this morning, tell Abbie her hat is a capital article; I don't think there is another like it in Norfolk; it goes to school nearly every day. It was nine weeks yesterday since I left Sterling, and this is the eleventh letter I have written home; beside those I have written from seventeen to twenty others since I came to Norfolk.

I have not felt tired once since I came here; good night, with love from Hattie.

* Calvin Fairbank (1816–1898), an abolitionist and Methodist minister, served nearly nineteen years in prison for assisting fugitive slaves on the Underground Railroad. At the time of his death the *Boston Globe* reported that "he was probably placed in jail more times for aiding in freeing the slaves than any other man in this country." *Boston Globe*, October 15, 1898.

Mission Home
Norfolk, Virginia
Dec. 19th 1868
Saturday Evening

Dear Parents,

Another Saturday night has come round, and really I am puzzled to know what has become of the week. Time does get away so fast down here that I sometimes almost want to stop the wheels for a little while. Christmas is almost at the door, I have been in Norfolk almost ten weeks, and yet it seems but a few days since I arrived. We have such a pleasant family-circle I believe we all enjoy ourselves very much; and there is merriment enough among us generally to keep out all fears of suffering from indigestion or any of its kindred ills. Today was a day for issuing clothing to the needy colored people from the rooms of the Freedmen's Bureau,* I went to the rooms this morning with one of my scholars to get some shoes &c. for her, also some things for one of my boys and his mother, and for another woman.

I never saw such a sight before, hundreds of men, women and children were waiting around the building, filling the sidewalks, crowding close around the door, all anxious to get something; it was with difficulty I could make my way through the multitude; a soldier guarding the door saw me attempting to approach, and with his cane he opened a passage right and left for me through them; in ten minutes I had received the attention I desired, and with my girl and the bundles made my exit through a rear-entrance and avoided the crowd. You ought to have seen one poor woman for whom I obtained articles, when she received them tonight; she is a soldier's widow, has one son a deformed boy, he is in my school; she has not yet received the bounty and pay which is due on her husband's account, and it is hard for her to struggle along. Miss Gleason saw her on the street this evening and asked her to come round by our house a few minutes, she did not know what we wanted of her, and when we gave her a dress and pair of shoes for herself, a coat, a pair of pants and

*The Freedmen's Bureau was established on March 3, 1865, to assist the formerly enslaved as they transitioned from slavery to freedom. Bureau officials worked with benevolent societies to provide for the physical needs of former slaves. Although the bureau was housed within the War Department, its work included providing material goods to destitute people, supervising labor contracts between African American workers and white employers, and operating schools and hospitals.

a pair of shoes for her boy, all which I obtained this morning, she was so thankful she hardly knew what to do.

I have had two of my large boys here nine or ten hours today, helping me number and record some books for our Sabbath School Library, they are two from my best class of boys in school, and they belong in my Sabbath class, both are good writers, and they have written today as steadily and faithfully as men.

I suppose we shall have a vacation during the Christmas holidays, it is the custom to suspend school for a week or ten days, for these days south are the greatest gala days of the year. I don't know whether I shall dismiss school entirely or not, some of my scholars want school right along, except just Christmas day; I have been laughing at them a little, I tell them I suppose they love their teacher so much they don't know how to have her away a few days; yes, they say it is so.

I spend about seven hours a day in my school-room; Miss Gleason laughs at me sometimes, she says she has a single bed she is going to send up to my school-house and have it put up in a closet off from my school-room, then she will send my meals up to me, and I shall not need to come home at all, I can stay there all the time.

Four evenings a week I spend two hours each evening in a Night School in the same building occupied by the Freedmen's Bureau; five of us from the family teach in this, and eight of my scholars come in and assist.

We have some laughable incidents in our Evening School, they afford us merriment when we get home. Last evening I walked one great boy the whole length of the hall for something; he did not mean to go at first, but when I took hold of his arm and told him he must come, he began to think I was in earnest, and he straightened up and walked along so comically he set the whole school to laughing, teachers, visitors, and all.

Wednesday, Dec. 23[d]

Great times these down in Dixie, every body flying round for Christmas—our scholars' thoughts so full of it, they have not room for much else. The Rev. Calvin Fairbanks that I mentioned in my last letter, stopped here until yesterday, he has gone onto Richmond, to be present at a New Year's celebration among the colored people. I suppose he is some one of my relations, for Mrs. Eager,[*] Mrs. Ebenezer Lampson's

[*]Nancy Eager (1792–1880) had a daughter, Polly Eager (1818–1892), who married Ebenezer G. Lampson (1814–1891) at Sterling in 1836.

mother, is a sort of cousin to him. He was a teacher in Kentucky, and he was in the habit of helping the slaves run away; he assisted some forty or more to get out of slavery; he was twice imprisoned, once four years and a half, and the second time thirteen.

I wrote again to Miss Waite last week; has she left Sterling yet? What is the weather up north? I saw rose-buds on bushes in a yard we pass to school one day this week. I have reached the foot of my last page, good night, with love from Hattie.

Mission Home
Norfolk, Virginia
Friday, Dec. 25th 1868

Dear Parents,

My this week's letter started for the North yesterday, so I suppose I may as well have another getting ready to follow. Christmas here seems like the *Fourth* of *July*, by the explosion of fire crackers and other kindred combustibles. I have been awake all night, in fact was out till half past one this morning, and then went out again at six. Do you wonder *where I was at?* as the children down here say. Well the colored people in some of these southern churches have a ceremony of Feet-washing, which they observe about once a year, either at Christmas or New Year, and it lasts nearly all night; they were to have it last night at the church where I teach in Sabbath School, and I wanted to see the performance. A party of four, two gentlemen of our northern friends, and two of us from the family went about ten o'clock; the church is some thirty or forty rods from our Home; the exercises were just commencing when we arrived, they held a prayer-meeting till twelve o'clock or later, then one of the leading colored men read the 13th Chapter of John and made remarks about it, and the feet-washing began.* Some few of the men with washbowls and towels passed along the half of the church occupied by the brethren, and washed the feet of those who desired it; in the same manner, two or three of the women officiated in their half of the church; the meeting was continued till morning, but we left at half past one. During the exercises of the first two hours, a few were continually passing out for supper which was served in a house a little way from the church; one of the brethren came to us and urged us to go out and get a cup of tea or coffee; we finally went

*In John 13, Jesus washes the feet of his disciples as an act of humility and service. Some Christian denominations observe the liturgical act of feet washing on holidays such as Christmas and Easter.

and found bread, cold chicken, crackers and cheese, and tea and coffee. Three of us planned last night to go to the Roman Catholic church this morning to witness the celebration of High Mass at six o'clock; so after I came in from the colored church, I just lay down on the sofa in the parlor till a little past five, then called the other two teachers, and we started out in time to see the mockery and mummery of the Romish church, which passes for worship. I felt indignant at the Priest and wished I could tear his robes from him; and at the same time, it made me feel sad to see intelligent-looking people so duped as to think such heathen-like performances worship. We came home about half past seven, then I went to the Post Office before breakfast, so I walked a mile and a half or something like it, this frosty morning before taking the first meal of the day. Yesterday and today pass for the coldest days we have experienced this winter as yet; the air was sharp before sunrise this morn, and made one sensible of possessing a nose.

Tuesday Dec. 29th

Recreation time with us here who are left behind, and we get up various performances for amusement. Miss Gleason, Mrs. Rogers, Miss Chappell, Miss Chase and myself constitute the household now, or rather the white portion of it. Miss Colburn and Miss Ward have gone to Richmond, Miss Kildare and Miss Twitchell* to Hampton.

How time gets away—it seems to me I never knew it fly so fast as it seems to down here—the school-year will be gone before I shall know it. My scholars bring me an apple now and then, and Saturday I was down in the kitchen, Miss Gleason was paring some nice Greenings for pies, she gave me four fine ones, and they were good. Oysters are a great article of food in Norfolk, and all the rest of the family eat them, but when they are served upon the table, something else always comes for me.

*Eliza H. Twitchell (1836–1917), of Saratoga Springs, New York, taught in Hampton and Norfolk, Virginia, Wilmington, North Carolina, and Savannah, Georgia, in the years 1866 to 1878. A testimonial from her pastor at the First Congregational Church in Saratoga Springs stated that she was "an active, devoted christian—rejoices in every opportunity of honoring her Divine Lord & Master—by acts of charity, & labours of love—ever manifesting a self-sacrificing spirit—willing to spend & be spent in any way that shall advance the kingdom of the Blessed God, our Saviour—and with a kind heart & benevolent spirit, added to her natural and acquired endowments." He continued that "her heart pants to be engaged" in teaching freedpeople in the South. See testimonial of E. N. Sawtell, August 7, 1866, AMA Collection.

No one could be more faithful to look after the health, comfort and happiness of each teacher than Miss Gleason is; she spares herself no care or labor, in our behalf.

Has the box for me been sent from Sterling yet? I neither see it nor hear from it. I wrote to the rooms in New York to have it forwarded to me as soon as it arrived there. How do you all do? Write very soon. Good bye, with much love from Hattie.

Mission Teacher's Home
Norfolk, Virginia
Jan. 1st 1869

Dear Parents,

I presume my this week's letter has been read at home ere this time, and as it is New Year's Morn, or rather afternoon now, I may as well commence another. And first, a happy new year to you both; I hope you feel as well today as I do, if you do, you feel well enough. I don't think I would ask to feel any better than I have nearly all the time since I have been in Norfolk; I have not once been tired or weary. It rained here pouringly this morning but it is clearing away finely now; the colored people here are coming out in procession, &c. to celebrate their Emancipation.* I don't expect the southern whites like very well to see them parading the streets so independently, with music and banners, but they can not help themselves. There are some considerable smart colored people in Norfolk, some that can talk well, too, and there are some fine looking ones. The southerners just let us yankee teachers entirely alone, and that is all we ask of them. There are so many of us together that we make a little society by ourselves, and we have about fifteen or twenty acquaintances outside, who are from the north. A gentleman and his wife and four unmarried gentlemen are to take tea with us this afternoon.

Wednesday afternoon a span of horses and a large wagon with five or six soldiers in it backed up to our basement-door and landed two barrels

*The *Norfolk Virginian* reported on January 1, 1869, "To-day being the anniversary of the emancipation proclamation by President Lincoln, the day will be celebrated by the negro population of this city with a procession, speeches, etc. The matter has been kept close, and been but little talk of it outside their own immediate circles. Every precaution will be taken to insure that no disturbance of any kind will take place, and that the affair will be conducted decently and in order."

and two boxes. One of the boxes was quite large, it would hold considerable more than my large trunk, this was from Clinton, Mass., and was sent to me; I opened it yesterday and found it filled with clothing, books and papers for the colored people. One of the barrels was from Princeton, Mass. and contained clothing for the people. The Princeton people did not send it to any locality, but let the Association forward it where they chose. All the barrels and boxes were forwarded to us from the Rooms in New York.

I have just finished a long letter to the Clinton people, and now I have one to write to Princeton, for the donors desired to hear from the locality where their offerings were distributed; and as I am best acquainted with the place and people I must write the letter to them. The holidays will soon be over, we must resume our usual work again Monday; I have had school five mornings since vacation-time began; did not have school this morning, it was too much of a day for school.

Tuesday night when I went into my room, I found it deranged generally; I had been out during the afternoon, and again in the evening, and I suppose two of the ladies had a good time disarranging, or turning things topsy-turvy. It took me some time to rearrange it.

Saturday Evening, Jan. 2d

My two long letters to Clinton and Princeton started yesterday, now two other long ones to Wareham and Marion must be written early in the week. We had our expected company to tea last evening and passed a pleasant evening. Our four stray teachers have all come back from Richmond and Hampton today.

I received a letter from Aunt Nancy a few days ago, she was anxious to hear from you, she had received a letter from Mrs. Parker a few days before. Is Thomas Patten married to Mrs. Knowles?

Bishop Mitchell* is stopping with us over the Sabbath; he is a Bishop in the Methodist Church; he was a personal friend to President Lincoln, corresponded with him and held office under him; I have had considerable conversation with him this evening, and find him quite interesting; he regards the assassination of Lincoln as much of a Roman Catholic conspiracy, as of the rebels.

Some days ago I received some more Newspapers from Lizzie Bailey,

*James Mitchell (1818–1903), a minister from Indiana, served as Lincoln's colonization agent during the Civil War.

the Watchman & Reflector; tell her I wish she would write to me, I will answer; I want to hear all about our folks, Sunday School &c.

Wednesday Evening, Jan. 6th

Have you deep snows and immense snow-drifts up in Old Massachusetts? I judge from the northern papers that there is cold weather and piles of snow in the higher latitudes; I am not sorry that I am away from those regions. The winter here is so much more comfortable, it seems so much pleasanter to spend the days here than up in cold, snowy New-England.

If the southern people don't like us yankee school-marms, they show no disrespect to us either by look, word or act. We walk the streets any where and everywhere with perfect independence, and without the slightest fear of molestation.

I neither see nor hear anything about a box from Sterling yet; has one been sent to New York? I want to hear from home again. Do write soon, and write all the news. Good night, with love from Hattie.

Mission Teacher's Home
Norfolk, Va.
Jan. 9th 1869

Dear Parents,

Your letter from home was received this morning. I have written to New York today about the barrel and box, so I shall look for them next week. I have distributed considerable that came in the Clinton box, and given it where I think it was needed and will do good. One boy in my Sabbath-School class has not been for a long time; I found that his mother was a widow, and he had not suitable clothes to wear, I have fitted him out with a hat and a pair of pants, another boy in my Day School, who is deformed, and whose mother is a soldier's widow, has received a pair of pants and some pieces from which to have an outside garment made, to his mother I gave a hood and a tippet. To the boy in our home who makes our fires, &c., I gave a pair of rubber-boots, two pair of pants and a coat, to another small boy whose mother works in our family, and is quite poor, a jacket, something for some pants and two pair of stockings, to his mother two pair of stockings, a worsted hood, and sacque, to his sister, a dress-waist, sacque and worsted hood, to a girl in my school, a dress-waist, sacque and some under-clothing, to her sister a sacque, to another girl in my school, a scarf, sacque, and hood, to her widowed mother a little shawl and a hood, to the sexton of the church where I teach in Sabbath School, a coat; and thus the offerings from the north get scattered about; I have other things selected out for some others, and have quite a pile left, beside the books and papers that came in the box.

You would be quite amused sometimes to hear some of the observations of these people. One woman where I called a few days ago, was sorry it was so near night, she wanted to see better how I was favored, she inquired how old I was, if I was never married, and why not; she finally thought I was nice-looking, and she would not think I was more than twenty-five or thirty. One of my large girls said to me the other day, "Miss Buss, you go ahead of all the other teachers, I saw you on the street, and you looked right nice." I suppose she saw me wearing my velvet bonnet. Then she and some others were talking about the teachers, which were the best-looking, and she said to me "Miss Gleason, Mrs. Rodgers, Miss Chase and Miss Buss are the best-looking ones in the family, don't you think so?" One girl said to me "Miss Buss, the first time I saw you, I thought you was *ugly* (their word for homely) but now I think you is right pretty." I get flattered and complimented a great deal among them, I hope it will not turn my head.

Tuesday Night or rather Wednesday Morning

I shall scribble a little more in this letter and send it northward. Yesterday we had a pouring rain, I think it snowed in Massachusetts. Today, Miss Colburn has received a large box of clothing from Worcester for the colored people; they need it all, and more too. In the box was a nice pattern for a morning-dress for her, a present from Mayor Rice's wife.* I have ready for Wareham a letter of twelve pages written on sheets like this, nine pages are written to Marion, three more are to be copied. I want to write three more letters this week, and then I will stop till I begin another. When the Sterling things get to Norfolk, I suppose I shall have two more letters to write to those two Sunday-Schools. My needle does not get tired sewing, it remains undisturbed most of the time; with nine hours' teaching a day, letter-writing, work for Sunday Schools, and various other things that occupy time, sewing is left far in the back-ground.

*William W. Rice (1826–1896), a Republican, served as mayor of Worcester, Massachusetts, from 1860 to 1861. It is unclear who sent this package. Mayor Rice's first wife died in 1862, and he did not remarry until 1876.

It seems to me as if I had been thoroughly transformed into another person, since my long southern sickness, for I never feel fatigued, but ready for any undertaking that comes in the way. Good night, with love from Hattie.

Mission Teachers' Home
Norfolk, Va.
Jan. 16th 1869

Dear Parents,

I hoped the box and barrel from Sterling would have arrived here by this time, but I have not yet been favored with a view of them. It rained here pouringly night before last and nearly all day yesterday, and the latter part of last night again, but it has cleared away finely this morning, only the wind blows hard. The rain was like a warm spring rain north.

I wrote to New York again yesterday about the barrel and box, I presume they will get here after a while. I wish they had come before the close of last year, then there would have been no charges for transportation on them from New York here. Government would have brought them, but the Freedmen's Bureau, except for educational purposes, went out of existence the 1st of January.*

I am almost a daily wonder to the other teachers here, because I am never tired; I teach from two to four hours a day longer than they do, but they can't see but that I am just as fresh at night, as I am in the morning. I can sit up half the night, too, to write letters, and they can not perceive any difference in my life or energy the next day. I am very well indeed right straight along. The other teachers get tired out, some of them, or have severe colds, and are obliged to stay out of school some times; one was out eight days, and two of my boys took her school; the other teachers in the same building said they did well. I can never have an opportunity to stay long in my school-room alone, unless I lock the doors; if my scholars know I am there, some of them are sure to be there, too; and the large ones will never all leave at night till I do. I don't know how long they would stay, if I would remain. Sometimes I have a troop of them to escort me on my way home; last night there were six or eight great boys and girls came along nearly home with me.

*On July 25, 1868, Congress enacted a law that terminated all the bureau's functions except in education and the collection of claims, effective January 1, 1869.

I expect the Virginia chivalry feel "Ugh! see the yankee schoolmarm and her niggers."

Tuesday Evening, Jan. 19th

The barrel and box have arrived safe; they came this morning, and I opened the box and went through that after I came from school this afternoon, before going to Evening school; the barrel I have opened and gone through this evening since I came in from Night School. I unheaded the wrong end and was obliged to go through the whole before reaching the package from home. We shall have some squash pies and some fruit cake now. If any of us are sick, our Matron, Miss Gleason, is as good as a Doctor; she just devotes her whole time, care and energy to our comfort and happiness. One of our teachers had a severe cold and a hard cough, she was ill all the holidays and was out of school nearly two weeks; I began to feel a little anxious about her, lest she should not recover but drift into consumption;* but Miss Gleason attended to her case, and she has been back in school several days, and tonight she went to Night School again.

I received a letter this morning from Rev. C. L. Woodworth,† Boston, District Secretary of the American Missionary Association; he cautions me about doing too much and feels troubled lest I should overtax my strength. I wrote to him last week how I was situated and what I was doing, and he replied immediately, a very kind letter. I will endeavor to write to the Sterling Sabbath Schools in the course of a week or two.

Where are the Misses Waite this winter?

Miss Colburn fares pretty well; the Society in Worcester a few weeks ago sent her a $50.00 check as a present, and last week she received a box from Worcester filled for the colored people, and in it was a pattern of a nice material for a morning-dress, a present to her from the Mayor's wife in Worcester: I tell her I intend to be sent out by the Worcester people. The rest of us think we might write to those supporting us, and just give them hints about presents, how some people send them, and how acceptable they would be from others. With much love, good night from *Hattie*.

* In the nineteenth century, tuberculosis was known as "consumption."

† Rev. Charles L. Woodworth (1820–1898) served as a Congregational minister, chaplain of the Twenty-seventh Massachusetts Infantry, and for twenty-five years as secretary of the AMA. The letter to him that HB mentions here does not appear to survive in the AMA Collection.

Mission Teachers' Home
Norfolk, Va.
Jan. 22[d] 1869

Dear Parents,

I do not suppose you have planted peas in Massachusetts yet, but some of the people in this vicinity have. The fig-buds have started on a tree in our yard, and every day I pass a yard in which are rosebushes covered with green leaves, and I think I noticed some buds one day recently. This is such a winter as I like; it has been more comfortable so far than the one I spent in South Carolina. How much better I do feel than I did last winter, shivering nearly all the time, so shriveled and shrunken, and frozen almost, with cold. I received some more papers yesterday from Lizzie Bailey; I read them and then give them to some of the colored people.

I did not leave my school-room tonight till nearly six o'clock; it seemed as if some of my pupils did not want to leave then. Miss Gleason reminded me, on my arrival home, that the days were growing longer, that soon it would not be dark as early, and she supposed, of course, I would remain till dark. Well, if I can benefit my pupils, I like to stay with them. The time does get away so fast here! what becomes of it?

Sunday Evening, Jan. 24th

A southern Baptist white minister from Georgia or Alabama preached this afternoon in the colored Baptist church, which is my special field of labor; he was a fine looking man (Rev. Dr. Curry)* and he gave us an excellent sermon, I was quite interested. I was also very much surprised to see about a dozen white men present, I suppose they were from the Baptist church next door but one to us.

I think I feel thankful every day for the strength and vigorous health I enjoy here. There are but three of us in the family who really seem equal in health to whatever comes along. Miss Gleason the Matron drives through every thing and seems very well; Mrs. Rodger, an excellent, unassuming woman, quietly works along night and day at whatever is to be done, and the teacher from Sterling, Mass., never gets tired; the other

*Jabez L. M. Curry (1825–1903) grew up in Alabama and graduated from the University of Georgia and Harvard Law School before serving in the US House of Representatives, the Confederate Congress, and the Confederate army. After the Civil War he entered the ministry and served as president of Howard College in Alabama (now Samford University) from 1865 to 1868. He lectured widely in the South in favor of state support for education.

teachers sometimes say they wish they could see her tired once; they believe she must get tired but will not own it; but positively, I have not once been tired since I have been in Norfolk.

Miss Colburn can not endure much, she often complains of being tired, yet she teaches four hours a day less than I do. Miss Chappell and Miss Twitchell undertook to teach evenings, but one was obliged to give it up entirely, and the other has been in Night School but little. Miss Kildare is frequently taking cold and coughing hard, she is thoughtless about taking care of her health; Miss Ward, the teacher down stairs at my school-building, often wishes she did not feel obliged to go back to school afternoons, we are the only two who teach an afternoon session in our schools; Miss Chase, another teacher often complains of being tired. My school is really the pleasantest and most agreeable school of all, and I might well teach more hours.

I wrote to Rev. C. L. Woodworth of Boston week before last giving him a particular account [of] how I was situated and how occupied; he answered my letter at once and said there was only one thing in it that troubled him, and that was the amount of labor I was performing; he wished me continually to remember that I was not made of iron. I do remember it, but while there is so much to be done I can do no less than what I feel fully able to perform; and so long as I can come home at nine o'clock in the evening, and feel just as fresh and just as ready for another school session as I did when I first went into the field in the morning, I do not think I am in much danger of overdoing.

Wednesday Evening

This morning I received a long letter from Mrs. Bodfish of Wareham; the Wareham people are getting a box ready to send to me. Two more papers were received from Lizzie Bailey yesterday. We went visiting yesterday, seven of our family and six out of the family; we all went to one place, had dinner between three and four, viz. chicken-stew, roast-turkey, roast pork, fried oysters, stewed oysters, mashed potatoes, mashed turnips, sweet potatoes, bread and butter, pickles, apple-pie and mince-pie; did we have enough? We went to Pinner's Point,* about three miles the other side of the Portsmouth shore.

Mr. Williams, the Methodist Minister who preached such an excellent Thanksgiving sermon here, has owned a large farm there, he has just sold

*Pinner's Point is north of Portsmouth on the Elizabeth River, across from Norfolk.

it now, and will move from it in a few weeks; he was very anxious to have us visit their place before he left, and appointed yesterday as the day. He came in to the Ferry with a span of large horses and a great open wagon and carried eight of us out to his house, at night the negro driver brought eleven of us back; two gentlemen had come back before.

I have a letter to your Sunday School partly written, I think I shall send it in my letter home next week, also one to my own Sunday School.

What becomes of Aunt Esther's house and other property? Splendid morning this, Thursday morning! Good bye, with love from Hattie.

Mission Teachers' Home
Norfolk, Va.
Feb. 7th 1869
Sabbath Evening

Dear Parents,

I wonder what kind of winter you are having in the Old Bay State. From the statements in the papers, I should judge the winter thus far had been a mild one throughout the country. I have not spent such a winter since 1855, have not suffered so little from cold weather, any one winter since then; I scarcely realize that we have had any winter; there have not been more than three or four mornings that I have experienced much discomfort, washing, dressing and combing my hair in a room without a fire in the morning.

We have had three or four inches of snow once, that is all. Norfolk, Norfolk for me, so long as the weather, climate and every thing else suit me as well as now. Don't you wish you were here away from the cold and snow-storms? I could select locations here where I would like to live; you might not like southern society and Virginia chivalry, but we do not have those; we have more Northern acquaintances here now than we have time to favor with much attention. In the white Northern Methodist Church and the colored Baptist Church where I attend I have opportunities of hearing good preaching.

Tuesday Evening, Feb. 9th

Two letters were received this morning, one good long one from Lizzie Bailey; (tell her I like to get such letters, I hope she will write again;) the other was from Aunt Pratt.*

It seems Mrs. Parker has visited you and stopped over night; I guess

* Several women with the surname Pratt lived in Sterling.

you had a good time; I wonder which talked the faster. I am glad Lizzie and Abbie Bailey come in so often to see you.

Yesterday two barrels filled with books, papers and clothing reached me from Wareham; I have opened them this evening and been through both since I came from Night School; there are some good articles of clothing among them.

I like to get these boxes and barrels; they are needed, and they do good, but it affords us some work to open, distribute, and write the letters back north again. I am finishing this letter home now, and after this I shall finish one to Clara Lowe McKinney,* then I shall retire for the rest of the night. I am so well here, and I feel so vigorous and energetic nearly all the time, that I think it is worth a great deal.

As Lizzie Bailey had received my note and Sunday-School letter, I conclude my large package all reached home safely. Squash pies are good, we have had some two or three times. This letter may be shorter than some of mine, but it may tell just as much news. Good night, with much love from Hattie.

Mission Teachers' Home
Norfolk, Va.
Feb. 11th 1869
Thursday Evening

Dear Parents,

I do not believe you have enjoyed such a day in Massachusetts today as this has been here in Norfolk. The weather has been truly delightful, so sunny and warm; I am writing this evening away from a fire, and I do not feel uncomfortable. The colored people's societies or lodges (whatever they call them) of Freemasons and Oddfellows have been marching through the streets in their regalia this afternoon, and really they made quite a display; they were preceded by a Band of Music, and their dress and adornings were in good order. Their hall is a short distance from my school-room, and they were preparing for performances when I went to school this afternoon; they passed our seat of learning between four and five.†

*In the 1860 census, HB was listed as living in Freedom, Illinois, in the home of James and Francis Cole. Also part of the household was a twenty-five-year-old servant named Clara Low.

†The *Norfolk Virginian* reported on February 12, 1869, "The negro Odd Fellows celebrated some anniversary of their order yesterday, in a procession,

Friday Evening

Another school-week gone! the time does get away so fast here! I never knew it seem to move on so rapidly! I can not half begin to do what I want to accomplish. One of the best young men in my Night-class left some days ago for Boston. He was to be in a hotel in that place, as waiter.

Saturday, Feb. 12th

This has seemed like a spring day in April. The buds are putting out on the trees, the grass is starting up, and it seems as if winter was over. I learn that some people had peas up some days ago. Miss Gleason and I have taken quite a walk this afternoon, we went out about four, made one call upon a family of northern people, and did not get home till half past six. We visited a garden and green-house a little way out of the city; the place will be beautiful in a few weeks; the gentleman was at his green-house, he invited us in, and treated us politely; he was a fine-looking young man but during the war was a rebel and his place was confiscated. I suppose it has since been restored to him.* We have foggy nights and mornings here in Norfolk a great deal, but they are quite bracing to me, I suppose because the fog is from salt-water.

Wednesday Morning

I have but a few minutes this morning to write, and then I find my ink is nearly gone. The books, papers, and clothing that came to me from Wareham, filling two barrels, are nearly disposed of. The colored people here, many of them have a hard time to live; they are at the mercy of the whites in many respects. Rents are enormous, and they receive small pay for their work. I send you one of the Norfolk daily papers. This paper has softened down its tones relative to political matters very much since I

---

headed by Slaughter's brass band from Petersburg. . . . The number of members in the procession was quiet [*sic*] large, and the appearance, dress, equipments, etc., highly creditable."

*In 1862, Congress enacted the Second Confiscation Act, which allowed for the seizure of property of persons in rebellion against the United States. Beginning in December 1863, Lincoln allowed Confederates to take an oath of future loyalty, after which they would receive "restoration of all rights of property, except as to slaves, and in property cases where rights of third parties shall have intervened." Andrew Johnson's pardons after the Civil War also restored most petitioners' property rights.

came here last October. I am quite amused oftentimes to watch the progress of the change. I think the more intelligent and the sensible southerners begin to see where they are, and that they really need northern energy and northern capital to help build them up.

I hope another letter from home will soon reach me. No more time. Good by, with love from *Hattie.*

Mission Teachers' Home
Norfolk, Va.
Feb. 23d 1869

Dear Parents,

I wonder how the weather seems up in the Old Bay State tonight. With us, I think the winter is over and gone; the grass is growing up green like the last of April, I saw a plum tree blossoming out today. Things are coming up in the gardens—I had no fire in my school-room today, and was warm enough. A Mr. Cobb* and his wife from Chicago arrived here last Thursday night and stopped with us over Sunday; he is a Congregationalist minister and acts as an agent for the American Missionary Association, collecting funds for the Society; he stated that during the last five or six years he had collected over $60,000. for the Association. He is traveling through the South now, visiting many of the teachers and schools, particularly those teachers sent from the West.

Thursday Morning

I have only a few minutes to write this morning.

A Rev. Mr. Woodruff (Methodist minister) and his wife from New York stopped with us over Sunday; they also arrived last Thursday, so we had quite a company.

Now we are every day expecting some of the Officers of the A.M.A. from New York to visit us. The weather is colder again, but not very cold. One of our teachers said she saw some lettuce in a garden yesterday nearly large enough to eat.

I can not write longer. I want to hear from home again. Yesterday I received a long letter from Princeton; my letter to them is going the rounds; they ask me to write again.

I am ever so well. Good bye, with love from Hattie.

* Henry N. Cobb's affiliation with the AMA spanned several decades. Dozens of letters from him, dated 1848 to 1871, are held in the AMA Collection.

[The following letter is on AMA stationery.]

Norfolk, Va.
Feb. 27th 1869

Dear Parents,

I heard from quite near, if not directly from home, today. Miss Colburn received a letter from Mrs. Ruggles; I think it is about time I received one from the next door above. An old gentleman from Bristol, R.I. is stopping with us over Sunday; he supports in the work one of our teachers here. He has been traveling farther south, in company with one of the Officers of the A.M.A., visiting Teachers' Homes and Schools; they both arrived here last evening, but the other gentleman left this afternoon for Hampton.

The Southern chivalry last week made manifest their high moral stand, and the F.F.V's.,[*] their qualifications for superior honors, by holding a three days' chicken-fight just out of this city. Twenty-one fowls were brought from North Carolina and matched against twenty-one from Virginia, and it required three days for these twenty-one pairs of Chanticleers to get through this fighting. From the reports read daily in the newspapers, and heard from other sources, I should judge there were bettings, quarrelings, drinking and such other accompanying vices as we might suppose would be in attendance at such a barbarous scene.

A few of my boys ran away from school the first day at recess to see what was to be seen; I gave them a severe reproof and told them no one with Christian principles in full exercise in his heart would be engaged in such a degrading show; they did not go again, but I learned afterwards that crowds of people went, and some who rank among the first; also that some of the leading men here were in the habit of raising game-fowls for such fights. The fowls fight like savages, I should judge, fight after their eyes are both put out, fight till they are obliged to lie down and die.

Wednesday Morn. March 3[d]

I have every day, for some time been looking for a letter from home, but it does not come yet. I hope mother, you have not again been so unwise as to take straw again of the straw man, to sew.[†] If you can not have what you need without doing that and working nights as you did last year I will spend my money for you, and wear my old clothes.

[*] First Families of Virginia.

[†] Sewing straw may have had to do with making straw hats and bonnets.

We have had two or three cold days again, but now the weather is moderating down once more. Is it spring up in Massachusetts? or does winter still hold sway? I like the climate of Norfolk so much, and it seems so nice to be comfortable in the winter, and to feel so well. When I come in from Night School, after teaching nine or ten hours a day, I generally feel almost as fresh and as ready for a new session of school, as when I first go before my pupils in the morning. Good bye for this time, with much love from Hattie.

Mission Teachers' Home
Norfolk, Va.
Thursday Mar. 4th

Dear Parents,

After looking for a letter nearly a month, it came this morning. I expected you had that old straw round again, as I did not hear from home for so long. I sent a letter home last week, and have sent one every week. I do not think I am doing too much, I can not do half enough, I wish I could do ten times as much. I am startled when I learn what efforts the Roman Catholics are making among these people. Unless Duty calls me out of this field, I shall not leave it so long as I can be sustained in it. *The Sisters, of something,* have their Institutions here in Norfolk, one of them is but a little way from my school-room; sometimes when seated on my platform, I see some of them walking on their grounds. If you were to see how I consume the viands of the table, and how elastic and vigorous I am, you would not think I was suffering from my labors. I did not come into this work to see how little I could do, and receive my salary, but how much I could accomplish.

Tuesday, March 9th

Well, I suppose I have reached the advanced age of forty-three years, and yet I do not feel more than sixteen. I hope you will not sit up nights at work as you did last spring. I am glad Lizzie and Abbie Bailey come in to see you so often. Did not Aunt Esther leave a will? I suppose the spring will bring its usual changes in Sterling, in the lines of moving and marrying.

I like Norfolk as well as ever, and should enjoy living here, if I could only choose my locality, and have a colony of my own choice settled around me.

Did father sell the old horse? I hope so, instead of wintering him, and being bothered to take care of him. Is the Thayer place sold? Has Mrs. Holbrook abandoned all idea of selling her place?

How is Mrs. Harris this winter? I suppose some one will buy the Enos Loring* place.

It is almost five months since I left home, it does not seem half so long.

I wish I could speak to the heart of every one in the country, of the importance of this work among the Freedmen and of the necessity of contributing liberally for its continuance.

Good night, with love from Hattie.

Mission Teachers' Home
Norfolk, Va.
March 13th 1869
Saturday between 12 & 1

Dear Parents,

I believe I have finished up my Saturday morning's mending and odd stitches, and having now nearly half an hour to wait for dinner, I may as well commence a letter home.

This [is] a very delightful day, almost summer-like. How much pleasanter to me is a winter and spring here than in cold, snowy New England, and how much better I do feel. The others in the family here have been prophesying all winter that I would soon break down, that I could not hold out as I was doing, teaching so many hours a day, and then frequently sitting up quite late at night writing, and Mr. Woodworth, too, wrote me a letter of kind advice, expressing much anxiety lest I should overdo; but I am well and strong yet, there is not a stronger one in our family, and I think, so far as health is concerned, there are six or seven weaker ones. Tuesday night this week I wrote till one o'clock and Wednesday night till two. Last week Thursday, Friday, Saturday and Sunday I wrote and read till nearly twelve.

I wish I could write to every Evangelical Church at the North, so as to arouse them to the importance of contributing money and sending hosts of efficient teachers among these Freedmen. If we do not instruct them, Rome will secure multitudes of them in her idolatrous worship. I tell my pupils just what the Roman Catholics are, how artful, how deceitful, what they have done in the past, and what they would do now if they only had the power.

There was a wedding here in one of the colored churches, Thursday

*Enos Loring (ca. 1779–1856) had been a farmer in Sterling. His widow, Rebecca (b. ca. 1789), had just died on February 23, 1869.

night this week; it was in rather high life among their people. The church was full, I should think a thousand people were present, there were five bridesmaids all dressed in white, the bride was arrayed in light blue, all appeared very well; the ceremony was rather long, being somewhat of the Episcopal form.

One of our teachers, Miss Chappell from the western part of New-York, yesterday received a telegraphic despatch informing her of the death of a sister.*

Tuesday Eve, March 16th

Half past eleven—I have just come in from a Concert of Sacred Music, given by fourteen colored people, and it was very good indeed. Seven men and seven women from the choirs in the two Baptist and one of the Methodist (colored) churches composed the company of singers. The Leader (a large, fat, quite dark negro), three other men, and two of the women were from Mr. Henson's choir. They had no instrument, but they kept excellent time, and articulated very distinctly.

I send home some specimens of penmanship, &c., to show you what some of my scholars can do.† The boy who drew the steamboat wants to learn to be a machinist; I wish I could get him a good place to serve as an apprentice. He is nearly seventeen, a smart boy, has very little color.

Miss Chappell did not go home to attend her sister's funeral.

Yesterday morning I received a letter from Marion, and in the afternoon a barrel of clothing and books came to me from that place. Is it cold up north? Don't sit up nights sewing straw.

Good night, or morning rather, it is past. I have written two other letters since I came in from Concert.

Much love from Hattie.

Mission Teachers' Home
Norfolk, Va.
March 26th 1869

Dear Parents,

My letter for home this week started yesterday, and I suppose it will reach you tomorrow morning. One of their *rebel Captains* was buried

* Helen M. Hyde (1840–1869) died on March 12.

† These are no longer in the collection.

here in Norfolk today, and they made quite a parade over him.* He was a Freemason, and Oddfellow and Chief of the Fire Department, so there was a long procession. The funeral services were at the Episcopal Church a few doors from us, on our street. The corpse was carried to the grave on one of the Hose-carriages of the Fire companies. I had a view of the whole procession on their way to the grave, when I came from school about five o'clock. I suppose I felt as much sympathy for them, as they would for us, following a noble northern soldier in like manner.

We have had a regular spring rain tonight, warm and pouring. We closed our Night School tonight, so we shall have no more night-teaching. I was not expected to teach in Night-School at all, but I have been all winter, teaching nine and ten hours a day sometimes, and have gone through well and strong.

Saturday Morn.

I have just received a good, long letter from Miss Esther Waite; it seems she has remained in Sterling all winter. You have snow yet, and deep still, in some places; I like winter here in Norfolk much better than in cold, snowy New England.

Wednesday Morn. March 31st

We close school today for a vacation of a week and a half. Miss Doxy† a teacher from somewhere over on the eastern shore came to our Home Monday, she will stop with us till Friday. Miss Doxy and Miss Patten,‡ the lady with whom she is associated, have been in this work seven years; they first went to Beaufort, South Carolina, in March 1862. They had been associated together north about twenty years. Two teachers from Hampton were over to visit us yesterday, they came into the two schools in our building. Last night Rev. Mr. Gould and wife from Hartford,

*Edward Lakin (ca. 1834–1869) earned distinction as an officer in the Confederate navy and served as captain of Norfolk's United No. 1 Steam Fire-Engine after the Civil War.

†Mary Jane Doxey (1825–1875), from Brooklyn, New York, taught for ten years in Southern black schools in Washington, DC, and Norfolk, Newport News, and Eastville, Virginia.

‡Rachel G. C. Patten (b. 1810), of Brooklyn, New York, was one of the oldest Northern teachers in the South. She and Mary Jane Doxey were inseparable and taught in the same places.

Conn. arrived here, they will be visiting our schools today. We expect one or two teachers from Richmond some time this week. Next week I intend to visit the teachers at Portsmouth and at Hampton.

I think it about time for me to hear from home again. What news in Sterling? Did Thomas Patten and Mrs. Knowles really get married last autumn?

Miss Waite mentioned the appointment of three ladies on the School Committee, but she did not write who they were. I shall write to her this week.

I hope you are eating the jellies I made, and berries I canned, &c. How long did the Ginger Snaps last? Are you both well? I am ever so well.

Good bye, with love from Hattie.

Mission Teachers' Home
Norfolk, Va.
April 2^{d} 1869

Dear Parents,

I presume you received my this week's letter this morning. It is vacation here now; our schools closed Wednesday, and will not open again till Monday, April 12th. Several of my scholars did not want any vacation, so I had school yesterday morning and this morning for about a dozen of them.

Yesterday afternoon I went out a mile or two, one of the colored people took us (three other teachers and myself) into her garden; she had lettuce large enough to eat, onions, carrots and various other things. Pear trees, peach trees, cherry trees, and dwarf apple-trees are in blossom here. Miss Goodman,* one of the teachers from Richmond (having her home in Worcester) is spending a few days with us.

We expected the Portsmouth teachers over here to tea this afternoon. There are three ladies in Portsmouth teaching together there.

*Hannah W. Goodman (1832–1898), of Worcester, Massachusetts, taught in the public schools in Springfield, Massachusetts, for seven years and was regarded as "a faithful and successful teacher" and an "educated and devoted christian lady." From 1867 to 1873 she worked as a teacher in Macon and Savannah, Georgia, Wilmington, North Carolina, Hilton Head and Columbia, South Carolina, and Richmond, Virginia. See letters of recommendation of George B. Ide, November 19, 1866, and S. G. Buckingham, November 19, 1866, both in AMA Collection.

One Portsmouth teacher (Miss Bartlett)* and Miss Hancock† from Richmond, have come over, they will stay with us over night.

Saturday Morning

Miss Bartlett, who was here last night, first entered this work in November 1862, she then went to Beaufort, South Carolina, afterwards she was in Florida; she has now been in Portsmouth, Va. nearly five years.

Miss Hancock is the daughter of a Baptist Missionary in India; I met her in Boston three years ago last summer at the rooms of the Baptist Home Missionary Association. We have no southern society at all, but little care we for that; we do not desire it, in fact, we very much prefer our own.

I send a letter today to Miss Waite; I have written to her about those specimens of penmanship and that drawing by my scholars, which I have sent home. I presume she will call upon you, and ask to see them, before you receive this.

Tuesday, April 6th

This is a delightful day, and yesterday was one of the same kind, Miss Goodman of Worcester, who came here from Richmond last Wednesday, left us early this morning for her post of duty. Several of us went yesterday to the top of the Atlantic Hotel, a very large, nice and new hotel here in Norfolk; I counted the stairs, they numbered one hundred and twenty-one. The day was quite clear and the view from the top was very fine; all Norfolk and Portsmouth were before us, and the Elisabeth River with its many arms. We could almost see Chesapeake-Bay and Fortress Monroe, some fifteen or twenty miles distant.

This afternoon I expect to go to Hampton, to be gone a day or two, I think two of the other teachers will go with me.

The colored people are very fond of societies; I enclose a list of those among them in Norfolk, Portsmouth, and vicinity. Some are Freemasons, some Oddfellows, and various others are to help the sick and bury the dead.

Good morning, with much love from Hattie.

* On November 15, 1862, the *New York World* reported that Julia M. Bartlett (1828–1904) and several other ladies were heading to Port Royal "to prepare the colored people for the freedom to which the nation has called them." She later taught at Wayland Seminary, a school for freedmen and women in Washington, DC.

† Anne Bird Hancock (born in the East Indies in 1833), from Newburgh, New York, taught in Portsmouth, Virginia, in 1864 and 1865, and served as principal of a black school in Richmond from 1865 to 1870.

Mission Teachers' Home
Norfolk, Va.
Apr. 13th 1869

Dear Parents,

I wonder if the snowbanks north are so deep that a letter from home can neither be brought through nor over them? It is a long time since I heard from home, several weeks—I suspect that straw for sewing is the mischief—if I were there I would dispose of it at short notice. From northern papers, and letters received by others in the family, I should judge there was considerable snow in your section of country yet, and not very good travelling. The north and northeast winds that prevail here feel as if they came direct from deep snow banks. Sunday was a very rainy day here, I did not go out at all, only one Sabbath before have I remained within doors at Norfolk. The Norfolk paper stated that several inches of snow fell Sunday in Richmond and other places in Virginia. Has Miss Waite called upon you since she received my letter? Has she decided to go to Europe with Mr. & Mrs. Blake?

I went to Hampton a week ago today and came back Thursday morning. It is just a pleasant trip there of about twenty miles on the steamer. Near Hampton, seven years ago, occurred the important engagement between the Merrimac and the Monitor—I should like to witness such an engagement.*

I visited the Normal School† and was very much interested; about sixty of the better class of colored scholars are there being fitted for teachers. I expect to send some of mine there soon, I would like to take them all to the institution and teach them myself.

Wednesday Morning, Apr. 14th

I wonder when my next letter from home will arrive—I looked for one this morning, but it came not. One was received from Aunt Nancy, and another from Hampton. Aunt Nancy thinks of going to Sterling this spring; I hope she will; I shall write to her to be sure and go. She had received a letter from you not long before she wrote to me.

*On March 9, 1862, the USS *Monitor* and the CSS *Virginia* (formerly USS *Merrimack*) engaged in battle at Hampton Roads, Virginia, marking the first time in history that ironclad vessels fought one another. Although the battle ended in a draw, it changed naval warfare, forcing nations around the world to move away from the use of wooden warships.

†The normal school was a precursor to Hampton University.

Cold winds from the north still are blowing in Norfolk; we had warmer weather in February than March and April, thus far, have been. I am glad I am not in New England at this season; I think I very much prefer wintering in Norfolk. I have no more time to write today; my next letter must be longer. Good bye, with love from Hattie.

Mission Teachers' Home
Norfolk, Va.
April 17th 1869

Dear Parents,

I am beginning to think it very strange that I do not hear from home again; I think it is more than six weeks since I received a letter. I look for a missive every morning, but none comes from Sterling, except the one from Miss Waite two or three weeks ago.

I believe I wrote home a few weeks ago about attending a colored wedding;—a few of us attempted to attend another one last week Thursday evening, but we were too late, the ceremony was over when we arrived at the place; the wedding was in the Baptist meeting-house where I teach in Sunday School—we were in time to see the party leave the house and enter the carriages that stood waiting; I believe there were seven couples to escort the principal pair; the bride and her seven companions were all arrayed in white.

Monday Evening

Yesterday and today have been quite warm and summer-like. The leaves upon the trees are opening very rapidly, apple-orchards are beginning to blossom, and the young figs are appearing upon the trees in our back yard.

Tuesday Evening, April 20th

We are having a nice, warm rain, to help forward the growth of vegetation. Lilacs are in bloom, and many other kinds of flowers. Strawberries will soon be ripe; radishes are ready for the table.

Wednesday Morning

Morning after morning I look anxiously for a letter from home, but it is in vain, none arrives. I believe it is two months since I received a line from home—the last came some time in February. What does it mean that I hear nothing for so long? I begin to think something is the matter, but then I should think some one else would write. We are enjoying delightful weather, it seems as if we could almost see things grow. I shall like the early fruits and vegetables which we shall feast upon here next month, probably.

Has any one bought the Thayer house? What changes are there in Sterling? Providence permitting, I suppose I shall be there to see in the course of ten or eleven weeks. I intend to go to Wareham in August; I hope to come back to Norfolk or Hampton next year.

It is worth a great deal to escape our New England winters. Do let me hear from home.

Good bye, with love from Hattie.

Mission Teachers' Home
Norfolk, Va.
Apr. 24th 1869

Dear Parents,

I believe patient waiters receive attention at last. Your long-looked-for letter reached me this morning. I suspected that straw-sewing was some of the mischief. I do not believe you were much sorry to bid good bye to the snow-banks, I should not be. Had Mr. Heywood been sick long? A few months effect many changes in any place.

I received a letter yesterday from a young lady teacher, under the A.M.A., in Mississippi, who must have something of a missionary spirit to stay in that place. See what she writes.

"In reply to my request that he would put me in communication with some teacher of the freed people who could give me some advice as to how a temperance society should be organized and put in operation, Mr. [E. P.] Smith has sent me your name. I am living all alone in the wildest, most heathenish, God-forsaken place that can be found in the South, I believe. Almost every alternate man is a drunkard—black and white, and every alternate store a dram shop—shooting and stabbing are frequent, and deliberate murders occasional. I think a temperance society would be of the greatest benefit to the community, not only that, but I feel it my duty to do what I can toward organizing one, and yet I am very ignorant as to the ways and means.

Please give me all the advice and instruction in your power. There is no one here with whom I can plan and consult."

This young lady is a Miss Bullard* from Holliston, Mass.; I have writ-

*Harriet "Hattie" C. Bullard (1842–1928), of Holliston, Massachusetts, taught in AMA schools in Charleston, South Carolina, Raymond, Mississippi, and several cities in Alabama from 1865 to 1877. In a letter of recommendation

ten to her what I knew, and have also written to another lady to write to her.

Wednesday Morning, Apr. 28th

Summer-like weather we are enjoying now. The figs on a tree in our yard are of all sizes, from that of a grape to a full-grown plum. I heard a Baptist minister from New York preach Sabbath evening, and heard him lecture again last evening. Rev. Dr. Armitage preached in the church near us Sunday, and I just thought I would improve the opportunity to hear him; he lectured in the same church last night, to young men, subject—Money. I liked his sermon very much, and his lecture quite well.

But after all, I don't like to go into these southern white churches; though I feel quite independent, and do not care for the whole army of southerners, yet to go into their churches makes one think of a cat in a strange garret; only four times have I been inside a church of theirs.

My Sundays are generally as busy days as any, especially if I go to church morning, afternoon and evening, as I frequently do, beside attending to my three Sabbath School classes.

No more time for this letter; good bye with love from Hattie.

Mission Teachers' Home
Norfolk, Va.
May 1st 1869

Dear Parents,

I presume my this week's letter reached you yesterday morning. The weather here now is delightful. Roses, Snowballs and various other flowers are in bloom.

We went to another colored wedding one evening this week, two couples attended the bridal pair, all were very neatly dressed, and were very graceful.

Tuesday Evening, May 4th

I wonder what news there is up in the far-famed town of Sterling; I suppose if I reach the place a few weeks from now, I shall find some changes since I left, a few months ago. I hope Aunt Nancy will visit you soon; I have written to her to come as early in this month as she

---

J. T. Tucker, editor of the *Boston Recorder,* called her "an excellent teacher & christian helper." See J. T. Tucker to the Executive Committee of the AMA, August 24, 1864, AMA Collection.

could, and stay as long as possible. Who does occupy the house in which Aunt Esther lived? Who preaches for you, for us, and for the rest of the town?

I hope you are having the benefit of the berries, the currants and the jelly of last season; use them just as fast as you can conveniently, get the *cans* cleared, for if there are currants and berries this year, I expect to spend the month of July filling them again.

Where is Addison Bailey?* Does he stay in the house with Mr. Kidder? Has Miss Esther Waite gone to Europe? Does Mrs. Harris come down to our house often? Do you see Mrs. Parker often? Did Thomas Patten marry Mrs. Knowles? Has Mrs. Newhall had occasion to make up a new lot of Ginger Snaps? I suppose I must make some the next day after I get home. I hope you are not now troubled with a lame back; if so, you had better let house-cleaning alone.

I don't know as I think of any more questions just now. Good night, with love from Hattie.

Mission Teachers' Home
Norfolk, Va.
May 5th 1869

Dear Parents,

My this week's letter started for home today. This morning I received letters from Lizzie Bailey, Aunt Nancy, and Anna. I would not be surprised if you saw Aunt Nancy in Sterling by the time this letter reaches you, or soon after. Lizzie wrote me that the old horse was dead; I was hoping father had sold him before the winter set in. He might do to work, but he was a miserable roadster, always tripping; I like a horse with good, sure *understandings*.

Saturday Evening, May 8th

The weeks get away very fast, Saturday night comes round so often. Lizzie Bailey wrote to me that you was cleaning house, and getting all so prim. She had seen Mrs. Morse recently, and it seems that she does her own work; I am glad to know that she has so far recovered. A Methodist Presiding Elder is stopping with us over Sunday, a Mr. Nickerson, formerly from the state of New York. He will preach tomorrow at the Union Methodist Tabernacle in this place.

*Addison Bailey (1825–1903), of Sterling, Massachusetts, married Caroline McCollom in November 1867.

Monday Morning, May 10th

Your letter to Aunt Nancy came to me yesterday morning, you put it in the wrong envelope. I thought at first I would send it right on to her today, and then I concluded I had better send it back to you, and you could do as you pleased about sending it to her, if she had not already reached Sterling. I feared if she received it, she would not visit you at all, for Anna expects to move the middle of June, and from Aunt Nancy's last letter to me I inferred that she purposed making you a good visit, staying as long in June as she could, and be home at the last before their moving, to attend to her house. If you have a lame back, I hope she will come, and keep you still a little. I wish you would heed my preaching about lifting and driving on with everything, and not sparing yourself any more; I think you would reap good results from heeding my sage advice sometimes.

This is a lovely morning. I intend to write to Lizzie Bailey in my next letter home.

Much love to all. Good bye, with love from Hattie.

Mission Teachers' Home
Norfolk, Va.
May 15th 1869

Dear Parents,

I suppose my this week's letter reached you a little earlier in the week than usual.

I think you would be quite well pleased with the appearance of some things in and around Norfolk just now.

A great abundance of roses are in bloom, and a great many varieties there are, too. Peas and strawberries are in market, and many other articles from the garden.

We have had strawberries twice and they were delicious. We have plenty to eat, have good food, and that which is well cooked; somehow, when we come to the table, I am always troubled with a certain kind of consumption. I suppose the most of us will remain here some six weeks longer; if nothing prevents, I shall probably reach Sterling the first week in July.

We have had a very pleasant family circle, and it will come rather hard to break up and scatter, nevermore to gather in one group. One of our number will go to her home in Western New York the last of this month; she is to have a sister married early in June, and very soon after, she herself is going to Lyons, Iowa, to keep house for an unmarried brother.

Does Mrs. Rice's niece still remain with her? I have not learned much news from Sterling of late. When Aunt Nancy gets up there, I believe she will write to me, if no one else does. Use the jellies and the berries all the time while she is with you; make her some Washington pies, she is fond of them.

Tuesday, May 18th

We had green peas for dinner today, greens and strawberries, too. We had strawberries for dinner and for tea Sunday, and twice yesterday; we shall feast on them while they last.

The colored children in our different Sunday Schools have been holding a feast for several nights to raise a little money for helping the support of our schools; I went in last night, they were having a lively time; the ladies treated me to an ice-cream and a slice of cake. Tonight several of us are going to an Old Folks' Concert to be given by an Association of singers among the colored people of Norfolk.

Last Saturday afternoon, one of the other teachers and myself visited the three different cemeteries in Norfolk; the two belonging to the whites have a great deal of shrubbery and flowers in them.

Some of the monuments must have been quite expensive; I noticed one where three brothers had fallen in the late war. On another erected to an elderly man, among the many virtues enumerated were inscribed those of a *master*. I would not like to see such an one in a northern cemetery.

Virginia is to have an election the 6th of July; then, I suppose she will decide whether to remain under military rule, or come back into the Union and behave properly.*

Wednesday, May 19th

We had a stormy night last night, and it has rained the greater part of the morning. I went out to the Concert last evening, the most of it was very good, the house was crowded. Last Friday one of the Hampton Teachers was over here, we went out to a fine garden and green-house about a mile from our Home. I saw some dwarf-apple-trees covered with little apples in clusters.

*On July 6, 1869, voters in Virginia ratified a new state constitution that provided for universal manhood suffrage. On October 8 the commonwealth ratified the Fourteenth and Fifteenth Amendments, thus fulfilling the requirements for readmission to the Union.

How is Mrs. Harris. Remember me to all friends.

I supposed when Ella Roper* came from the south a year ago, she had left the work entirely; but I see by the Magazine that she is in Georgia this year.

Take care of your lame back, and heed my advice. Good bye, with love from Hattie.

Mission Teachers' Home
Norfolk, Va.
May 25th 1869

Dear Parents,

We are eating green peas and strawberries almost every day. I suppose peas in our garden at home are not more than just up. Has Aunt Nancy come to Sterling? If so, I think I shall soon hear tidings from that celebrated town. A great variety of flowers are in bloom here now. A few days ago I went into a garden and green-house about a mile from our Home, I never saw such an abundance of roses. Many of them were trained like little trees, some were grafted; on one little tree, white roses and deep crimson were in bloom. Early figs will be ripe here in June. I should like to attend that grand musical convention in Boston next month; I think that will be something worth hearing; there will be a multitude of people in the "Hub of the Universe" then.

Wednesday Morn.

Old Election-day at home. I suppose the last year's chicken will be roasted, and the plum-pudding baked for dinner. I don't know what we shall have, but something good, I presume. Quantities of strawberries, green peas and other vegetables are brought into Norfolk every day; a large part of them are shipped north on the Baltimore and New York steamers. This is a fine section of country for raising such articles for market. I think I shall go to Hampton again this week Friday.

One of our teachers, Miss Chace [Chase], leaves on the New York steamer tonight for her home in Western New York. I suppose we shall all leave in five weeks, or a little more.

The weather is beginning to grow warm, like summer; we are wearing summer dresses.

*Ella E. Roper (1841–1917), of Templeton, Massachusetts, taught in AMA schools on Roanoke Island, North Carolina, and in Macon, Georgia, and Wilmington, North Carolina, at different periods in the years 1864 to 1875.

Don't forget to eat up the berries and the jellies. When Aunt Nancy is there, make her some Washington Pies. I suppose about my first work at home will be to make up a quantity of Ginger Snaps.

Time is getting short. Good bye for this time, with love from Hattie.

Mission Teachers' Home
Norfolk, Va.
June 1st 1869

Dear Parents,

I suppose you are calling it summer with you now. It seems like July here. If it is as warm north as it is here, I hope father will not try to work out of doors at all; he will need to be very careful about exposure to heat this summer, his head will not bear much warmth from the sun.

I received a letter from Aunt Nancy this morning; she thinks she has a very nice family engaged to move into her house, and she intends to visit Sterling as soon as she can after getting settled down at housekeeping again.

I went to Hampton again last Friday afternoon, came back Saturday; we had a very pleasant time. We took over quite a quantity of flowers that our scholars brought to us for decorating the soldiers' graves. Saturday morning we visited the cemetery, it contains between five and six thousand graves, all neatly kept, and carefully numbered and registered. Mrs. Rodger wished to find the grave of an acquaintance, she succeeded, and placed a neat bouquet by the head-board. The ladies at the Normal School and the pupils were busy arranging flowers for the decoration which was to take place the latter part of the afternoon.*

After dinner, Mrs. Rodger and I rode down to Fortress Monroe, we went inside the Fort and walked about as long as we wished. The Fort is a strong one, and must have cost millions of money; I should like to know the exact sum.† I should not like to attempt to run by its guns in time of war; some of them are monsters, fifteen inches' bore, and throwing balls larger than our stove-tea-kettle, there are a large number of guns of various sizes.

*Now known as Memorial Day, Decoration Day was celebrated on May 30 from 1868 to 1970.

†The original estimated cost for building Fort Monroe was $816,814.96, and construction began in 1819. By 1834, $1,731,284.14 had been spent on the fort and the estimated cost had risen to $1,889,840. See Robert Arthur, *History of Fort Monroe* (Fort Monroe, VA: Coast Artillery School, 1930), 42, 46.

We passed the house in which Jeff. Davis was kept so long, and I just felt that I would like to have him there now, and some ten thousand more.* I am afraid a large number of them would go to the gallows if I was to sit as judge and pronounce sentence when they were tried for treason.

I keep looking for another letter from home, but it does not make its appearance.

Remember to use up the berries in sauce and in pies.

Good bye for this time, with love from Hattie.

[In 1868 and 1869 Buss sent twenty-five letters and eight monthly teacher's reports to the American Missionary Association. Most of these letters are cited elsewhere in this book; however, her letter of June 15, 1869, is included here in its entirety as it gives her thoughts at the conclusion of her time in Norfolk. It is worth noting the different tone in this official report as compared with the more optimistic tone of her letters to her parents.]

Mission Teachers' Home
Norfolk, Va.
June 15th 1869

Rev. E. P. Smith
Dear Sir,

I sit down to make my last report from this field, at least, for the present. It makes my heart sad as I contemplate the present condition of the colored people of Norfolk, and ask myself the question, what shall their future be?

O that the great mass could be thoroughly awakened to value their privileges as they ought, and to make those sacrifices which I feel confident they might make to insure their continuation! Norfolk has been a hard field, there have been many discouragements, but I have loved the work among this people, even more, than during my former years of labor, and I have been happy here, happy at school, in our Home, everywhere. I have been favored, too, with excellent health during the entire year.

*For his first four months of imprisonment, former Confederate president Jefferson Davis was held in a casemate at Fort Monroe (it can now be visited as part of the Casemate Museum). For the remainder of his imprisonment, from 1865 to 1867, he was held at Carroll Hall, a building at the fort that is no longer standing. Andrew Johnson pardoned Davis on Christmas Day, 1868.

I wish I were able to say that I had accomplished in and for my school what I attempted to do; but I am obliged to confess that the results fall far short of what I desired to see. I have endeavored, not so much to advance my pupils over a great amount of ground, as to teach them to think; I have striven to secure fixedness of attention, concentration of thought, association of ideas, and to lead them to find the connection of cause with effect. This is no light task—to subdue their volatile spirits, and control their impulsive temperaments sufficiently to insure the careful following out of even a very short train of thought, requires effort upon effort. But in all my experience as a teacher, I have ever found that if I would have a sure foundation laid for a clear understanding and good scholarship, it must be in the art of right thinking, and the careful and patient practice of the same. I can see that my pupils have been somewhat benefited in this respect, but I wish it were very much more.

There seems to me to be a great amount of vice in this city, and I often feel that the good we try to do our pupils is in a great measure counteracted by the evil influences to which they are subjected outside of the school-room. And yet, I would not be discouraged, oh no! for I fully believe that when good seed is carefully and prayerfully sown, God will, in his own time cause a harvest to be brought in.

The longer I am engaged in this work, and the more thoroughly I try to become acquainted with it, in its real nature, influences and prospects for the future, the more do I find to convince me that the great masses of this people are to be reached and elevated by the efforts of well-trained theologians and teachers of their own race. The more plainly, too, do I see the wisdom of concentrating Northern effort in thorough and systematic training schools, which shall become centres radiating a clear light, and exerting a powerful influence over vast areas.

I earnestly desire to continue in this work another year, and feel that if Providence were so to direct, I would be glad to labor in the Normal School at Hampton. I leave the desire with the Lord, assured that if it shall be the place for me, he will open the way for me to occupy it.

My scholars have been absent so much, last month and the first of this, picking strawberries and peas, that I have been obliged to give up the idea of an Exhibition, by which I hoped to realize a little for our Treasury.

yours truly, Harriette M. Buss.*

*For an unknown reason, HB spelled her name "Harriette" in her letters to the AMA.

5

Raleigh, North Carolina, 1869–1870

HARRIET PRESUMABLY returned home to Sterling during the summer of 1869. From there, she decided to move to Raleigh, North Carolina, to teach in a young Baptist school for freedmen and women led by Henry Martin Tupper (1831–1893). Tupper was the son of a farmer in Monson, Massachusetts. His parents were not Christians, but he converted to Christianity as an eighteen-year-old student. He graduated from Amherst College in 1859 and from the Newton Theological Institute, in Andover, Massachusetts, in 1862. As a student Tupper expressed a desire to serve as a missionary in Africa, and he taught "a large Sunday-school class of colored youth." Less than three weeks later, on July 14, 1862, he enlisted as a noncommissioned officer in the Thirty-sixth Massachusetts Infantry. According to one distant relative, "Ardent in temperament, and fired with an exalted love of country, he cast aside his bright prospects for the future and volunteered as a simple private in the 36th Mass. Vols. From that hour, his splendid talents, his noble patriotism, and his entire energies, have had no other end nor aim than his country's good and the salvation of her imperiled institutions."*

Tupper fought at Fredericksburg in December 1862 and in the Vicksburg Campaign the following spring. According to one biographical sketch, "In one engagement a shell burst so near his face that it scorched

**Cyclopedia of Eminent and Representative Men of the Carolinas of the Nineteenth Century*, 2 vols. (Madison, WI: Brant & Fuller, 1892), 2:430–32; J. A. Whitted, *A History of the Negro Baptists of North Carolina* (Raleigh, NC: Edwards & Broughton, 1908), 21, 148–49; Tupper, CMSR.

his flesh; but, though others at the right and the left were killed by the flying pieces, he was providentially spared to do his great life-work." Tupper led Christian meetings among his comrades, and although he was only an enlisted man, he performed the duties of a chaplain, writing letters for the sick and wounded. According to another early account, "During these years he embraced the opportunity for becoming acquainted with the colored people who flocked to the camps." Indeed, Tupper had empathy for the African Americans he met during the war. He lamented that so many Union soldiers "are so desponding and have such false ideas of the negro." When Lincoln issued his Emancipation Proclamation on January 1, 1863, Tupper rejoiced in his diary that he was "much cheered" and "think it will prove one of the most eventful and memorable days of this century." Tupper would live according to principles of racial equality for the rest of his life. A black Baptist minister later wrote, "It was the good fortune of North Carolina to have as its first volunteer Rev. Henry Martin Tupper, who, in the special Providence of God, saw much of the needs of the colored people while fighting in behalf of the Union and the freedom of the Negro."*

By August 1863 Tupper had become quite ill, suffering from chills, diarrhea, coughs, and a sore side, and on January 17, 1864, he was transferred to the Veteran Reserve Corps (formerly known as the Invalid Corps). Eight days later he married Sarah Baker Leonard, of Stafford, Connecticut, to whom he had been "devotedly attached" before he left for the service. Shortly after the close of the war, he received a commission from the American Baptist Home Mission Society to travel into the former Confederacy to serve as a missionary for former slaves—a call he saw as a "divine command." Tupper selected Raleigh as his destination, in part because he believed the climate there would be beneficial to his recovery from illness during army life. When he received his discharge from the army on July 14, 1865, he and Sarah prepared to depart for the South. "I desire to labor for the colored people of the South as a preacher, missionary, and perhaps to some extent as an instructor . . . in case young men were found wishing to enter the ministry, and requiring study," he wrote on July 21, 1865, "as it seems to me that attention should be given at once to raising up and educating a colored ministry, and this to some

* *Cyclopedia,* 430–32; Whitted, *History of the Negro Baptists,* 21, 148–49; Tupper, CMSR; Tupper diary entries for January 3 and 13, 1863, Henry M. Tupper Diary, Shaw University Archives, Raleigh, NC.

Henry M. Tupper. (Courtesy of Shaw University)

extent must be accomplished by ministers and missionaries who reside with them."*

Henry and Sarah departed New England on October 1 and arrived in Raleigh on October 10. On October 11 he called on a local Baptist minister to explain his mission. That pastor told Tupper he should "go back North to his Yankee friends" and then said to Sarah, "I hope, young woman, you have brought a generous supply of handkerchiefs with you, for you will certainly need them." The Tuppers nevertheless decided to forge ahead. According to one black Baptist preacher, "Without waiting for further recognition he at once commenced his work among the

*Tupper, CMSR; *History of the Thirty-Sixth Regiment Massachusetts Volunteers, 1862–1865* (Boston: Rockwell & Churchill, 1884), 352; *Cyclopedia*, 432–33; Whitted, *History of the Negro Baptists*, 21–22, 149–50; Clara Barnes Jenkins, "An Historical Study of Shaw University, 1865–1963" (EdD diss., University of Pittsburgh, 1965), 35–37.

Sarah Baker Leonard Tupper. (Courtesy of Shaw University)

colored people, whose condition he found pitiable in the extreme. They were poor and destitute; many of them were refugees who had followed the army, and were literally houseless and homeless." Tupper worked with the Freedmen's Bureau to help procure food and clothing for the formerly enslaved. Most of the Tuppers' work, according to Buss, was among "the poorest classes of freedmen, principally the refugees from other places."*

Tupper had nowhere to lead religious meetings other than "under the shelter of a neighboring tree or in the low, dark, comfortless cabins." On December 1, 1865, he wrote in his diary, "Visited six families; held a prayer meeting; heard my theological class." Thus, wrote a black Baptist preacher, "Shaw University was started in a very humble way in a negro cabin on the outskirts of the city." Soon Tupper took five hundred dollars he had saved as a soldier and purchased a lot at the corner of Blount and Cabarrus Streets, where in the summer of 1866 he and his "faithful followers" built a two-story wooden church and school (in 1867, dormitories were opened on the second floor). It was good that Tupper came to the area. As Harriet's future roommate, Esther P. Hayes, reported from Raleigh in 1867, "The colored people are very anxious to have schools but

*Whitted, *History of the Negro Baptists,* 21–22, 149–50; Jenkins, "Historical Study," 37–39; *National Baptist* (Philadelphia), February 23, 1871.

First Shaw University building. (From H. L. Morehouse, *H. M. Tupper, D.D.: A Narrative of Twenty-Five Years' Work in the South, 1865–1880* [n.p., 1890])

have no teachers. They are willing to do something for the support of a teacher." In time, several teachers from the New England Freedmen's Aid Society came to open a day school, and Tupper's black theology students assisted in teaching its five hundred to six hundred students.*

Tupper announced in the *Biblical Recorder* that the Raleigh Baptist Institute for the Education of Colored Men for the Ministry would open its second session on October 17, 1869. "The school is under the direction and auspices of the American Baptist Home Missionary [*sic*] Society, and that the design of the school may be fully carried out, and its influence and usefulness as widely extended as possible, we earnestly and cordially invite Baptists throughout the State to assist in giving information and selecting colored men of good moral and religious character to attend this school." Those who could provide "evidence of having been

*Whitted, *History of the Negro Baptists,* 150; Jenkins, "Historical Study," 40–41; Esther P. Hayes to E. P. Smith, November 28, 1867, AMA Collection; H. L. Morehouse, *H. M. Tupper, D.D.: A Narrative of Twenty-Five Years' Work in the South, 1865–1880* (n.p., 1890), 7–11; Wilmoth A. Carter, *Shaw's Universe: A Monument to Educational Innovation* (Rockville, MD: D.C. National Publishing, 1973), 2–3.

called to preach the Gospel, and are anxious to qualify themselves for the work, board, lodging, and tuition will be furnished free of expense." He continued, "The importance of this effort to raise up an educated colored ministry cannot be over-estimated." As a word of warning, Tupper added: "Other denominations are actively engaged in establishing churches and educating men for the ministry and it is currently reported that the Catholics have in Rome one or two hundred colored men in course of training to become religious teachers in the South, and if we, as a denomination, maintain our ascendency among the colored people, we must at once enter the field with our united strength and by selecting the best men, intellectually, and morally, and by giving them a good thorough practical education, thus train up a ministry that will be fully competent to preach the gospel and take charge of the churches."*

In 1870 Tupper began allowing black girls to attend the school, recognizing that their education would be important for the black community of the state. That same year, Tupper decided to purchase the home of Daniel M. Barringer, ex-minister to Spain, which was for sale for $13,000. Tupper sought pledges of support from wealthy Northerners. Elijah Shaw (1819–1896), of Wales, Massachusetts, told Tupper he would "mortgage the house over his head" to help the Raleigh Institute and immediately pledged $5,000 toward the purchase of the property (Shaw ended up providing at least $10,000 to the school). The school would come to be known as the Shaw Collegiate Institute in 1870 and Shaw University in 1875.†

Harriet arrived in Raleigh in October 1869 ready to join Tupper in his work of educating freedmen and preparing them for Christian ministry. Her "own Association of churches" in Massachusetts sent their contributions directly to the American Baptist Home Mission Society to support her salary and expenses.‡

Raleigh, N.C. Oct. 29th 1869

Dear Parents,

I suppose you will soon be looking for a letter from the Old North State, so I will at once proceed to have it penned and on its way. I am safe at Raleigh, and cozily established, comfortably too. We left New York

* *Biblical Recorder* (Raleigh, NC), October 20, 1869.

† Jenkins, "Historical Study," 43, 48.

‡ HB to E. P. Smith, October 23, 1869, AMA Collection.

The Tuppers' home. (From H. L. Morehouse, *H. M. Tupper, D.D.: A Narrative of Twenty-Five Years' Work in the South, 1865–1880* [n.p., 1890])

at half-past nine Tuesday evening, passed through Washington at sunrise Wednesday morning, saw the Capitol at a very short distance, came down the river in a boat to Acquia Creek some fifty or sixty miles, then *on to Richmond,* not by Greely's command, but because we chose to go.* We passed through Richmond Wednesday afternoon, reached Greensboro between 12 & 1 at night, and there we separated, Mr. Ruggles and wife taking the train for Charlotte and I the one for Raleigh; I arrived in Raleigh at sunrise yesterday morning, and soon proceeded to Mr. Tupper's; Mrs. Tupper prepared me a nice breakfast, and then I lay down on the lounge and had a long nap. Today I have taken my place in school, Mr. Tupper being very glad to pass it into my hands. My home is with two teachers from Portsmouth, N.H. who are sent out by the Boston Society, another one is expected soon, and then there will be four of us, we have a nice and neat one-story house of four comfortable rooms, and shall be very pleasantly situated.

Mr. Tupper is from Munson, Mass. and his wife from Wilbraham, I am very much pleased with them both, and should board with them if they only had the room to spare; their house is a low one with only two main rooms and some small spaces attached.

*In 1861 many Northerners, led by the *New York Tribune* editor, Horace Greeley, urged Lincoln to take the offensive with the cry, "On to Richmond!"

I shall not stop to write much this time, you may look for more particulars in my next letter.

I have arrived in safety, am not sick, but very well, and feeling quite rested.

Good night, with love from Hattie.

Raleigh, N.C.
Nov. 3^{d} 1869

Dear Parents,

I presume you have received one letter from Raleigh, which announced my safe arrival and pleasant establishment. I am feeling fully at home, and see nothing why I am not just as pleasantly, comfortably and happily situated as I was at Norfolk. I think I shall like Mr. & Mrs. Tupper very much, also Misses Philbrook and Haley,* the ladies with whom I live. Mr. Tupper is certainly a good man for *me* to teach with, for you know I would not be domineered over, nor bear dictation in my work, from any one, and he just gives my department all into my own hands, and lets me have my own way, and he seems glad to pass it over to me; if I ask him how this or that is to be done or arranged, it is always to be just as I think best.

He graduated at the Baptist Theological Institution at Newton, Mass. in 1862, then enlisted as a private and served in the army till the close of the war. After the war he came to Raleigh, and has been at work here ever since; he seems an incessant worker, and he has certainly begun a good work here. He has established a colored Baptist church, (which now numbers nearly two hundred members) in which a discipline is enforced like the discipline of northern churches, he has collected funds and received aid from various sources for the erection of a large building for meetings and school-purposes, and he superintends all the work himself. A large room on the first floor has been finished and used as a place of worship, two small rooms in the rear are the school-rooms of Miss Philbrook and Miss Haley, on the second floor, in the central part of the rear (our building is long and wide) is the school-room for our students of the Raleigh Baptist Institute, on each side of this are their sleeping-rooms, which they keep in order themselves; the front part of this floor is now being finished for the regular place of worship, and a church-tower is being erected, Mr. Tupper is busy as a bee all the time, the lumber, the

*Elizabeth A. Philbrook (ca. 1821–ca. 1872) and Caroline C. Haley (1836–1899) were both from Portsmouth, New Hampshire.

placing of every timber, and every thing else is under his eye; he has just bought another lot adjoining this, bought it under the direction of the American Baptist Home Mission Society, and soon he will go about the erection of another large building, particularly for our school. He makes arrangements for the boarding of his pupils, purchases all their rations, has a colored woman in a small house near his cook for them, his wife overseeing somewhat, and so he seems to have plenty of irons in the fire. With all these duties, beside his duties as Pastor, and with a school on his hands that should receive seven hours instruction a day, you may judge he was ready to give me a cordial welcome, and glad to pass over to me some considerable portion of his work.

Our students are ordained colored Ministers, and young men endeavoring to fit themselves to be teachers and preachers; Mr. T. has them in the school-room in the morning an hour before breakfast, I have them from nine till half-past one, then he has them again from three till five. They ask me questions in their Bible lesson that put one to careful thinking, and he told me today that they asked him questions in the Theological Department equal to those raised by the students at Newton. I wish you could spend a morning in my school-room, I know you would be interested. I think I shall be better satisfied with my work among the Freedmen here, than in any other place where I have previously been. My work seems easy as play, there is no constant fretting of nerves by the wear and tear of discipline; a more polite and respectful class of students you never saw, they are eager to gain knowledge, they give me close attention, hang upon my words, and seem to drink in all the instruction I give them; they anticipate my wishes too, and seem happy to render me any polite attention.

I am having some bedding made for them now, I have selected some eighty or ninety yards of ten-cent calicoes, and have cut nine comforters for single beds, two pounds of cotton are to be put in each one. You would be amused to hear my students practice Elocution with me, or to see them follow me in Gymnastic exercises; I have three ordained Ministers among them.

I had a class of girls in Sunday school Sunday morning, and after morning service I had a Bible class of men and women, I took up the same chapter Mr. Tupper had read, dwelt upon his text, and followed out the ideas he had advanced; one of them told me I preached as good as brother Tupper, I laughed at Mrs. Tupper about rivaling her husband, she said she did not know about my coming down here and preaching the first Sunday as good as brother Tupper. Mr. Tupper said one of the class told him they had had two good sermons that day. The people seem very much attached to him, they have been sounding his praises to me since I came among them; one says he is the best man in the world, another says he has many crowns up yonder,* and so they eulogize him. I should think he had a very happy faculty of guiding and controlling them. Mrs. Tupper is one of those lovable women that you feel drawn towards at once; I did not go up there today, but I have been up to see her almost every day; it is nearly half a mile up to her house; our school is about as far from our home as the Post-Office in Sterling is from our house.

I wish you could see how nice and cozy we are at our little home, the two ladies are very kind, they are Unitarian ladies, but they teach at Mr. Tupper's Sabbath School; Miss Haley is full of life, she keeps us laughing so at home, that we shall not be likely to suffer from dyspepsia. I should think she was about twenty-five. Miss Philbrook is older, she may be as old as I am. They have a friend with them now, a Miss. Boardman from Portsmouth, N.H., she arrived Saturday, she is quite deaf, but very pleasant, has come down for a visit, and to improve her health; Monday she insisted upon taking a piece of sewing she found I had to do, and doing it herself.

What weather are you having at home? Has it snowed since I came away? I have heard of its snowing in Philadelphia. Raleigh is not a compact city, but open and pleasant, the locality is on high land, the air has been sharp and frosty since I came; Mrs. Tupper says she does not know of a more healthy place than this. I have been in several stores since I came, and have been very politely treated at every one; they must know us yankees the moment we speak, but they have probably learned that it is policy to treat us well. Mr. Tupper went to the depot a week ago tonight, thinking I might arrive then, Miss Haley went too, looking for Miss Boardman; the conductor saw Mr. T. and said to him "Nobody for you tonight, Mr. Tupper, no Northerners aboard."

We have had callers tonight, two or three southern women. Two Northern teachers called today, and two others called one day before this week.

It is after twelve. Good night. Love from Hattie.

[P.S.] Love to Lizzie & Abbie.

*The New Testament teaches that Christians will receive crowns of righteousness in heaven.

Raleigh Baptist Institute
Elm Cottage
Saturday Evening, Nov. 6th 1869

Dear Parents,

I wish that for a little while you could be transferred to Raleigh, N.C. We have such nice, cozy times here, are so comfortable, and enjoy ourselves so well. Misses Philbrook and Haley are excellent housekeepers; we live well, have good palatable, wholesome fair, and plenty of it. Last Saturday they made some pies out of my squash, the dark colored, and the pies were good too, we have had some currant-tarts, of my currants; we eat a great deal of cornbread, and the way they make it, I like it very much. I don't believe I could be more pleasantly situated than I am. The lady stopping with us is very agreeable, a lady of property, but with good common-sense ideas.

We have all been to the State House today, and there I met Gen. Fisher* (Adj. Gen., I believe) Mrs. Ruggle's Cousin, I liked his appearance; we also met Mr. Ashley,† the one that I wrote about from Norfolk, who was at Wilmington two years ago, and whose life was in danger for so many weeks; he is now the State Superintendent of Schools in North Carolina.

We went into the State House Library, and I learned that I could take books therefrom, so I selected "Massachusetts in the Civil War" by Gen. Schouler.‡ I was very much interested at the Asylum; the gentleman who escorted us about was very polite—he had several blind pupils go through with some exercises—a little boy seven or eight years of age sang for us, he was a very smart, fine looking boy, only he was blind—a young man with a beautiful face, and a good head sang and played the piano—a young lady sang and played also, and a class of girls sang, all very finely; two blind girls read to us, and one worked out mentally an example in

*Abiel W. Fisher (ca. 1835–1895) had been born in Vermont and served in the Fourth Vermont Infantry. After the Civil War he settled in North Carolina, where he served as adjutant general from 1868 to 1872.

†Rev. Samuel S. Ashley (1819–1887), a Republican from Northborough, Massachusetts, and an alumnus of Oberlin College, served as superintendent of public instruction in North Carolina from 1868 to 1871. See John L. Bell, "Samuel Stanford Ashley, Carpetbagger and Educator," *North Carolina Historical Review* 72 (October 1995): 456–83.

‡The book was *A History of Massachusetts in the Civil War,* by William Schouler, 2 vols. (Boston: E. P. Dutton, 1868).

Multiplication which I gave her, there were three figures in the number to be multiplied and three in the multiplier. I ran it through myself and she soon gave me the correct answer. The exercises by deaf and dumb pupils also interested me very much; a daughter of one of those Siamese twins* was one of them; a very smart, bright-looking boy of eight or nine years went through some interesting exercises; the teacher told us he was about the smartest boy he ever saw; and one of the worst. I think Raleigh quite a pleasant city, but not very large. It amuses me to see how very polite the merchants are to us.

Monday Evening, Nov. 8th

I did not want to come to Raleigh, I was anxious to be located in Washington, but since my arrival here, I am more and more convinced that this is just the place; there is a field here for an immense amount of good to be done. I never before felt that any teaching of mine might result in so much good as here. Five of our students are ordained Ministers, one of them is almost white, is from the North, and is Pastor† of the 1st colored Baptist Church in Raleigh. (Mr. Tupper's is the 2d) They are all so polite, so respectful and attentive that it is a pleasure to appear before them as teacher, I have no labor at all in discipline, and in recitations they are all attention, they seem to hang upon my words, eager to catch every idea. In the Bible lesson they raise questions that would surprise you; they indicate such careful thought, and when one asks a question, the answers and the quotations from Scripture that others will give would surprise you, too. Mr. Tupper says, in asking deep, knotty questions, they equal the students at Newton. We have an interesting Sabbath School; Mr. Tupper has just slipped off the superintendence of it into my hands, and he sits down and takes a class. Mrs. Tupper says the Roman Catholics have never made much effort here until this year, now they are putting forth great exertions. We shall work against them in good earnest, and endeavor to prepare our students to meet them in argument and resist their influence. Mr. T. says they are endeavoring to gain power in the Government, and the Governor and other officials have taken pews at the

*The famous Siamese twins Chang and Eng Bunker (1811–1874) were both married, and they had twenty-one children between them, some of whom toured with their fathers. They settled in Mount Airy, North Carolina.

† Rev. William Warwick, sometimes spelled "Warrick" (1810–1883), of Philadelphia, pastored the First Baptist Church (Colored) in Raleigh from 1867 to 1874. Warwick was in Tupper's first class in Raleigh in 1865. See Jenkins, "Historical Study," 40.

Romish church. Mr. T. will stand fast and firm to resist Jesuitism, he says his ancestors far back were among the French Huguenots, against whom was perpetrated the massacre of St. Bartholomew's Day;* they afterwards fled to some of the islands on the coast of Scotland.

You may look for a long letter from me next week Wednesday, or Thanksgiving morning. I have written to Aunt Nancy to go up Tuesday, and that by Mr. Bartlett's team she could be brought to our door between five and six P.M. Bake the peas [pies?] Tuesday. Remember to use that can of white cherries in pies and sauce while she is up, give Lizzie and Abbie a bowl of them. Have quince and citron, too, for Aunt Nancy and Mary. There is a paper in a box-lid up on my bureau, will you give it to Mrs. Winn? The lid belongs to the box you carried to Mrs. Butterick. Put that cake of soap up in my chamber. The key to my bureau drawer is in a little box at the right hand corner of the lower one, please keep it there. Good night, with lots of love from Hattie

[P.S.] Are your dresses finished?

Raleigh Baptist Institute
Elm Cottage, Nov. 13th/69
Saturday Evening

Dear Parents,

I suppose when this reaches you, Aunt Nancy & Mary will be with you, and you will all be making ready to do justice to a Thanksgiving dinner. Well, we people down here in *North Car'liny* are going to have a Thanksgiving dinner too, and if you have roast turkey, I think we shall also. Misses Philbrook and Haley are excellent housekeepers, and they have a wonderful faculty of having good, nice food, on an economical plan.

Their friend, Miss Boardman, stopping with them a few weeks, is a very pleasant lady. We four have fine times; the others are all Unitarians, the old style Unitarians, but, we have no quarrelling, no controversy.

What do you think we had for dinner today? Roast beef-steak stuffed, and it was delicious; you take a large thick slice of beef-steak, cover it with dressing, roll it up, then sew up the ends, or tie them up, or put skewers through to keep them secure, then roast it an hour as you would a roasting-piece. I think I shall have some when I get home again. We have

*The Massacre of St. Bartholomew's Day, which occurred in Paris, France, on August 24–25, 1752, was a mass killing of French Huguenots by Roman Catholic nobles, instigated by Catherine de Medici.

breakfast about eight in the morning, dinner somewhere from two till three, and then between six and seven we usually have a cup of nice choc [blank space] bread and butter, and some kind of cake. We do not set the table for this meal, but take it in our hands sitting round the stove in the parlor, and we are generally kept laughing enough to prevent dyspepsia.

My room is a nice little nook, cozy as you please, I wish you could see it, you would say it looked comfortable. I have a pretty little parlor-stove in it, Mr. Tupper went with me to select it, have a cheap bedstead, red and white straw matting on the floor, I put that down today, a piece of wool-carpeting by the fire, a wash-stand manufactured out of a barrel with a board fitted on the top, which one of my students fixed, a large dry-goods box fitted up by this same student with shelves and a door, to take the place of a bureau, and soon I shall have a small wardrobe which he is now making, and a little table which he will make next week. For a bed I have a nice matress; Mr. Tupper had four large matresses sent down for the school, he kept two for the use of teachers, and the other two he sold and took the proceeds to buy the calico and cotton for the comforters I am having made for the students. Our students all occupy single beds. Mrs. Tupper and I both say this is the best arrangement. Mr. Tupper intends to have two other lady teachers, besides myself, another year, I have already written to one to know if she does not wish to come.

The first night I spent in Raleigh my matress was laid on a large table; I don't know that I was ever laid out on a table, but it made no difference to me, I slept soundly.

I made a pillow-tick of brown wiggin I had, and filled it with husks, I also made a curtain to hang around my barrel-wash-stand, of this same brown wiggin. If the ladies of Sterling in our church should send a box or barrel to us, I think I should like to have my comforter on the large bed in my chamber put in, and perhaps that Patch-spread in the little entry chamber.

I hear about the Ku Klux* in some parts of the state, but we do not fear them here. Mr. Tupper says he has been here four years, he has walked the street at all hours of the night before twelve o'clock, and he has never been molested; they know he is an old soldier and they do not meddle with him. I think nearly every person in Raleigh, white or black, knows

*The Ku Klux Klan first formed in the South during Reconstruction to terrorize African Americans and Republicans after the Civil War. President Ulysses S. Grant helped destroy the "first" Klan in the early 1870s. A new Klan emerged in the second decade of the twentieth century.

Mr. Tupper. There are military forces stationed here.* I would not ask to be treated any more politely anywhere than I am when I go to the stores, as I have frequent occasion to do; at book-stores, dry-goods, or those for other wares, it is all the same; pleasant and polite, ready to show me goods when I only go to examine and price them, and tell them I have not come to buy; they must know I am from the North, for a quick, energetic yankee woman is known at once South, our rapid gait, and elastic step would betray us, if nothing else did; but furthermore they know I am associated with Mr. Tupper in his school, for I look out various things for the school and the students, and they are perfectly willing to let anything go and have it charged to Mr. Tupper. When I looked out the material for comforters, I went to two dry-goods stores, told them what I wanted, and for what purpose, and that Mr. T. would want them charged to him till he could dispose of some matresses, the proceeds of which were to balance the bills; it would be all right, was the reply.

I was very politely treated all the way to Raleigh, at Richmond where we changed cars, a gentleman helped me carry my load into the car; at Greensboro, the Conductor on the train I left directed another to shew me into the room in the depot, then he came and purchased my ticket to Raleigh, obtained checks for my baggage, aided me to the cars, carried part of my bundles and saw me comfortably seated, this was the middle of the night, and I appreciated his aid.

I liked the appearance of Richmond very well, should think it a pretty city. So I should think of Washington—the Capitol is a fine building.

We passed Mt. Vernon on our way down the river from Washington, saw the tomb of Washington in the distance—the bell of the boat tolled as we passed it; I learned that this is always the custom.† I have not time to write near all I want to in this letter; if this reaches you Wednesday, you may look for another Thursday morning. I intend to write to Lizzie and Abbie in my next; much love to them.

I want to hear from home—and I shall certainly expect a letter after Aunt Nancy and Mary reach Sterling. Remember to give them some of my fruit-cake. See to it, Mother, that you do not sit up late at night to

*On the postwar military occupation of the South, see Gregory P. Downs, *After Appomattox: Military Occupation and the Ends of War* (Cambridge, MA: Harvard University Press, 2015).

†In a naval custom first established in 1801, vessels on the Potomac River passing George Washington's tomb at Mount Vernon pay tribute to the former president by tolling a bell.

work, retire early, and get your rest. I hope father will have some outside windows for the back windows in the sitting-room. Good bye, with lots of love from Hattie.

Raleigh Baptist Institute
Elm Cottage, Nov. 15th 1869

Dear Parents, & All,

I suppose one of my letters started for home this morning, and I intend to have this start tomorrow morning, so as to reach you before you eat your Thanksgiving dinner. The other ladies expect a barrel today, filled with good things for Thanksgiving, from their friends in Portsmouth, N.H.

I fancy we shall have as good a Thanksgiving dinner down South, as you will up North. I am not to have much leisure down here, I find. Mondays, Tuesdays, Thursdays and Fridays I have the students under my training from nine A.M. till half past one P.M., in this time I teach them Elocution, Orthography, Arithmetic, Penmanship, Grammar and Geography. Wednesday mornings I do not go in school, but Wednesday afternoons I have them in Composition, Declamation, a Bible Lesson and general exercises. Their sleeping-rooms open off from the school-room, they take care of their rooms, but I look after them to see that they keep them in order, teach them how to fix them up and make them as decent and comfortable as possible, &c. &c. Monday afternoons I meet the women of both the colored Baptist churches in Raleigh for a Bible lesson and prayer-meeting and other afternoons there is plenty to do; frequently I go to the stores, and for several afternoons I have been attending to the comforters we are having made; some of the colored women meet in the church and quilt them under my direction.

Sundays will be as busy as other days for me; at half past nine in the morning I go to Sunday School at Mr. Tupper's church, superintend the school, remain through the morning service and then from twelve till one I have a Bible class of men, women and children, after that I go home to dinner, and at two go a mile to attend Sabbath School at the other Baptist church. The Minister is a Northern man almost white, he is one of our students and seems delighted to be in school. Yesterday when I went in, he wanted me to take charge of the school and do just as I did at Mr. Tupper's, or as I would up North; he introduced me to the school as Miss Buss, a lady from Massachusetts, and one of the best teachers in the country, (didn't I feel flattered!) I expect I will have to superintend his Sunday School too. The quantities of letters that I will have to write will not be a small item, four or five must be written every month to the Wachusett Baptist Association, beside a host of others. Dr. Simmons* has just sent me a letter, wanting me to write to a Sunday School out West, and a few days ago he wrote down to us, wanting Mr. Tupper and myself to find some rich Baptist North, to endow our Institute with $25000.00, I wonder who the rich Baptist will be.

I do not get time to go up to Mrs. Tupper's as often as I would like, I would like to go up there every day, she is a lovely woman, stays close at home, having a fine baby not quite a year old.†

On our way from Washington to Richmond, we met a southern woman travelling with her son, the boy was about six years old, weighed about 275 lbs., I never saw such a specimen of humanity, such limbs and such a body. They had been North, in Canada and in the New England States, the woman thought she passed through Sterling from Fitchburg to Worcester. Her home was on the James River, and during the war she was between the two armies; she said her husband was a Union man; the Union army took all their cattle, horses and hogs, took down their outbuildings, took away everything except their house and land, but her husband bore it as all right; soldiers from both armies were frequently coming to her house, one day a deserter was dragged from her piazza and shot; she said she became so accustomed to seeing dead men, seeing them almost every day, that it seemed as if her heart became hardened to it. She had two brothers engaged in the war, one in the Union army, and one in the Confederate.‡

A Baptist Minister and his wife from Pennsylvania are stopping in Raleigh a few weeks; they are going to live about five miles from here; they were in school a few mornings ago, and seemed very much interested. Mr. Conover (that is their name) preached for Mr. Tupper a week ago yes-

*James B. Simmons (1825–1905) served as corresponding secretary of the American Baptist Home Mission Society. Starting in 1869 he devoted significant energy toward missions and education for African Americans in the South.

† Elizabeth Tupper was born in Raleigh on February 6, 1869. She married Dewitt Ballard in 1893 and died in Philadelphia on January 23, 1932.

‡ This may have been a member of the Rowland family of Charles City County, Virginia, who had moved to the area from New Jersey more than a decade before the Civil War. We thank Judy Ledbetter, of the Richard M. Bowman Center for Local History in Charles City County, for assisting us with this information.

terday afternoon, and yesterday afternoon he preached for Mr. Warwick, the Pastor of the other colored Baptist church; I liked him very well. Mrs. Conover has been a teacher and thinks she shall endeavor to teach the Freedmen near them when they get settled in their home.

If a box or barrel should be sent here from Sterling, will you put in my britannica [Britannia] tea-spoons? I think they are done up in a paper and laid in one end of that little long basket on one of the shelves in my closet. If not there they must be in one of my bureau drawers, the front side.

I hope you will keep both kerosene cans filled, I rinsed the other one the day I left home, and intended to take it down and have it filled, but had not time, I left the can in the little front chamber. Miss Haley is chopping apple for Thanksgiving mince pies.

Good night, with much love from Hattie.

Raleigh Baptist Institute
Elm Cottage, Nov. 16th/69
Tuesday Evening

Dear Parents,

I expect I have two letters on the way to you; one started yesterday morning and will probably reach you tomorrow morning, the other started this morning and should make its entrance into Sterling Thursday morning. I am wondering if Aunt Nancy and Mary are with you tonight, if so, I imagine you are having a good time; I don't think I would object to being there, too, for a while. Our turkey for Thanksgiving is out in the coop, he was brought from market this morning and shut up, but in a few minutes he was missing, our colored woman went after him, soon caught him and brought him back, he again made his escape in a short time, and a second time she captured him and placed him in another coop with some chickens where I believe he has since remained; if he has any premonition of his doom, I don't blame him for breaking through his prison-walls.

I wonder if Deacon Breck* has received a letter from me; I sent him one with my Donation offering in time for the Donation visit of our people to Mr. Atkinson. By the way, have you got your little pail home from there? You remember I carried it down to Mrs. Atkinson with something in it.

*Possibly Charles C. Breck (1811–1904), a farmer and abolitionist from Sterling, Massachusetts.

Thanksgiving Evening

The day is nearly ended, and with us down here, it has been a pleasant one, both out of doors and in the house. In the morning I was busy marking little slips to sew on the different articles of bedding in our Institute; the other three were all busy in the kitchen, and Julia, our colored woman, too, so I took my implements and established myself in the kitchen. Our dinner-table was set in the parlor and at quarter past three we four sat down to a very nice dinner. First, we had a fine roast turkey, mashed Irish potatoes, baked sweet potatoes, squash, onions, sweet-pickles, spiced currants and cranberry-sauce, next, a nice plum-pudding appeared, then mince-pie and squash pie (from some of my dried squash) came into place, and after these, apples, candy, raisins, and two kinds of nuts. Do you think it possible for us to make out a dinner from such a bill of fare. We ate very heartily; I believe we all said we never ate so much at any one meal before; we sat at table over an hour. By the way, the Portsmouth ladies had a barrel come this morning filled with good things. Tonight we have said we never acted so bad at Thanksgiving before, and we never had so good a one. I finished the edges of one of the students' comforters this afternoon; this evening I had a party in my room, (the other three) and we all cut up various antics. First, two of them came fantastically rigged up, one of them wearing a mask; then they went back and came in usual array; after we had exhausted various other resources of merriment, one of them took a kitchen chair, placed it [on] top of my large trunk in one corner of the room perched herself in it with a Jewsharp and entertained the rest with *thrillingest* music, to which we practiced the *most modernest* dances we knew, the steps of which had never been taken nor the figures witnessed outside of our room. From the time we sat down to dinner till the close of the day, our mouths were kept stretched, either by eating or laughing. There is no danger of our having the Dyspepsia.

Tuesday, Nov. 23d

My lunch for my journey lasted through, and more, too. We ate boiled chestnuts on the way, and I had quite a lot left when I arrived here, they lasted us some days. I did not think you were going to put them all in. I had Mrs. Ruggles take half of one of my mince pies, and I had a whole one left when I entered Raleigh, we ate that for dinner at Mr. Tupper's, the first day of my stay in this city. Some other things I had left were devoured at Elm Cottage.

The night I left home, we waited down at the Junction for the Nashua-train nearly an hour; if I could have had that time at home, and the part of the next day when I was not occupied in New York, I might have accomplished a few more things that I wished to leave done.

Your letter containing the one from Norfolk arrived one day last week; I shall soon look for another, either from home, or from Aunt Nancy. I was glad to hear from home, and to hear that you were better. I intended to write to Lizzie and Abbie in this letter, but have not time, I must go up in town this afternoon; think I shall get time to write with my next letter home. Mr. Tupper has given me a list of about twenty names for me to write letters for him, and I have as many of my own that I want to write soon. They seem to have an idea who I am at three or four stores, where I go every day or two, and they are just as obliging and as ready to do me a favor, as they would be at any stores North.

We had for dinner today young partridges stuffed and roasted, and nice apple-dumplings; we have a good table all of the time, and I pay $5.00 a week for my board and washing. I hope some societies at the North will send us some bedding, we need it for our Students. A new one came today and more are coming, and we have none too much bedding for those we now have. If a box is sent from Sterling, you can just put in the rest of that dark squash, we should all like it. I told the ladies you were not going to use it yourself, and they said "Tell her we will use it." Good bye, with love from Hattie.

Raleigh Baptist Institute
Elm Cottage, Nov. 27th/69

Dear Parents,

Your letter, with Aunt Nancy's and Mary's was received one day this week. I am so glad they came up and you all had such a nice Thanksgiving. I suppose you received my letter yesterday and learned what a nice Thanksgiving we had down here in North Car'lina. I believe all have written home what a good time they had; one says she wrote, that *four spinsters never had a better time.*

Didn't I write home how Mr. Warwick, the colored Baptist Minister here introduced me to his Sunday School? Before I left his church that day, he told his people that I was a thorough Baptist woman, warp and filling.*

I hope some of our Northern friends will send us some bedding for our Institute soon, we haven't enough for what pupils we now have, and

* In weaving, warp and fill (sometimes called "weft" or "woof") are the lengthwise and transverse pieces of yarn or thread, respectively, used to make fabric.

we are soon to have more. Several of the students say they want more bed-clothing, they sleep cold. I give them as much as I can, and I am getting more ready as fast as I can. I have tonight finished the ninth comforter that I have had made, next week I shall have two more quilted, and after that I think I shall get two more ready sometime, out of the material I have; then I must stop, till somebody sends us some money to use for our school. If I had the money at my disposal, I could buy good, thick, soft and warm dark gray blankets for $4.00, $4.50, $5.00 and $5.50 a pair, and out of a pair I could make three for single beds. If I had it, I would like to spend $75.00 or $100.00 at once, to make our students decently tidy and comfortable in their rooms, and to prepare for several others that have made application for admission.

Mr. Tupper is receiving letters of application every few days; we might have fifty students as well as eighteen, if we could only accommodate them. Those old-fashioned home-made coverlets make excellent outside coverings for our students beds, one makes two good ones.

We four independent women hired a carriage, horses and a driver today for an hour, took Mrs. Tupper and baby in, and rode out from Raleigh about three miles on the road by which *Sherman's army* marched in, some four years ago last spring;* the rails they threw down into the mud to make a hard road still remain. We enjoyed our ride very much, it was such a lovely day, the weather has been quite summer-like a part of the day, but it will not last long. If I had three, four or half a dozen pair of hands, I could keep them all busy for a while, there are so many things that want to be done all at once,—letters to be written to Sunday Schools, Churches and individuals, telling them of our work, our wants, our plans, and asking them to aid us (this is no small item, for we have numbers to write) and our scholars to be cared for.

Yesterday in a book-store, I was introduced to the Minister of the white Baptist Church in Raleigh;† he appeared very gentlemanly and friendly, invited me to come to his church, said the seats were all free,

*Raleigh surrendered to the Union general William T. Sherman on April 13, 1865.

†Thomas H. Pritchard, sometimes spelled "Prichard" (1832–1896), had recently become the pastor of the white Baptist church in Raleigh, where he served from 1868 to 1874. He was regarded as an "able, eloquent and truly christian divine." He married Francis G. Brinson in 1858 and by 1870 had three children. He later served as president of Wake Forest College from 1879 to 1882. Quotation from *Daily North Carolinian* (Raleigh), February 13, 1868.

inquired where I boarded, said his wife was away now, but when she returned he should call; he called his little girl across from the other side of the store and introduced her, and he seemed disposed to chat quite a while in quite a cordial manner—I was surprised. I believe he lectured to our students last winter, and I presume he will again this winter.

We four are all going to hear him at his church tomorrow evening. His predecessor here was a bitter rebel, the colored people tell me what curses he used to ask for in his prayers, upon the yankees, during the war. I don't know how the Raleigh people feel, but I was never more politely treated at stores and places of business than I have been here ever since I came. I have been to several stores at different times merely to look at articles that we should need, and to price them, and I am always treated with all the attention and obliging spirit I could desire. We four all went into the store of a Union man who went through the lines during the war, and were weighed one day this week; I weighed four or four and a half more pounds than I did down at Mr. Sanborn's* a few days before I left home, so you see I am not pining away; I believe all the others had gained in weight, too, since leaving the North; we are all daily troubled with Consumption of Food, to such an extent that it causes this gain in weight.

Monday Evening

I have just received a letter from Miss Colburn; she and another lady are in Newton, Georgia; she seems to like [it] very much and to be very happy; they are 22 miles from a railroad, in a quiet place; she writes that she [would] rather be there than in Savannah. When we rode out Saturday, we passed planters' houses, about as elegant and imposing in their appearance as the Higgins house below Samuel's. Several cotton-fields were by the roadside, the cotton-bolls were open and their white contents ready to be gathered. Yesterday was a nice day, I attended to Sabbath School at half-past nine in the morning, (I superintend and Mr. Tupper sits down and teaches a class, that is his wish), after Sunday School staid through the morning service, then had a Bible-class till one, went home, took a lunch, walked a mile to the other church, had a Bible class there for an hour, came back to Mr. Tupper's church for the afternoon service commencing at three, after meeting went up to Mr. Tupper's (nearly half a mile) came back, had supper and went half a mile to the white Baptist church at seven o'clock. I was never better in health than I am now. Good night. Lots of love from Hattie.

*James C. Sanborn (1837–1916) was a retail grocer in Sterling, Massachusetts.

[On a separate piece of paper]

Mother, if the ladies of Sterling should send anything to us, suppose you put in that thinnest, poorest blanket on my bed. I should double it and spread it over my matress. This is the fourth article I have named, viz. the comforter (mine) on the large bed in my chamber, my half dozen tea-spoons in the basket on the shelf in my closet, the rest of that dark dried squash, and this old blanket.

Raleigh Baptist Institute
Elm Cottage, Dec. 6th 1869

Dear Parents,

I suppose my last week's letter reached you Friday morning, and if another one is to reach you this week Friday, it is time one was being penned. I am so busy all of the time, and there is so much to be done for a few weeks now, that I could keep half a dozen pairs of hands employed, if I had them to use.

Last week Tuesday evening we all attended an Exhibition at the Deaf, Dumb and Blind Asylum; it was quite interesting. I send you one of the Programmes. Some of the little blind boys and girls sung very finely.*

I have sent a letter to Richmond for Miss Goodman to come to Raleigh during the Christmas vacation; she is from Worcester and is in a school like this; I hope she will come, the other ladies wished me to invite her. I wonder if any of the churches to which I have written will send us any clothing and bedding. If they should send us a box or barrel from Sterling, you might put in that overcoat of father's that he gave me, mark the price on it; I could sell it here, and the money would do to buy you a bonnet or a dress, sometime. You remember that brown coat that once I was going to rip to pieces and have a sacque of it, or a basque.

Tuesday Evening, Dec. 7th

I shall not spin out a long letter this time, for my hours are too closely occupied. I think I have been fortunate last year and this to get into such good quarters, where I have no care only to attend to my own affairs.

How well I was at Norfolk, and I am just as well here; it seems sometimes as if I was made of iron; perhaps the iron I took after coming from South Carolina changed my constitution. We have such a nice board all of the time—had a great turkey roasted Saturday for Sunday and yesterday. I pay $5.00 a week for my board and washing, furnish my own room

*This program is included in the collection.

and find my own fuel, that is very reasonable for the South. I received four papers from Lizzie Bailey this morning. Remember me to her and to Abbie.

I suppose Aunt Nancy and Mary have gone home.

Good night, with love from Hattie.

Raleigh Baptist Institute
Monday Evening Dec. 13th

Dear Parents,

Monday has come round again, and I have no letter written for home yet. I sent one to the Office a few moments ago, which I had this evening written to Rev. Dr. Simmons of New York. A letter from Lizzie Bailey came to me this evening, it was written last Thursday, and she says Abbie wants to come in to your house when her letter is finished, so I suppose you had their company. I am not sorry that I am away from New England this winter, I have no fancy for freezing cold weather and snow a foot deep. I have seen a few flakes fall here two or three times in little squalls, but snow-storms are not the fashion in this locality, and I am glad they are not. We have but two or three days of cold weather at a time here, then it becomes warm again. Our thermometer tonight stood at sixty out of doors some time after sunset.

We have a sunset and a sunrise gun every day in this city; it is where the Military are encamped, I suppose. I generally rise in the morning very soon after I hear it. I am first up in the morning, and last to retire at night in our household. I have a fire and my room warm in five minutes after I leave my bed. I wish you could look into my room just now, and see if it has not about as cozy and comfortable an appearance as any room you ever saw. Lizzie writes that Mr. Smith* is failing fast; what new difficulty has appeared in his case? I thought he was getting along very well when I left home.

I suppose the pig will be made to yield up his life erelong now; I think with such cold weather and deep snow, I should not keep him to feed.

* On January 21, 1870, the *Massachusetts Spy*, of Worcester, reported: "Luther Smith, who fell from the staging attached to the armory building in Sterling, in July last, and struck on a picket which entered his head and entirely putting one eye out, died on Tuesday last. The wound in his head gradually healed up, and he so far recovered from the effects of the fall as to be able to walk around, but during the last four weeks his health has been gradually failing. Deceased was 42 years of age and leaves a wife and six children."

Do you see Mrs. Harris often? I suppose the snow will keep her housed up pretty close. Does Mrs. Moses Sawyer* stay in her house alone this winter? How is Mrs. Newhall? Did the snow drift in round our house? Who shoveled the paths?

Tuesday Evening

I have tonight received a letter from Miss Kildare at Wilmington. She teaches in a Col'd Orphan Asylum† this year, and likes her position very much. I am glad every day that I came to Raleigh. I did not want to come here, and did not intend to come, when the Board at New York first proposed it, if I could only persuade [them] to let me remain in Washington, or some place farther north than this point, but I think this was the place for me, after all.

The Roman Catholics in this city are having a great Fair this week to raise funds for something, I know not what; I believe it continues open all the week. I wish I had a Programme to send with this letter. Friday is to be particularly devoted to the colored people, they are very urgently invited to come and spend lots of money; I hope none will accept the invitation. Gov. Holden's daughters‡ are among those engaged in the Fair; the Gov. himself has taken a seat in their church.

The other three ladies from our house were intending to go to the Fair tonight, if it had been pleasant, but it is raining a little. They wanted me to go with them, but my duties were at Night School; furthermore, I should not go to a Roman Catholic Fair, if I were not engaged at Night School.

No money from my hand, with my knowledge or consent, helps these serpents in their artful plans.

It is time to go to the Evening School.

Good Night, with love from Hattie.

*Moses Sawyer (1813–1869) married Betsey Wilder Sawyer (1819–1906) in 1839, and they lived in Sterling, Massachusetts. Moses had recently died, on June 23, 1869.

†In 1869, Mary Kildare left Hampton Roads, writing, "I shall gladly go to any place you think best to send me, but I would greatly prefer doing missionary work as I know I am better adapted for it than teaching." A few years later, she wrote from Wilmington, "The work never was more interesting nor seemed more important to me than it does at present." See Kildare to E. P. Smith, August 28, 1869, and Kildare to E. M. Cravath, May 28, 1872, both in AMA Collection.

‡North Carolina governor William Woods Holden (1818–1892), a Republican, had eight children, six of them daughters.

Raleigh Baptist Institute
Dec. 20th 1869

Dear Parents,

I suppose snow, ice and cold weather are in the ascendant in New England; not so here in North Carolina. The ground freezes a little some nights, but the sun is generally warm the middle of the day. I saw roses in bloom but two or three weeks ago, as I passed some yards, and as recently as that, Chrysanthemums of various kinds were in bloom in Mrs. Tupper's yard, also in the grounds about the State House. Christmas Holidays commence soon; we shall have no more school after Thursday of this week, until the Monday succeeding New Year, unless I hear some recitations of those Students who remain here. Several of them will go home during the vacation, and more will come in after the Holidays are over.

If you could look into my room tonight, you would see a comforter partly bound, a lot of patchwork partly put together for the tops of three or four more (part of it the other teachers' scholars have sewed in school, after I cut and basted it for them, and part of it was sewed before) two coarse canvass bedticks nearly finished, half a dozen pairs of gray bed-blankets just bought and brought home today, which I shall cut apart and hem, (only twenty four ends to hem across) a piece of cloth for three pillow-cases, and a lot of sheets and pillow-cases brought in by the woman who washes and irons them, ready for a change of the students' beds Thursday.

I have taught them, so that most of them make up their beds in a very neat manner, nearly as well as I would, and keep their rooms tolerably tidy; I don't know but their rooms look as well as the same number of white students would have theirs, with no more in them, and no better accommodations. If they get a sheet on wrong side up, or their spreads turned about I send them to make a change; if I find a broom standing down, some one must go and hang it up, and so on; their rooms are inspected by me every day while they are in school, and as they all open off from the school-room, it is quite easy to look after them. They take their meals nearly half a mile away, in a house right by Mr. Tupper's yard; the boarding arrangements are all under Mr. Tupper's and his wife's direction.

They have a Debating Society, which meets once a week; I went in last Friday evening, and really I was quite interested; they were much pleased that I came in. Their question for discussion was this, "Which exerts the greater influence over man, the hope of reward, or the fear of punishment?" Ten of them spoke, most of them with considerable spirit, and though they departed somewhat from the question, or took it sometimes in a limited sense, yet, they did as well as white youth who had enjoyed no better advantages than theirs would have done. They decided to continue the discussion another week; and then desired me to make some remarks to them; I told them it was too late that night (nine o'clock) but I would take up the question the next morning, explain its terms, and give them some suggestions about conducting a debate, which might help them some next time. I did so, and some of them thought they received lots of light, and they could do so much better next time—I expect to hear an extra discussion Thursday night, for I have promised to go over the explanation again Thursday. I have been amused to have some of them try to find out which side of the question I favored, they want to know if their side isn't the right one; I tell them I shall wait till after the question is decided before I give them my views. I should like to see the same number of white students together anywhere that would constantly treat a lady teacher with any more politeness and respect than these students of ours do; I do not believe they can be found.

I have tonight received a letter from Mr. Bowers* of Clinton which is quite cheering; his people are making up a box to send me, and among other things, they propose to send a Communion Service of plated ware, if I desire it. In my November letter to the churches, I wrote about the baptism of four, and the communion at Mr. Tupper's church the first Sabbath in the month, I mentioned that there was no silver ware, but a china pitcher, glass goblets and white earthen plates served the purpose.

I am glad these are coming. I think the people here will be so glad of them. I shall write to Clinton tomorrow. I wonder if Deacon Breck received a letter from me the first week in November—I sent a letter to him containing my portion for our Donation-Visit to Mr. Atkinson, but I have never learned whether it was received, or not. We have all received an invitation out to dine Christmas at the Bureau Superintendent's;† the others are not going, I have accepted, on condition Miss Goodman does not come from Richmond. *Our* Christmas turkey is in the pen. Good night with much love from Hattie.

*Charles M. Bowers (1817–1907) was a Baptist clergyman in Clinton, Massachusetts.

†Rev. Henry C. Vogell (1806–1887), former chaplain of the Sixty-first New York Volunteers, served as the Freedmen Bureau's superintendent of education in North Carolina from 1868 to 1870.

Raleigh Baptist Institute
Dec. 25th 1869

Dear Parents,

I suppose I may wish you a joyous Christmas, inasmuch as it is Christmas Morn, though I have not yet retired for the day before Christmas. It was midnight of the 24th, two hours and a half ago, so I suppose the day is fairly commenced. I am full of business just now; Christmas is the great day of the year down this way. Mr. Tupper's people are having what they call a Fair to raise money for the Church. They sent over for me yesterday morning before I was ready to leave the house, I was wanted to tell them how to trim the room and arrange the tables. I responded to their call, tarried with them long enough to get them well started, came back, went up town of several errands, home again, over to the church awhile, home to dinner, over to the church, up in town with a Committee of the Students to buy a Present for Mr. Tupper from the School, also with a Committee from the other Baptist Church (colored) to buy their Pastor and wife a Christmas Present, back to church, home to supper, then over to the church till nearly midnight, and home again, since which time I have attended to several things—written several notes, sorted over and counted the money taken at the Fair tonight, &c. &c.*

One of my Students personated Santa Claus, and he carried it out finely, affording much amusement to the children, two others of our Students made speeches, and they did well, too, I felt rather proud to be their *school-ma'm*.

Saturday Evening

It has rained pouringly here all day. All of us at our house had Christmas presents this morning, we all made each other a little gift; we had each seen all the gifts for the others, except our own—and this morning we had clean napkins spread at our several plates, and then we went just before breakfast was ready, one at a time, and placed our offerings under the different napkins, then, after seating ourselves at table, we all lifted up our napkins and discovered the treasures underneath—a nice glove-case from Miss Boardman, and a pretty work-basket from Misses Philbrook and Haley were at my plate. We had a lively time at table, arose and made speeches, drank toasts, and various other things. Miss

*According to a cashbook in the Shaw University Archives, the fair raised $29.52.

Philbrook is a perfect mimic, she can sing, talk, or act like almost any one, and she affords the rest of us much merriment. After breakfast I went over to church, looked after the Fair a little, which was to continue through the day, came home, dressed to go out to dine, and a little before one o'clock the carriage came for me; five Raleigh teachers among the Freedmen board at the Bureau Superintendent's home, two Baptist teachers from Newbern were there, two other Raleigh teachers outside of their home, were there, and Mr. Tupper and myself; we had a nice dinner, a pleasant time, and at six o'clock the carriage brought us home; it rained so hard Mrs. Tupper did not go to take the baby out. The money from the Fair today has been brought to me tonight; the Festival will probably be continued Monday. Two papers from Lizzie Bailey have been received this week.

Monday Morn, Dec. 27th

It is still raining, was a damp, disagreeable day all yesterday, but I think it will be fair after a time. The Festival is to be continued all today, tomorrow and tomorrow evening.

Our School-present to Mr. Tupper was a nice gold pen and case—price $4.50—but the jeweler let us have it for $3.95; he was very much pleased with it, said nothing could have suited him better. Mr. Warwick, the colored Minister of the other Baptist Church, gave fifty cents towards it, some students gave twenty-five cents, some fifteen, and some ten cents, each; their school-mistress gave what she had in mind to do, towards it. The present from Mr. Warwick's people to him and his wife was a silver revolving butter-dish—$8.00. I should have advised them to purchase something different, but their Committee could not select any thing else they were so charmed with this.

Mr. Tupper's people are contributing to make him and his wife a New Year's Present; I suggested the idea to them, and that the women should make Mrs. T. a present; and the men, Mr. T.—but some of the men wanted it the other way, that their gift should be to Mrs. Tupper, and the women's to Mr. Tupper, so it will be this way. I believe they are trying to see which will raise the most; I suppose I shall make the purchases Friday.

I am glad every day, that I came to Raleigh; I was never better satisfied, or happier in any place where I have taught. We certainly have some very interesting young men and youth among our students; and there is a pleasure felt, in seeing those so long trampled under foot, developing by our instructions into useful and worthy members of society, which we do not experience in any other teaching.

Good bye, with love from Hattie.

Raleigh Baptist Institute
Jan. 7th 1870

Dear Parents,

Are you buried up in snow-drifts at home? I hear of great snow-storms up North; I am glad they do not reach us. School has opened again this week with several new students, and more to come; all the former ones, but one, are back, and we expect him.

One of the older ones went away the last of November, he is now back again; he brought me two apples, and day before yesterday, when I was fixing something for one of the rooms, he exclaimed, "Miss Buss, I believe you is the smartest woman ever I see; I've thought of it lots since I've been away." Yankee ways of driving ahead with anything and everything are new to these people; they are not accustomed to seeing a white woman putting her hand to all sorts of work, and moving it onward, and it surprises them. They frequently say to me, "You does too much," "You works too hard." One student brought a vest to me one day, and asked me to mend it, another asked me to cut and make a pair of pants for him—the vest I undertook, but the other job was outside my empire. Mrs. Tupper says a colored man came to her once with a whole suit of clothes he wanted her to make.

Saturday, Jan. 8th

I think I have not mentioned that the box from Clinton arrived one day this week, and a welcome box it was, too. It came just at the very time—I was trying to fit up beds for new students, and I had not enough to do with; the bedding in the Clinton box just helped me nicely through. A Communion Service came in the box, which seems to afford Mr. & Mrs. Tupper as much happiness as if it were a present to *them* of solid silver. I told the people about it at the Wednesday evening prayer-meeting; I thought I would test them a little, I told them it was sent from a Northern Church for me to give to whatever church I saw fit, that it was here in my possession, and I was wondering whether they wanted it more than any other church; you should have seen their faces light up, and heard their eager exclamations as they took a vote whether they desired it or not; one man said he would speak for it twice, then another said "It is ours now, ain't it, we done voted for it?" He had previously said to me "Of course you'll give it to our church, because you belongs to this church while you is in Raleigh."

One of our students [Thomas Noel] is from Arkansas, an Episcopalian, but I think he is wheeling around slowly, and will yet be a Baptist, if we let him alone, let him study and investigate for himself. I tell the other students not to attack his views. He is a fine fellow, quite dark, and very smart; Mr. Tupper and I both think he will make his mark in the world. He came to our school from the Episcopal school for the Freedmen in this city, and they have been trying to get him back; I tell him when he finds teachers that care more for his interests than we do, or will do better by him, he may go; he thinks he shall stay where he is. He has been instructed by several different teachers before us, and from some of them he receives good letters, particularly from his Captain in the army. He said to me one day, "Miss Buss, I thought my teachers before used to do a great-deal, but I never had any do like you do." He was in the Union Army three years, enlisting when he was eighteen, and he has the upright form, the erect bearing, the manly gait, and the firm tread of a true soldier. I have in school, ten or fifteen minutes every day, an exercise in military drill, and I give this into his hands; it interests and amuses me to see him manage the men, he does it with so much promptness and dignity, and the other students seem to like it. I open the door from our schoolroom into a large room which is to be the church-room when finished, and send them in there. His commands—Right dress—Front—Right, about, face—Front, face Left, face—Left dress—Mark time March—Counter march—Halt—File to the left, &c, &c are all given like a regular Captain, he explains each order, shows them how to obey it promptly, and then requires it done. When he gets them pretty well-trained I am going to have Mr. Tupper in some day to see them manoeuver, I would not be surprised if the student could handle his men as well as Mr. T. himself, though he too is a veteran soldier of three years' service, and understands military tactics well.

Monday Evening, Jan. 10th

I received a letter from Aunt Nancy and Mary last week; I trust the silk handkerchiefs for father, and the cloth for some nice, long night-dresses for mother, reached you safely last Tuesday or Wednesday. I hope I shall hear from home again soon. Tell Lizzie and Abbie I will write to them again some day, when I get my family of twenty-five or so all cared for; I am seeing my way through quite well now.

We had a baptism yesterday, one of our students, and a middle-aged woman. The student was here last winter with Mr. Tupper, but was a Presbyterian, Mr. T. let him alone, did not try to influence him at all; this autumn he thought he would go to Charlotte to the Presbyterian Theological School* there, as he could receive some aid in that school, the same as many of our students are aided by Baptist Churches North. He remained there but a few days, became a decided Baptist, and took his way back here at once. Last week two others from that same school came to ours, they had turned Baptists and been baptized by the colored Baptist Minister in Charlotte; today one of them told me he could write back to the School, and half of the students would leave and come here, for they are dissatisfied with the management there, and they charged him before he left to write back just how it was here.

One student presented me a very neat little penknife today.

Yesterday I went to Sabbath School in the morning, superintended it as usual, staid through the morning service, walked a mile and a half to the Baptism, came back again, walked a mile in another direction to superintend my other Sabbath-School and attend to my Bible Class at two o'clock, then came back to Mr. T's Church to the afternoon exercise, went home, and attended church in the evening. One man told me yesterday he liked to look at me, I asked him why, "Cause I thinks you is a good woman, you follows up our race so close, and tries to taught us."

It seems to me no one occupying the position I have, and seeing the influence which labor in a school like ours must exercise over the future, could help being deeply interested in the work, and desiring to continue in it. Several of my pupils are six-footers or nearly that in height, they can look over their school-ma'am's head very easily, but not so easily walk over her rules. Two of them are now at work in Arithmetic by my light, while I am writing. Good night, with much love from Hattie.

Raleigh Baptist Institute
Saturday Evening, Jan. 15th 1870

Dear Parents,

Another Saturday night has come round, I never saw the weeks get away so fast as they have seemed to since I have been in Raleigh. Your letter and one from Deacon Breck reached me yesterday morning. I am glad you have received my New Year offerings all safe. I don't advise you

*The Charlotte Presbyterian Church established the Freedmen's College of North Carolina in 1867. Today the institution is known as Johnson C. Smith University.

mother to take such a long walk again; it is too far for you to walk up to the Old Place. The handkerchiefs were bought at Hewins & Hollis;* already hemmed.

I have not been away from the house today; we have had pouring showers since the middle of the forenoon. A very nice colored woman made me quite a visit before breakfast this morning, she was in my room nearly an hour; before breakfast was over three of my students came for extra lessons; they are three among our most promising pupils, I have given each of them a class in school, and so I take them for extra lessons Monday evenings and Saturday mornings; one of them is the one who was baptized last Sunday, another is the one who gives the others military drill, and the third is one of the new ones from Charlotte; I am specially fitting them for teachers, that while they are studying for the Ministry, they may help themselves by teaching during our vacations. They seem to feel that it is very nice to have extra lessons. I am not wearing myself out by any means, I am doing my work by the strength derived from what I eat, not by diminishing the already acquired forces of my muscular or my nervous systems. I weigh some pounds more than I did when I left home. It amuses me sometimes to read my letters from New York; Dr. Simmons will write "I am afraid you are doing too much, and remember overwork is a sin," and perhaps before he gets through, he will name something more he wants me to do.

I think, mother, you had better practice before you preach to me, let that old straw-sewing alone, and not wear yourself all down by sewing straw till midnight, and then just be able to drag around all summer. I expect I shall travel some while I am North this summer, and carry the wants of the Freedmen, and particularly of our Raleigh Institute, before some Baptist Churches in New England, and perhaps before some in New York. If I work for the Society in this way, and by correspondence while I am North, my salary continues the same as when I am here. Mr. & Mrs. Tupper will not go North this summer; he hopes to put up another building for our school this season, and while he is doing that I shall be asking Northern aid,—I think I shall get considerable, too. The Wachusett Baptist Association have paid over all the money they voted at the meeting in South Gardner in September, to raise towards sending me South under the direction of the Baptist Home Missionary Society; it has all been forwarded to New York, except fifty dollars ($50.00) which the Fitchburg Church sent directly to me a few weeks ago.

* Hewins and Hollis sold "fine shirts and gents' furnishing goods" in Boston.

Monday Evening, Jan. 17th

I presume the Sterling people will send something to me soon, for Deacon Breck wrote that Deacon Fairbanks had presented the Church with a new Communion Service at New Year, and now he thought they would send the old one to me for some colored church, if I desired it. I shall write for it. If they send an offering, a barrel will cost less transportation than a box of the same size because it can be more easily handled. You need not send the comforter now, the winter is half gone, but the old blanket, the spread and the spoons that I wrote for some time ago, I would like. A barrel should be directed thus—

Miss H. M. Buss
Care of Rev. H. M. Tupper
Raleigh, North Carolina
Via New York—Steamer, Portsmouth, Va.
Care of Agent of Seaboard and R. Railroad

A gentleman from New York addressed the people at Mr. Tupper's Church last evening, and he will speak to them again tomorrow evening; he is a Mr. Bourne,* one of the originators of the African Christian Civilization Society;† his father, years ago was a Presbyterian Minister in Virginia, and began there to preach against slavery; he afterwards went North and was one of the prime movers of the anti-slavery organization in our country. He warned the colored people against the Roman Catholics, told them what Roman Priests were desiring and aiming to do in this country, and he will tell them more tomorrow night. He is connected with the Protestant Union; I talked with him after the meeting; he says he fears the power of Romanism in this country must yet go down in

*Theodore Bourne (1821–1910), son of Rev. George Bourne (1780–1845), graduated from Union Theological Seminary and was an ordained Presbyterian minister. Bourne was the first secretary of the African Civilization Society and became well known for his support of the colonization movement.

† Founded by the famous black preacher Henry Highland Garnet in the 1850s and incorporated in the state of New York in 1863, the African Civilization Society sought to bring about "the civilization and Christianization of Africa, and of the descendants of African ancestors in any portion of the world, wherever dispersed." The society also hoped to ensure "the elevation of the condition of the colored population of our own country and other lands." See Jonathan W. White, ed., *To Address You As My Friend: African Americans' Letters to Abraham Lincoln* (Chapel Hill: University of North Carolina Press, 2021), 189–93.

blood, and he thinks Providence has freed the colored people that they may be educated and help save our nation from this foe. He has been traveling through the Southern states, and he says, from what he has seen, he is inclined to believe that the foreign soldiers in our army burned up and destroyed Protestant churches in the South as far as they could, being so instructed by their priests. The people that Mr. Tupper and I teach are well warned against Roman Catholics; some of them tell me sometimes what the priest in this city has said to them, and what they have said to him in reply, and I should judge he had better let them alone. One said to him one day "I want you to tell me how you are going to get me out of purgatory after I'm dead." Mr. Tupper has been here four years, and he has schooled his church members pretty well. Good night. Love from Hattie.

Raleigh Baptist Institute
Jan. 21st 1870

Dear Parents,

I can scarcely realize that Friday night has come round again. I suppose my this week's letter will not reach you till tomorrow morning, for it was a day behind time in being mailed. I have two events to chronicle for today, the first, that *Miss Dix*,* the long-celebrated Philanthropist, called in my school this morning. She called upon me when I was on a plantation on Hilton Head Island, S.C. in 1864, called with Mrs. Russell. She is now stopping in Raleigh a few days, and she came this morning with a Southern Baptist man, Mr. Palmer,† the Superintendent of the Deaf, Dumb & Blind Asylum in Raleigh.

* Dorothea Dix (1802–1887) was a renowned reformer dedicated to improving conditions for the mentally ill. During the Civil War, she served as superintendent of Army nurses. In January 1870, she visited several hospitals in the South. Of her visit to Raleigh she later wrote, "The citizens and public functionaries have met me with such unmistakable cordiality that I needs must put out of my mind the terrible past during the rebellion and take up the line of work where I left it in 1860. Strange to say, none are heartier in welcoming me home to North Carolina than the Democrats and Confederates, so that my plans are accepted and acted upon with an alacrity that hourly surprises me." See Dorothy Clarke Wilson, *Stranger and Traveler: The Story of Dorothea Dix, American Reformer* (Boston: Little, Brown, 1975), 315; and Thomas J. Brown, *Dorothea Dix: New England Reformer* (Cambridge, MA: Harvard University Press, 1998), 332–33.

† Wesley Jones Palmer (1834–1888) served as principal of the institution from 1860 to 1869, when he moved to Belleville, Canada, to assume the leadership of the Institution for the Deaf and Dumb there.

They both made some remarks to our students, and gave them good advice. Mr. Palmer told them what a good teacher Mr. Tupper was, what an earnest worker; I don't know what he might have told them about Mr. T's Associate Teacher, if she had not been there to hear.

Well now for the second event—I met with quite a little loss this afternoon, and one which I can not easily replace, one of my left, upper double teeth. It is but a few days since I was saying that for aught I knew my teeth were all sound; but within three or four days this one has commenced aching, and I was satisfied there was a defect about it that would keep it aching; the other ladies advised me to have it out, and Misses Philbrook and Haley told me of a good dentist here in Raleigh to whom they had been; Mr. Tupper said he would go with me, so this morning I decided to go this afternoon; he went home and told his wife he was going to the dentist's with me to have a tooth extracted, and she told him he wasn't going, she was going herself, for she wanted him to attend to her teeth, and she was glad to have an opportunity of going with some one. Mr. Tupper remained at home taking care of the baby, and she accompanied me, the other three ladies went too—(quite an array) I told them they might laugh at me all they wanted to. I was intending to take gas, for I expected the tooth would have long prongs and be difficult to extract (as it proved) but the dentist had no gas, and if the poor tooth was removed at all, I must fully realize what a pleasant operation it was. He thought at first it was a sound tooth, but by trying it a little he found it gave me pain, and prepared for business.

It did hurt some, that is certain, it required some strength and three or four pulls to separate it from its place among its neighbors, but I kept still, held the chair firmly with both hands and uttered no sound, and glad was I when it was laid before me. It had three long prongs, and there was quite a defect in one side of it.

I liked the appearance and manner of the dentist very much, he was very gentle and careful, yet steady and firm; I think no one could have removed it giving me less pain; but didn't it seem as if he was pulling my head off, and as if the bones grated and snapped?

The idea of paying one a dollar for pulling your head apart—only I havn't paid it yet, for when I gave him a bill he could not change it, and he said "Well, never mind you can step in some other time," before I left I said "Wouldn't you like to take my name, so as to know whether I come in to pay it, or not?" "Well" he said "I can take your name, but I guess there is no doubt but that you will pay, the ladies are generally honest, but the men we look after." Some other day I shall go with Mrs. Tupper to have two or three of her teeth filled.

This evening I have been over to school to hear the students engage in a discussion; they did very well, Mr. Tupper was quite pleased with the ability which they displayed, he pointed out some of their errors, and then they wanted me to make some remarks, too, which I of course did. Their Schoolma'am is never to be ignored, she must always be brought into notice. If I were the Queen and these students were my courtiers, I do not think they could pay me more deference.

Saturday

I was able to sleep well last night, no grumbling tooth disturbed me, sending telegrams through my head over all the lines of nerves; the cavity left seems to me partly large enough for a cart and oxen to be driven in. The ranks are broken, my first tooth has given out and fallen, whether the rest will make haste to follow like a flock of sheep their leader over the wall, though but to perish on the other side, or not, I can not say. We have all been out riding today, rode to the Insane Asylum in Raleigh, thence to the Deaf, Dumb & Blind Asylum, called on Miss Dix, then rode out to the rebel cemetery and home.* During the last two or three weeks, we have had several days that were almost summer-like; two days I had no fire, and one or two evenings I needed none in my room.

Monday Evening, Jan. 24th

I sent six letters to the P.O. last Wednesday night, and I shall send three more tonight, two more tomorrow, and several more, ere the week closes. I am very well. Good night, with love from Hattie.

Raleigh Baptist Institute
Saturday Evening, Jan. 29th

Dear Parents,

It seems as if Monday morning was scarcely past ere it is Saturday night. My time is occupied, almost every moment, but I do not think I have a hard time, there is none of that wearing upon the nervous system that there would be, or always is, in disciplining a school of restless, mischievous spirits. Our school now numbers twenty-seven and another student is to enter Monday morning. I went over to the school-room last evening to attend the Students' Discussion, their question was this, "Resolved that the works of Nature are more to be admired than the works of Art"; about twelve spoke upon the question, and every one of them

*The Confederate cemetery at Oakwood Cemetery now contains the remains of nearly fifteen hundred Confederate soldiers. The Ladies' Memorial Association of Wake County acquired the deed to the property in 1867.

advanced some argument of weight. If you could spend a day in school, I know you would feel much interested, you could not help it. I have been here now three months and feel quite established. One of my students said to me the other day "Miss Buss, you knows more about business now than a great many men that are doing business." We expect Dr. Simmons from New York to be here next week.

Sunday Evening

My usual Sabbath work is done, I have superintended two Sabbath Schools, taught two Bible classes, and attended meeting three times. A little cluster of purple violets and other flowers are blooming on my mantel-piece, they were brought to me today by a girl in Sunday School, she said her aunt sent them.

Monday Evening

I hear from time to time of the outrages committed by the Ku Klux in some two or three of the back counties of North Carolina, but we know nothing of disturbances here in Raleigh; I feel no more fear here than I would at home. There is a Military encampment here about half a mile from us. The Ku Klux generally do their work in back places, away from railroads and centres of trade. Two railroads pass through Raleigh. Mr. Tupper said a short time ago that he now went to bed and slept as he would North, but the first two or three years he was here, he slept like a soldier with his gun at hand. He does not wonder that Southerners despise a class of Northerners that there are scattered among them, neither do I; they are rash, unprincipled men, mere nobodies up North.

Mr. Tupper's course is a very prudent one, while he is an earnest Republican, he here lets politics alone, simply doing his work as a Minister and Teacher. I think he commands the respect and confidence of many of the Southern people, particularly the businessmen. Good night, with love from Hattie.

Raleigh Baptist Institute
Feb. 4th 1870

Dear Parents,

It does not seem possible that another Friday night has come round, but I suppose it has. Dr. Simmons from New York was here yesterday, he left last night to go on farther South. He talks as if he expected me to stay here right along; well, that will just suit me, if the A.B.H.M. Society*

*The American Baptist Home Mission Society was organized in Washington, DC, in 1832 to raise and support Baptist missionaries through local con-

choose to appoint me to this field; I like Raleigh, I like our School, and if I must teach with a man at the head, I rather teach with Mr. Tupper than with any other, for I do pretty much as I have a mind, and that I will do anywhere, but some teachers of the masculine gender might attempt to show off a little authority and try to be absolute, which, by the way, would not be so easily carried out with me, as it might be with some others.

I wonder what the weather is up North today—I imagine you may be having a North-East snow-storm, we are having a driving rain, it comes pattering against and streaming down my window-panes. There is lettuce up in our garden nearly or quite large enough to eat.

Monday Evening, Feb. 7th

Have you just enjoyed a severe snow-storm up North? I imagine so, from the weather we have had here, cold storms of rain and sleet. It is raining now fast, rained yesterday nearly all day, rained so fast that I did not go up to my second Sabbath-School. There was a good attendance at my morning Sunday School, if the weather was unfavorable—69 scholars and 11 teachers; my teachers, except Mr. Tupper and one man are principally from our students, three or four of them go up to the other Sabbath School and take classes for me there; Mr. Warwick the Minister, also, has a son and daughter who teach classes. His daughter comes to me twice a week to recite Latin, she seems like quite a nice girl.

My students begin to ask me if I shall go North this summer, when I say I expect to—"Well you will come back again, won't you?" is the next question, when I tell them I don't know, if I do not come, probably some one else will—then it is, "I want to know if you won't come back, I want you to come back, I want you to stay as long as I stay." I said to some of them a few days ago, when they were talking to me about coming back, I expected they would have to get up a petition to my father and mother to consent to my returning, "We'll all do that" was the reply. One was earnest today to know if I did not think I would come back, I said yes, if nothing prevented—that I would like to stay here ten years—"That will suit me," he answered, "I want to stay ten years, and I want you to stay as long as I do." You can imagine the satisfaction there is in trying to help upward a class of students who thus appreciate what you are trying to do for them. And beyond this, there is a satisfaction in the thought that they will go forth and in the centres of other circles stand to communicate to waiting

---

gregations, with the goal of spreading the Protestant Christian faith, teaching morals, and establishing churches and schools in North America.

numbers the knowledge we have imparted unto them. They will disseminate far and wide among their people the light we bear to them. We mean to labor to make them firm in the defense of Bible truth, strong to meet and to grapple with the monster Popery, who is trying every art to make long strides among their people. At every convenient opportunity, I tell them of the Roman Catholic Church, of its history, its nature, deeds, deceit, and designs. The whole phalanx of priests might feel flattered if they heard some of my reports of them and their church.

One student tells me he has been to several different teachers from the North before coming here, and he thought they were all good, but he never had any take that interest in their race and work for them as I do. He is an Episcopalian, or he thinks he is, and hopes he may yet be a Minister; this *Baptist* Institution will not, of course, serve up the right kind of Theology for him, but he begins to think he can't leave this school for any other while I remain here. These people, remember, speak out like children, ever [even?] when they become men and women.

I hope I shall hear from Sterling again soon. You can tell Winny Knowles his papers were very acceptable to the children among whom they were distributed.

This is the 27th letter I have written since the opening of this year, and only five have I received. I shall stop some time, if no one writes to me. Good night, with love from Hattie.

Raleigh Baptist Institute
Saturday Evening, Feb. 12th 1870

Dear Parents,

I wonder if time gets away as fast up in Massachusetts as it does down here in North Carolina. I never saw anything like it, it seems as if it was Saturday night as soon as Monday morning was well begun. The weather is mild and the air balmy with us; a large apricot tree in our garden is in bloom, the shrubs about in the yards are in full blossom. I do so much like wintering here, away from severe cold weather and deep snow-drifts. In the Watchman & Reflector of January 27th I saw a little article quoted from the *Biblical Recorder* of North Carolina, speaking quite favorably and in a friendly manner of our Institute.* I think there is a friendly feeling existing among many of the whites towards our School. At the Book-

*On January 5, 1870, the *Biblical Recorder*, of Raleigh, published a short piece: "Elder Tupper's Church and his Theological school, the Raleigh Institute, are both in a prosperous condition. Recent baptisms 22, students, 20."

store where I purchase all our books and stationery, they always seem very friendly, and are ready to order any thing I wish. An old gentleman of the Firm has a very benign countenance, he sometimes inquires after our School, if we are not having a good one this session.

Tell Lizzie Bailey I read her papers and then give them to Mr. Warrick, the colored Baptist Minister.

Sunday Evening, Feb. 13th

My usual Sunday work is done, and my records of the two Sabbath Schools under my charge are about finished. I get more and more interested every week in my week-day labors, and enjoy more and more every Sunday my Sabbath duties. My work now is very well systematized, both Schools have the same lesson every Sunday, and Saturday night I have a Teachers' Bible Class in our school-room, in which I meet the teachers of both Sabbath Schools and go over the lesson for the next day; in this way the teachers, the greater part of whom are our students, are prepared to teach their classes; and each Sunday, at the close of the School-exercises, I review each school in the whole lesson.

Some eight or ten of our students teach classes at Mr. Tupper's church, and two or three of those same ones teach classes for me in the other Sunday School. My Bible classes are not very large, usually ranging from ten to twenty at each school, but they are very interesting; in those, I take up the chapter, or a part of the chapter which contained the morning's text, explain the chapter, and dwell particularly upon the text, endeavoring to follow out the sermon, and illustrate and impress more deeply the teachings of text and sermon. You should see their interest, see them lean forward, as if hanging upon the words I utter, and eager to catch every one, that none be lost. Mr. Tupper has most of the students who do not teach classes in his Sunday morning class, but several of them come again into one or both of mine, at 12 and at 2.

Tuesday, Feb. 15th

We have had one good letter this week, one man North, a friend of Mr. Tupper's, worth $150,000.00 or $200,000.00 stands ready to give $10,000.00 to our Institute; we would like ten such offerings; we would soon have our School on a good basis.

We have had one young man in school a few weeks that North might pass for a white man; four or five others are quite light, one of them, a youth of nineteen or twenty is about as lovely in character as any pupil I ever had. One of our smartest men, who is an ordained minister and has a church some fourteen or fifteen miles distant, to which he goes every

Friday afternoon, came to me yesterday quite anxious for me to give him a Bible lesson; he says "If you will, sometimes, I will be so glad, I have to preach every Sunday, and I get no Bible teaching, I lose [love?] all the Bible class lessons here." He walks back Sunday nights or Monday mornings; I shall certainly find time to give him a lesson every week.

The petitions of our students are quite amusing sometimes; one asked me today to write a sermon for him, and a few days ago another one wanted me to write a political speech for him to send to some political gathering; I declined both, having already on my hands all the duties I can well perform. I am looking every day now for letters from home and from Aunt Nancy. Good night, with love from Hattie.

Wednesday Morn.

This letter should have been mailed last night, but it rained pouringly. I suppose now it will not reach you till Saturday morning. My letters home are generally mailed Monday night, Tuesday night, or Wednesday night.

Raleigh Baptist Institute
Thursday Eve, Feb. 17th 1870

Dear Parents,

After waiting a long time, I at length received another letter from home this morning, also one from Aunt Nancy and Mary. I had not heard of Mr. Smith's death; Lizzie Bailey wrote to me some weeks ago, how ill he was. What does Mrs. Smith do? It will be hard for her with her little family.

I suppose my this week's letter is on its way to you, and will probably reach you Saturday morning. I would like the Spread that I had last year; my bedstead is a double one, and quite a broad one. I was invited by Mr. Palmer to attend an Exhibition of the colored Deaf, Dumb and Blind pupils of the Asylum this evening; Mr. Tupper has gone. I want to have our students go there some Saturday. It is raining fast, it seems very much like April.

If you have any coverlets, spreads, or anything you want to contribute to our Institute, send it along. I think I could sell that *brown coat*, mark the price on it, if you send it. I hope you are using the fruits and berries I dried and canned; don't have a meal without sauce of some kind; use them all up; a plenty more can be put up next summer. If I should travel considerable while I am North during our vacation, I intend to stay at home enough to attend to this department, and several others. Plans are now being devised and partially executed for enlarging our work here very much next year. I believe Mr. Tupper and the Bureau Superintendent, under the direction of Rev. Dr. Simmons of New York, have this morning bargained for a fine piece of property here in Raleigh, a beautiful locality for our School, and a few acres of land attached. I am so glad! I want this Institute to amount to something, and I think it will.

A few days ago I had one of my hoarse colds that affect my voice so forcibly, rendering it so sweet and musical; for a remedy, one night, I cut up two raw onions, sprinkled a little sugar over them, and added nearly all the juice of a lemon, then ate the compound: it was effective; I shall try it again if I have occasion. I send this letter earlier so that you may get it before a barrel starts. The Britannia tea-spoons, that old blanket on my bed, and the wide spread are what I want. Love from Hattie.

[P.S.] Father and Mother both be very careful on the ice and slippery snow; don't fall.

Shaw Collegiate Institute
Raleigh, N.C. Feb. 18th 1870
Saturday Evening

Dear Parents,

Has the spring opened in New-England? We had potatoes planted yesterday. Next week we shall plant some peas. I wish I had a quantity of good garden seeds of all kinds from the north. Scholars keep coming in to our School, and it continually becomes more and more interesting. I always thought teaching was my life-work; I longed for it, I aimed and planned for it as soon as I knew what a school was; but I never felt so completely in my element, so fully satisfied that I was just where the Lord sent me, as I do here. There is such a wide field of usefulness, so many ways of doing good, that not a moment need be lost.

We teach everything, religion, morals, science, various kinds of work, system, order, neatness, and how to live so as to be tidy, decent and respectable; and our teachings afford results, we daily see them. Line upon line and precept upon precept do I give in my departments, till I bring things up somewhere to my mind. I wish you could see our work in its different phases for a few days, you would become deeply interested, you could not help it. To have so many around me looking up to me for instruction of all kinds, and to find that my teachings are eagerly received, well appreciated, and reduced to practice, thrills my heart as I never had it thrilled before.

Every act of our pupils towards us says to us "You are our friends, you have come to do us good, we can trust you, we can follow your directions, feeling confident that they will tend to our best interests." One student told me a few days ago, that one year ago he did not think anything of going to school, or that he would ever get an education, and said he "If I had been told that any white lady would ever have done for me as you do, I would not have believed it."

To hear these students pray for their teachers will move one's heart, if anything could do it. If their prayers are all answered, we shall have a large amount of *true* wisdom in this world, and shall wear bright crowns in the next. I was at one of their prayer-meetings tonight, and I believe every one that prayed, prayed earnestly for their teachers.

I have a class of six in Physiology, yesterday I set them all to drawing figures of human skeletons on the blackboards; they were rather disjointed and deformed, but for their first effort I thought they succeeded remarkably well.

Monday Evening, Feb. 20th

It seems like spring here, the mocking-birds sing every morning in trees near our window, they have sung nearly all winter. Hyacinths and Crocuses are in bloom on our grounds. Four new names added to our list of pupils today.

Baby Tupper has just given me a kiss for Grandma Buss; she is getting over the whooping cough. Mrs. Tupper sends her best respects; she kept [to] her room a week and a half, sick with a severe cold, but she is about the house again overseeing her work. Miss Hayes* and Miss Lathrop† are

*Esther Perkins Hayes (1829–1902) was a teacher in Limerick, Maine, who moved to Raleigh about November 1867 to teach at the Washington School. Upon visiting her school in 1870 one newspaper stated, "We were gratified to see the proficiency of the pupils. We examined all the classes and saw that she had not labored in vain." Another paper praised Hayes's "rare industry, earnestness and judgment," calling her "one of the most successful and popular teachers in the South." Following her death, the black Congregational church in Raleigh dedicated the Esther P. Hayes Memorial Parsonage in her honor. *Raleigh Daily Standard,* June 22, 1870; *Raleigh Weekly Era,* June 24, 1875; *Raleigh News and Observer,* November 29, 1907; *Raleigh Times,* November 27, 1907.

†Miss M. A. Lathrop (b. 1841) was an African American teacher from Thompson, Connecticut, who, like HB, was supported by the American Baptist Home Mission Society. Lathrop was at Shaw for the 1870–71 and 1871–72 school years and thus overlapped with HB for a year. It is worth noting that HB was now sharing a room with a black woman. Although Northern mission-

preparing to go to Dreamland, so I must prepare my letter for the close. I suppose you see Lizzie and Abbie often, remember me to them, and to all the neighbors.

Good night, with much love from Hattie.

Raleigh Baptist Institute
Thursday Evening, March 3d

Dear Parents,

I hear you are having cold weather up North. It is cool down here, but yet, Peach trees are unfolding their blossoms and people are beginning to make gardens. I received a letter from Aunt Nancy this morning, she wishes you could find time to write to her once in a while.

I have managed School myself this week, Mr. Tupper started for New York at 1 o'clock Monday morning, he went on business and returned last night the middle of the night, today he looked in upon us about five minutes, then left. Plans are in operation to greatly enlarge our work here another year, and I think they will be successful. Mr. Shaw, who was here week before last has given $10,000.00 for our Institute.

Mr. Tupper now usually teaches the students four hours a day and I teach them seven. Monday night and Tuesday night I went up and staid with Mrs. Tupper; she is one of the loveliest women I ever met; I like her better and better all the time; I am so glad there is a prospect of having a nice place in Raleigh next year, where we shall all live in one family, Mr. Tupper's people and I, and one or two other teachers that we hope to have.

Sabbath Evening

We have had another rainy Sunday, and the trees are all icy. Rev. Dr. Simmons came here Friday night on his way back from New Orleans, and has tarried here since. A Baptist Missionary from Mexico was with him. The Missionary from Mexico is an Englishman by birth, he went to Mexico in 1852, when he was but fifteen years of age; he has since become a Baptist, and is laboring among the Roman Catholics, distributing

---

ary societies urged their teachers to "dispossess [their] thoughts of the vulgar prejudice against color" and to treat African Americans "as if they were white," racial prejudice often persisted. In Natchez, Mississippi, in 1866, a local AMA superintendent would not allow black teachers to room with white teachers. If they wanted to live in the society's residence, they had to agree to "room with the domestics." See Foner, *Reconstruction*, 145.

Bibles among them, and leading them to the light; he has been quite successful, and he has two brothers engaged in the same work. He talked to our colored people this afternoon, telling them about Mexico and the Roman Catholics. If our people do not beware of Popery, it will not be for lack of instruction, for they receive it from Mr. Tupper and myself, and various other sources.

I suppose Dr. Simmons has effected something for our work in Raleigh.

Monday Evening

I enclosed a leaf about one of our students, for whom I have solicited aid, and I hope I may receive something for him. He is one who tries to help himself, and knows nothing about my writing to ask assistance for him.

I enclose a note to Mrs. Harris asking aid from her, and I believe she will give him something. I should like to place fifty dollars in his hands tomorrow morning, I think he would make a wise use of it.

I suppose I can soon say I am forty-four years old—is it possible? I don't feel any older than I did at sixteen. One student thought one day I was fifty, another one laughed at him well, said I wasn't more than twenty-eight or thirty; not exact guessers either of them.

Good night, with love from Hattie.

Ps. If you get any money to send to me for this student, have it in as few bills as possible, and put it in an envelope within an envelope, or get a Post-Office money Order on the Raleigh Post Office for the amount.

[The leaf she enclosed follows.]

Mother, do you not believe that your church, society and Sabbath School would contribute something to aid one of our students? He is the young man from Arkansas, of whom I have written once or twice; is about twenty-four years of age, and has served his country three years, in the Union Army—name, Thomas Noel,* is a member of an Episcopal

*Thomas Noel was nineteen years old when he enlisted as a private in the Fifty-fourth US Colored Infantry (not to be confused with the Fifty-fourth Massachusetts Infantry) at Pine Bluffs, Arkansas, on September 15, 1863. His CMSR (which spells his name Noal) gives his occupation as farmer. In February 1865 Noel was promoted to corporal; however, in January 1866 he was reduced to the ranks. In March 1866 he was again promoted to corporal. He mustered out of the service at Little Rock, Arkansas, on September 15, 1866. Standing five feet, eight inches tall, Noal was described in his enlistment record as having "black" complexion and hair and "brown" eyes.

church, and is striving to fit himself for a teacher, and for a man of usefulness among his people. He is now in debt some twenty or twenty-five dollars for board, and is quite troubled about it, for he has been disappointed about some money that he was expecting from his home, with which he purposed to defray his expenses. He is one of our best students, and one of our most promising young men; Mr. Tupper and I both think highly of him and feel that he will make his mark in the world. Our Baptist Home Mission Society assists most of our students who are members of Baptist Churches, and are studying for the Ministry, to the amount of fifty dollars a year, towards paying for their board; but as Noel comes outside of these arrangements, he can not receive aid from this source. And yet, we have not a student that I would sooner aid than him; I am anxious to have him assisted as much as any other one of our pupils. I shall aid him some myself, and hope that friends in the North to whom I write in his behalf, will be inclined to respond promptly and cheerfully with offerings sufficient to relieve him from his present embarrassment.

I feel that he is worthy of liberal aid, aside from his three years' service in the Union Army, in defense of our country's liberty, and *that* I am sure commends him to our notice.

I have never had a pupil that I would sooner assist; I think I never had one of better principles, one who had a nicer sense of honor and propriety, or one of finer sensibilities and who seemed to have a better or more delicate appreciation of kindness and sympathy, in proposition to his advantage, than Thomas Noel.

He is one of those who try to help themselves, he knows nothing about my seeking help for him.

I should be very happy, in the course of a few days, to place in his hands a contribution from New England that would relieve him from his present anxieties; and I believe no one thus contributing would feel any the poorer. It is very important, for the good of our country, and for the true elevation of the colored people, that this race should have well-educated and good men of their own for leaders among them. The student of whom I write gives much promise of being a man of just this class.

Raleigh Baptist Institute
Friday Evening, March 11th/70

Dear Parents,

I suppose my this week's letter reached you this morning. I hope you will find some who will be interested for that student of whom I wrote, and sufficiently interested to send me a contribution for him. Mrs. Harris could easily give a liberal sum, if she felt like it. Fifty dollars would pay his board in our Institute during our school-year of between eight and nine months.

Mr. Tupper and I have a prospect of being provided for in our old age. ?? One student said to me one day this week, he had thought about it a great deal, and he had made up his mind to this, that if he outlived us, and we should either of us ever come to want, or be poor, he would do all he could to help take care of us. Mrs. Tupper wants to know what is to become of her and the baby, she thinks they are left out in the cold. It was the same student that I think I wrote about in my last letter.

Did I not mention how one came to me one Saturday morning recently when I went over to the school-room, wanting instruction about something? This same one always wants to be taught some new idea when I am within call; I said to him that Saturday morning, "What did you do before I came?" "Well" said he, "I know how I had to get along, but you are here to teach me now. I prayed to the Lord last year for your coming, and the Lord told me you was coming."

Monday Evening, March 14th

Almost the middle of March; it does not seem as if it was nearly five months since I left home. I never knew time to get away more rapidly, and I think I never passed a happier five months than these spent in Raleigh. In three months more, I presume I shall be thinking about coming North. If I am as well when I reach home, as I am now and have been all the time here, you may expect to see me *drive round* and *tear about* as I did last summer. I am busy all the time, but I seldom get tired.

A School like ours does not wear upon the nervous system like one composed of restless, ungovernable spirits, where the stern work of disciplining all the time is like holding with your utmost strength a wild, head-strong, and hard-bitted colt.

One of the members of our school is one of the colored Policemen of Raleigh; one Saturday night recently he came to the door and left two nice North Carolina Shad for me; I was not at home, but had gone to meet my Saturday night Bible-class of teachers—he was very particular to leave word that they were for me, and also to leave his own name. A few mornings afterwards, he brought a string of small fish to me, there were a dozen on the string, I don't know what they were, but they were very good.

I think some of our students, perhaps nearly all or quite the whole, would do almost any thing for me that it was possible for them to do.

They so appreciate my efforts in their behalf, that it is only a pleasure to teach them.

From Lizzie Bailey's letters, I judge that some of the Sterling people are dancing enough this winter to have a gay time, if that makes gayety. I rather *seek* enjoyment in my work than in that kind of amusement, and I imagine I am much more likely to *find* it. I go to Mrs. Tupper's every opportunity I have; I am so glad there is a good prospect of our all living in our house next year, and near our church and school-building, too.

I don't believe teachers often work in School more harmoniously than Mr. Tupper and I do. We are both interested to do all in our power for the permanent good of this race. Good night, with love from Hattie.

Raleigh Baptist Institute
Tuesday Evening, March 29th/70

Dear Parents,

If you received my last letter, you have learned that I am sole manager of affairs in this Institute now. Mr. Tupper may be North till the first of May. I hope he will come to Sterling, I know you will be glad to see him, and will give him the best the house affords. He will come to see you, if his travels take him that way. I stay with Mrs. Tupper every night, and shall do so, till a brother and a sister whom she is expecting in a few days, arrive. The barrel came last Friday; I had it carried right up to Mrs. Tupper's, and kept all things eatable there. She says she done voted to have all things that you sent, and so she had them. She talks about her mother Buss' dried apple, pumpkin, &c. The apples were good, she liked those much, and hoped I would help myself to some of her Massachusetts' apples. This morning a couple of nice shad were brought to me, sent by the same student (one of the Raleigh Policemen) who sent the others, they were brought up to Mrs. Tupper's.

I eat a little at Mrs. T's in the morning, drink a cup of tea and come to school at seven, come home to breakfast at eight. I have not time to write much now, only that I am very well, better than when I first came down last October. Good night, with love from Hattie.

Raleigh Bap. Institute
Saturday Eve, April 2d/70

Dear Parents,

I suppose you will have no objections to hearing directly from me. I think it quite probable you may see Mr. Tupper next week or week after.

He was to be in Hartford today, after which he was going to Holioke, Northampton, Athol, Fitchburg, and Worcester. In going from Fitchburg to Worcester, he will pass through Sterling, and he told me he should stop to see you if he went that way; I presume he will stop with you over night. You can learn from him whether he wishes me for an Associate Teacher another year, or not. I wish you could give him a lot of dried apple to bring home; I don't suppose, however, he could carry it about with him.

Sunday Evening, Apr. 3ᵈ

I have staid with Mrs. Tupper, and been a kind of guard for her, I suppose, every night, till last Friday; her brother and his wife* arrived that night, they will probably stay several weeks. If Mr. Tupper should call upon you this week, you can tell him school goes along finely; the students are all very respectful and obedient to their school ma'am. I expect they will all be glad to see him back, for I believe *my rule* is a little sterner than his.

His church is getting along well, some of the members say Brother Tupper left the care of the church pretty much with me, or in other words left me in his shoes. Mrs. Tupper thinks I am standing in large shoes, if I have his.

Will you succeed in obtaining anything to aid the student of whom I wrote—Thomas Noel? He needs it now to help him pay for board, for which he is indebted, and about which he is troubled. Money which he has not received was to be sent to him from Arkansas. I hope you will obtain something for him in Sterling, and that it will come to me very soon.

It has been a rainy day here, I presume it has snowed with you. Good night, with love from Hattie.

Raleigh Baptist Institute
Friday, April 8ᵗʰ 1870

Dear Parents,

If you have received my letters, I presume you are now looking for Mr. Tupper every day. We have just heard from him, he is in Connecticut and expects to remain in that state for a while longer; he thinks now that he will not be in Worcester and vicinity until the 20ᵗʰ of this month.

*Sarah Tupper (1834–1924) had four brothers, three of whom were still living at this time. It is unclear which brother visited.

You need not be surprised, however, any day to see him. In his mission of traveling in behalf of this Institute, he may suddenly change his plans and route. If he should happen round at our house about the last of his being North, I wish you could give him a good lot of dried apple to bring home. Mrs. Tupper thinks much of the dried squash. School goes along very pleasantly and orderly; I have had five visitors today. I judge you are having a cold, backward spring North, by the reports that come to us from various sources. Mr. Tupper seems to think the weather is cold and unpleasant, and he would be glad to get back to the sunny South.

Sunday Evening, Apr. 10th

Ten o'clock—it is raining fast, has been a rainy day, though ceasing at times, for a little while. I have been through my Sunday-work, and did not get much wet any part of the day. We have had a large number of stormy Sabbaths since the commencement of this year. I think there have been three so stormy that I did not go to my afternoon Sabbath-School.

Monday Evening, Apr. 11th

I think it about time that I heard from home again. I enclose with this a letter to Mr. Tupper; if he should visit you, as I hope he may before he returns, you can give it to him. Is there any news in Sterling? How many new neighbors do you have this spring?

I suppose Lizzie and Abbie Bailey are as kind and neighborly as ever. I am very sorry to have Dr. Lord* leave town. I am sure I should not like to call upon any other physician. Good night, with love from Hattie.

Raleigh Baptist Institute
Saturday Evening, Apr. 16th 1870

Dear Parents,

I wonder what the aspect of the country is at home tonight, and what the progress of events. Apple trees, Cherry trees and Lilacs are in bloom here. If Mr. Tupper has not yet reached Sterling, I suppose you are thinking every day that he may call upon you.

I attended an Exhibition last night, of one of the colored schools in Raleigh; it was very good. If you could spend a few days among these people and children in their meetings and schools, I think you would get very much interested. Our Institute misses Mr. Tupper very much, but

*Friend and Harriet Lord moved to Newton, Massachusetts, in 1870.

everything goes along finely. One student wanted to know this morning if I wasn't coming back next autumn; he said if I did not come back, he wouldn't come back to school; it was one that I supposed cared as little who his teachers were, as any of the pupils. A few days ago I was showing one who is a carpenter how to do something for Mrs. Tupper, and I said I believed I could be a carpenter if I tried, "Yes ma'am I *know* you could, you could be any thing you were a mind to be" was his reply.

Sunday Evening, Apr. 17th

We hear often from Mr. Tupper; I can not say when he will reach Sterling, but probably some day this week or next.

The Policeman who is one of our pupils brought round another nice pair of shad for me yesterday, that was the third pair he has sent or brought to me, and they have cost as high as a dollar a pair.

When am I to get another letter from home? How are all the neighbors? I enclose in this another note to Mr. Tupper; if he should call, just give them to him, don't forget it.

Good night, with love from Hattie.

Raleigh Baptist Institute
Tuesday Eve, Apr. 26th 1870

Dear Parents,

If Mr. Tupper has not called upon you ere this letter reaches you, I think you will not see him while he is North this time. I shall be quite disappointed if he is not able to visit you, and I think you will feel some disappointed if you do not see him.

He intended when he left Raleigh, to go to see you, and he has intended all the time since he left, to see you ere he came back. But his last letter implied that he might not have the time. He wants to get back here this week Friday night if possible, so as to close the bargain for the place under contract, on Saturday.

The place we expect to have for our Institute, I consider one of the finest in Raleigh; the locality is high and pleasant, the house large and good, with modern improvements; the grounds are beautiful, tastefully laid out, and adorned with flowers and shrubbery, and several acres of land are attached sufficient for fruit and vegetable-gardens, in which the students could work and raise supplies for the table. The site is a very short distance from the building in which we now teach. Mr. Tupper is collecting money North to help make up the balance required to pay for it. The friend of his who was South a few weeks ago will give several thousand dollars, the Freedmen's Bureau will aid considerable, and the balance, our Baptist Home Mission Society called him North to solicit from individuals and churches. He has been to Windsor, Vt. to Mr. E. Lamson's;* Mrs. Eager gave him fifty dollars.

If you have obtained any money for our Episcopal student, Noel, and do not have an opportunity to send it to me by Mr. Tupper, just keep it at home for me; send me word how much it is, and I will pay him the amount from my own money, and just replace it when I get home. Checks come to me from New York whenever I ask for them; and the Bank here cashes them at once.

One student inquired particularly today if I was going home at vacation. He says "Don't you go, I want you to stay here, I am afraid if you go North you won't come back again; I want to go up there, I'll go and tell your folks you are not coming home, and I'll carry them a heap of letters."

Shouldn't you think I would stay here through the summer, now???

Our sick student is still sick, unable to sit up, but I hope he may be better in a few days; his roommate, a slight, short youth, is an excellent nurse, and takes good care of him.

I am very well, get along with every thing finely. Good night, with love from Hattie.

Raleigh Baptist Institute
Monday Evening, May 2[d] 1870

Dear Parents,

You did not see Mr. Tupper, after all, while he was North. I am sorry he could not stop to see you, for I wanted you to see him so much. He passed through Sterling one day, from Worcester to Fitchburg, passed through on the noon train; had he known just how the trains ran, I think he would have stopped off till the five o'clock train. He went to Clinton also, saw Mr. Bowers. He meant to stop and see you, but the weather and travelling were so unpleasant while he was North, he had no time to spare. He did not even go to see two sisters of his who live but few miles from a railroad over which he passed two or three times. He arrived home safe Saturday night. His church was full last night, every seat was occupied, and more too.

*Several generations of men in the Lamson family had the first initial E. It is unclear which one this was.

This morning, he informed me that I must run the school this month, for he should have other business. I think I can do it.

Two of the students want me to take them North, when I come—Noel for one, and his roommate, a little short, slender youth of twenty or so, almost white. They are nice young students, I would not be ashamed of them North or South. I think Noel's roommate has one of the loveliest dispositions I ever saw manifested by any one; I have not seen him vexed at all but once since I have been here.

Noel is getting better fast now; but he was quite sick for a few days; I scarcely knew how it would terminate with him; the students were all very good and kind to him. He said one day, that if his mother were here, she could not do more for him than I did.

I did what I could for him myself, and taught the others how to do.

"Are you going North this summer?" "You will come back next autumn, won't you?" are questions that are proposed to me almost every day.

If nothing prevents, I presume you will see me at home some time next month. It does not seem possible that it can be six months and a little more, since I left home—where has the time gone? It has sped away on lightning wings—I never knew time to get away so fast. I had a letter from Aunt Nancy a few days ago; she wrote that she had recently heard from you, and you had been having one of your lame backs.

I wish, mother, you would not lift every thing, as you do, and expose yourself to all weathers so much.

Wednesday, May 4th

The American Baptist Home Mission Society now own one of the finest situations in Raleigh; the business has been finished this week—I am so glad! *Shaw Collegiate Seminary* will probably be the name of our School now. Mr. Shaw, a friend of Mr. Tupper's gave $5000.00 right out towards it, bought for himself a part of the land worth $2000.00 and is to pay $5000.00 more in annual installments.

Mr. Tupper went to Windsor, Vt. While he was north, saw Mrs. Eager, she gave him $40.00 and Flora Lamson* gave $10.00 so he obtained fifty there. I presume I will be expected to travel some while I am north and solicit money. Our Home here and School-rooms must now be furnished. I am very well—can eat any time, and like a pig, too. Good bye, with love from Hattie.

* Flora Lamson (1840–1916) was originally from Newton, Massachusetts, but was living in Windsor, Vermont, by 1870.

Shaw Collegiate Seminary
Raleigh, N.C. May 14th 1870

Dear Parents,

I suppose I shall not send many more letters home, ere I present myself there in person. I have begun to get ready to leave Raleigh for a few months;—have had several bed-blankets washed up to be packed away, and this morning had one of the rooms cleared, ready to store the things away in. This month here is much like June at home, so if we go North the early part of June, we may have two Junes this year. Tell Abbie Bailey that one morning when I wore her great hat to school, one of the students asked me if I had seen the sun that morning.

What became of your little minister, Mr. Kent, when Dr. Lord's people moved away? I can't say how long I may stay at home when I first get home, but I should not wonder if the Society wanted me to travel round collecting money the first thing; I should like to do that part of the time, but I intend to stay at home in July. I shall want Mrs. Butterick to do some dressmaking at once.

Saturday Evening

I have just had a little plate of strawberries, the first of the season. This afternoon I walked by *our new place* in Raleigh—it is perfectly charming there. I walk past it and look at it whenever it is convenient. Noel does not get well very fast, it is like the frog getting out of the well, jumping up three feet and falling back two; I sent him to the Doctor's this morning, he worries considerable, and feels troubled because he is in debt, and incurring more expenses that he don't know how he can ever pay; and he is so far from home, and the money he expected from Arkansas does not come to him.

Sunday Evening

Just after meeting was out this afternoon I was called up to Noel's room by his roommate who was somewhat alarmed about him. I hurried up and found him in a strange condition; I did not know what to do for him, and I sent for Mr. Tupper; we neither of us knew what was the matter with him, or what to do for him—at first, it seemed as if he could not speak, but in a few minutes he began to talk in quite a delirious manner, said he was going to die, his time had come; we did not know but it was so, and sent for the Doctor forthwith; we feared he was having a congestive chill, or some kind of a fit; the Doctor said he had a chill at first, and delirium which often followed, came on before the fever, an unusual occurrence; he was very wild and delirious most of the time for two or three hours, but at ten o'clock tonight, I left him comparatively quiet, and left special instructions with two or three students how to manage him, what to do for him, and to be sure that some one was up with him and awake all night.

Monday

Noel is better today, but he appears to me as if it would take him some time to get up again; the Doctor has been in to see him this morning, and thinks it probable he will have another chill tomorrow. His extra expenses, to the Doctor, for medicine and other things, have now been some seventeen dollars, and how much more they may be, I can not say. I wish I had fifty dollars for him, I think it would help him gain, as much as medicine. I like the appearance of the physician who has the care of him, he is a young man, but seems very kind and gentlemanly.

I received a letter from New York this morning, informing me that the Board had voted for me to devote myself vigorously during vacation, to collecting funds for this Institution. I presume I shall travel some of the

The Barringer House. (From H. L. Morehouse, *H. M. Tupper, D.D.: A Narrative of Twenty-Five Years' Work in the South, 1865–1880* [n.p., 1890])

time, and probably write many letters, perhaps solicit contributions some through several of our Baptist papers.

I expect to have a busy vacation, but I feel ready for it; I am not worn and tired and fretted by disciplining a set of wild scholars; I have had none of that to do.

Do you want to know how smart I am? One of our youngest, and most awkward students said Saturday, he knew the reason I was never married, it was because there was nobody smart enough!!!

Rather bad to be so smart, isn't it?

Good by for this time. With love from Hattie.

6

Raleigh, North Carolina, 1870–1871

HARRIET RETURNED home to Massachusetts at some point in mid-1870. In September, she delivered a speech at the meeting of the Wachusett Baptist Association. According to a report in the *Massachusetts Spy*, "Miss Harriet M. Buss of Sterling gave a very interesting and thrilling account of her three years labor in Raleigh, N.C., as a teacher among the freedmen, who are being educated for the ministry, and the favorable consideration of the churches was asked in her aid." Her requests for financial support for Shaw Collegiate Institute appear to have been successful. The *Spy* reported, "Gratifying responses and pledges followed from representatives of many of the churches present, pledging various sums in her aid as a worthy agent of the [Baptist] home missionary association at the south."*

The contours of Harriet's speech are probably present in a letter she published in the *National Baptist* a few months later. She explained the history of Shaw Collegiate Institute, telling how Tupper had started a church and school in his home in Raleigh in 1865 and that by May 1870 it had grown to "nearly forty pupils, a part or all of the time, the majority of whom were connected with Baptist Churches, and were preparing for the ministry." Harriet thought it was "quite an advantage to the pupils" that Tupper ran both a church and a school, "for in this they learn how to conduct meetings properly, how to manage a Sabbath school, and how to be efficient leaders and guides of a Church." She described how Tupper often allowed the students to preach, take part in services, or lead Sabbath school.

* *Massachusetts Spy* (Worcester), September 23, 1870.

Harriet explained that the vision of the Home Mission Society was for Shaw to become a permanent institution that combined the training offered by colleges and theological seminaries in a single institution. An "encouraging" amount of financial assistance had already been contributed toward Shaw, but she urged readers of the *National Baptist* that "liberal aid from interested friends will be needed to carry on the work to completion" and to meet the needs of the students and teachers. She asked for contributions of money, bedding, and "serviceable" secondhand clothing for men, women, and children. "We can sell such clothing to the colored people for something near its real value, and as a general rule it is better for them to buy it, than to have it given to them. The money thus obtained helps to purchase some of the many things needed in our Institution."

By October 1870 Harriet was back in Raleigh. As the new school year was set to begin, between twenty and thirty students were enrolled, "all of whom, with two or three exceptions, are hopefully pious," she wrote to the *National Baptist*. "One of the latter, a young man of promise, has just found the Saviour, and another has serious religious impressions. Fifteen or sixteen of the students are already ordained, or are hoping to become preachers of the Gospel; others are preparing themselves to teach. Some twenty or more new pupils are expected soon to enter the school."*

Raleigh, N.C.
Friday P.M. Oct. 7th/70

Dear Parents,

I presume you will like to hear from this part of the country as soon as possible.

I had a good journey all the way, and arrived here safely Wednesday afternoon between five and six. Mr. Tupper met me at the cars before I had time to reach the platform.

Mrs. Tupper has been wishing me here ever since she came. I think I received about as cordial a welcome from all sources as I ever did anywhere.

We are full of business of all kinds. I can not write much of a letter this time, for I am in a hurry to go up town of [on?] an errand, and then I am going to see Noel, the student who was so sick last spring. Poor fellow! I

* *National Baptist* (Philadelphia), February 23, 1871.

don't think he will live long; the Doctor pronounces him in consumption. He may live several months, and he may not live one. So far away from his home and friends in Arkansas, without money to help himself, it is rather hard for him! He is with some very nice colored people about half a mile from us; I think they take good care of him, and I shall go to see him as often as I can.

I will write a better letter next time.

Good by, with much love from Hattie.

Shaw Collegiate Institute
Raleigh, N.C.
Tuesday, Oct. 11th 1870

Dear Parents,

I wonder if it is raining in Massachusetts as it is here just now. The water comes pouring down in earnest. I hope you have not needed to bring any water from abroad, since I came away.

I found Thompson in Connecticut quite a pleasant place, or I think it would have been in a fair day. The village is two miles from the station; I rode each way in a covered carriage. Rev. Mr. Sperry* and his family were expecting me, they gave me a cordial welcome, and made my stay with them very pleasant. I reached their home between eleven and twelve, and left a few minutes before six, so I had dinner and tea with them. The colored woman appeared to be a very nice lady, is about twenty-nine; they spoke of her in very high terms, and said she was much esteemed in their church. She will probably arrive here next week Friday, will teach a school in our building, next room to our school-room and board with us at our Teachers' Home. We are full of business; Mrs. Tupper has had a hard time since she came, getting our house cleaned and fit for yankees to live in. Miss E. P. Hayes from Limerick, Maine, a teacher under the American Missionary Association, who has been in Raleigh three years, and has spent the summer here, came to Mrs. Tupper after her return, and wanted to board with us this year; Mrs. Tupper told her she must wait till I came, it would be just as I said; so the next day after I arrived she was informed of my coming, and came to inquire if she might room with me. I was glad to have her, for I liked her very much last year, and I expected before I went home, she would want to board with us this year. She moved her quarters last Friday night, and Satur-

*Burton Sperry (1827–1887) was a clergyman in Thompson, Connecticut.

day morning she made apple-pies, and I made pickles; I put up a gallon jar of little tomatoes, and a gallon-jar of sliced tomatoes for sweet pickles. I also tried a few figs, and we find they are very nice pickled, so this Saturday figs and tomatoes will again be disposed of in the pickle line [lime?].

The chamber Miss Hayes and I have is about twenty-two feet by fifteen, there are five windows in it, do you suppose it is large enough so that we shall not need to quarrel?

I have undertaken to superintend the students working out-of-doors one hour every pleasant day, from one o'clock till two. I began with them yesterday; the grounds about the house are to be kept in order. The front yard, the flower garden and the shrubbery need a great deal of attention just now, for they have been lying neglected for some months. The work for our Institution building has commenced; the ground is now being broken for one wing, and the bricks are bought.

Tell Mrs. Newhall her cake and pie were very nice; I ate one piece of mince pie on the way, and brought the other to Mr. & Mrs. Tupper, her cake too, I brought here, and we have all liked it very much. I only ate one little piece of cake on the way down, did not want anything sweet.

I have carried Noel some of the apples, pears and plums that I brought, and I wish I had more for him. He may live some months, but if he should not live a week, it would not surprise me. I wish he could go home, or his mother could come to him and take care of him. We this morning heard of the death of one of our best students. He belonged to Georgia, was a fine young man, and gave promise of much usefulness; he seemed so happy in our school and was anticipating so much! I have wondered why I did not hear from him while at home, and was wondering how soon he would come into school again; but we shall teach him no more.

Three or four kinds of roses are in bloom in our garden; I should like to arrange a fine lot and hand in at home. I believe baby Tupper knew me when I came back; she is not afraid of us, and affords us considerable amusement.

The old gentleman at the bookstore in this city seemed quite friendly when I went in after my return.

If it has rained at home as it has here today, there will be plenty of water in the well.

Have you had the apples picked?

Good night, with love from Hattie.

Shaw Collegiate Institute
Raleigh, N.C. Oct. 13th 1870
Thursday Evening

Dear Parents,

I wonder if Lizzie and Abbie are keeping you company tonight. Miss Hayes and I are sitting before a little fire in an open fireplace in our chamber. I think I shall like her very much for a roommate.

The free public schools for white and colored pupils are going into operation now in North Carolina, each class by themselves.*

While he was north and knew nothing about it, Mr. Tupper was nominated and elected Chairman of the School Committee of Raleigh; this Committee control the money and employ the teachers for both the white and colored public schools. I think this shows that the people of this city have confidence in him.

Saturday Evening

Miss Hayes has made pies and doughnuts today, and I have made pickles. Last Saturday and today I have put up two one-gallon jars of tomatoes, sweet pickles, and two jars of whole tomatoes; I have also made this week a small jar of fig pickles and we all like them very much.

Monday Evening

It has been pleasant weather here nearly every day since I came. I expect our colored teacher from Thompson will arrive this week Friday; she will have one of the public colored schools, teaching it in our building.

I am getting the grounds around our house cleared up and improved somewhat, but it will take some days yet to bring all into order; the students work well, and do just what I tell them to do. A few nights ago there was a very singular and splendid appearance of northern lights, as bright a crimson as the clouds at sunset sometimes are. I am quite at home in Mrs. Tupper's family; I am to go over the house, get what I want to eat, and do as I would at home; we have a very pleasant little circle, four

* Article 9, section 2, of the North Carolina state constitution of 1868 required the state legislature to "provide by taxation and otherwise, for a general and uniform system of public schools, wherein tuition shall be free of charge to all of the children of the State between the ages of six and twenty-one years." On the creation of public schools for African Americans after the Civil War, see Green, *Educational Reconstruction;* Anderson, *Education of Blacks,* chap. 1; and Williams, *Self-Taught,* 71–77, 155–76.

of us and the baby. I am glad Miss Hayes wanted to come here; I shall try and persuade her to write a letter to your Sabbath School—she is a Congregationalist. Tell Lizzie and Abbie to write to me, I want to hear the news.

Good night, with love from Hattie.

Shaw Collegiate Institute
Raleigh, N.C. Dec. 16th 1870

Dear Parents,

I judge by the sharpness of the air that you are having winter up north in good earnest. I should think the wind came direct from a snow-bank of huge dimensions. Perhaps you are enjoying a furious snow-storm, such as is natural to New-England. Well, for my part, I would choose never to see another snow-storm; the appearance of the clouds, indicating one far to the north is sufficient for me.

Miss Hayes and I are both sitting over our stove writing letters. We have a large airtight stove up in our great chamber, and it soon warms up the room. Mr. Tupper has commenced teaching this week, and he takes three classes off my hands, and forms one or two new ones, but I have all my time occupied now.

Yesterday I received two good letters, one from the Rev. Dr. Moss* of Philadelphia; I was formerly acquainted with him and his wife in Worcester, when he was Pastor of the First Baptist Church; now he is Editor of a paper called "The National Baptist."

My second letter was from the Rev. Dr. Bowers informing me that a box containing fifty sheets, several comforters, and other things, had started for me from Clinton. I shall not be long getting to the bottom of it after it arrives. I have taken to working out of doors a while every day, between one and two o'clock, and I like the arrangement much; I believe it does me good.

Saturday Evening, Dec. 17th

I have this evening finished my brown winter dress. Our vacation begins next Friday noon. We are to have a Fair at Mr. Tupper's Church

*Rev. Dr. Lemuel Moss (1829–1904) was a Baptist minister who served as the editor of several Baptist publications, including the *National Baptist*, published by the American Baptist Publication Society in Philadelphia and advertised as "a first-class religious and family newspaper." He later served as president of Indiana State University and Chicago University.

all through the holidays, and we must get ready for some twenty or more new scholars to enter after New Year, so I imagine I shall not be very idle.

Monday Evening, Dec. 19th

I enclose a letter from Miss Hayes to your Sunday School; I don't know what she has written, but I presume it is interesting. Good night, with love from Hattie

[Separate scrap without a year]

Dec. 19th

One of our students has today handed Mr. Tupper, towards our Institution, a little roll of specie ($3.90) which he earned and treasured when he was a slave, and has kept ever since; there was a gold dollar, three silver half-dollars, five quarters, a ten-cent piece and a five-cent piece. Hasn't he shown some interest in our work?*

Shaw Collegiate Institute
Raleigh, N.C. Jan. 7th 1871
Saturday Evening

Dear Parents,

I suppose things move along in Sterling, just about the same as usual. Have deep snows fallen yet? Ours has all disappeared. A barrel from Groton Junction is on its way to us; we received a letter this morning, stating that it started last Saturday.

Miss Hayes returned last night from Smithfield. I presume Lizzie and Abbie are in often to see you. From Lizzie's last letter, I should think *dancing* was the order of the day with a certain class; I wonder if they expect to dance in the next world. Marking sheets and other bedclothes occupies my leisure moments—not a small job to go through the piles that stare me in the face. I don't teach Night School any more; Mr. Tupper was not willing I should, he said I would not live the year through, or not much more, if I did not stop. I don't feel any signs of decay.

Monday Evening, Jan. 9th

I think it about time for me to get another letter from home. Tell Lizzie and Abbie I will endeavor to write to them next time, but it is too

*In the antebellum period some slaves worked at night to make things that they could sell. In other cases, some slave owners permitted them to save some of the money they earned when they were rented out to local whites.

Miss E. P. Hayes. (Courtesy of the Kislak Center for Special Collections, Rare Books and Manuscripts, University of Pennsylvania)

late tonight. I have sewed the marks on four comforters, and made nineteen pen-wipers this evening. The pen wipers would not do for a Fancy Fair, (though, when I was making them, I threatened sending them north to one) but I guess they will answer the purpose for which they were manufactured.

Mr. Tupper received a letter from a southern white Baptist Minister, a few days ago, recommending a colored man to our School, and stating that he himself would call to see us. One day last week I gave a southerner a polite invitation to visit our School, and he told me he would like to visit it. Winter will soon be half gone, and then all gone, and spring will be here. Time goes faster and faster, it seems as if it moved with railroad speed. How do you endure the winter? Is father pinched up with the cold weather?

Good night, with love from Hattie.

Shaw Collegiate Institute
Raleigh, N.C. Jan. 14th 1871
Saturday Evening

Dear Parents,

I hardly think you are enjoying weather at such a temperature as we are; we have scarcely needed a fire this evening. Groton Junction barrel has arrived today, so I have had something to keep me busy out of school. A barrel and a box are on their way from Mystic Bridge, Ct., to Mr. Tupper. Fitchburg people intend to send me another barrel next month. I wish I had that brown overcoat that father gave me three or four years ago, down here; I could sell it to one of our best students; he wants one very much. A nice overcoat came in one of my boxes or barrels, I sold it to one of our ministers for eight dollars; it cost him half a dollar for new buttons and twist, and half a dollar to have it fixed, (Miss Lathrop, being a tailoress, repaired it for him) so that he obtained a good garment for nine dollars; I heard him say today he would not sell it for twenty-five dollars.

Miss Hayes and I went visiting yesterday; we took tea and spent the evening with two teachers who keep house together about half a mile from us; they were here Thanksgiving day.

Monday Evening

Do you have any rains north? We had a drenching rain yesterday afternoon and last night. Two of our students and three other young men were baptized yesterday morning.

This morning I received a letter from Aunt Nancy and Mary, and they sent on your last letter to them, because they thought I did not get a letter from home very often.

I send a picture of Miss Hayes; it is tolerable, but it does not do her justice; she was very tired and almost sick when she had it taken, so that it has not her natural cheerful expression. What did you ever do with her letter to your Sunday School?

I intended to write to Lizzie and Abbie this time, but I had to write a letter to Groton Junction this evening, and it is too late now.

Good night, with much love to all, from Hattie.

[P.S.] I am glad the tea and coffee were so good.

Shaw Collegiate Institute
Raleigh, N.C. Feb. 13th 1871
Monday Evening

Dear Parents,

Would you call it winter with the flowers blossoming out of doors? The Crocuses begin to bloom in our front yard. Our students have been spading up the garden, we shall have potatoes planted in a few days. I don't know but another flood has commenced; it has been raining down here most of the time for the last three weeks, is pouring down now. Have the springs and wells been filled, up north yet?

I send several copies of the Minutes of the Baptist State Convention (colored) of North Carolina, you can keep one and give the other five to Lizzie Bailey; one is for her, one for Deacon Stuart, one for Deacon Fairbanks, one for Deacon Breck, and the other for Mr. Sanborn.

We have one student who would pass for a white man anywhere north; he has brown hair, gray eyes, and European features; he keeps Miss Hayes and my wood-box filled.

I have never in my life taught anywhere else, where I felt that I was doing the good I may do here. This field grows more and more interesting; I should be very unwilling to leave it now. I am getting a good supply of sheets, pillow-cases, towels, quilts and comforters for our Home; I do not intend to bring any bedclothes out with me next time. I have marked 19 sheets, 19 pillow-cases, and 13 bed quilts and comforters for our House, and I have several more to mark.

The bouquet I made for our dinner-table Thanksgiving day, still stands on the mantel-piece in our dining room; it has not had any water for six weeks.

Mrs. Morse wrote to me a few days ago; Clinton ladies want to send on the money to pay the freight on the box they sent.

Miss Hayes wants to know if you don't think she is a beautiful looking creature. Mrs. Tupper has kept [to] her room for several days, sick with a severe cold and Neuralgia in her face; the baby has the whooping cough, has had it about six weeks. I am blest with my usual health, such as I have had for the last four years. Good night, with love from Hattie.

Shaw Collegiate Ins.
Raleigh, N.C. Feb. 27th 71

Dear Parents,

You need not expect much of a letter this time, for I left the schoolroom at nine o'clock, and I have written two letters since I came home.

A letter received from Leominster this morning informs me that a barrel started from that place for us last Friday.

Yesterday was a warm day, I went to church morning and afternoon wearing my new black dress and sacque, with no shawl. Gardens are being planted here.

Miss Lathrop went visiting Saturday afternoon among some of the colored people near us, she told about peas being up two inches. I wish I had a quantity of nice garden seeds of all kinds for ours and the students' gardens; I hope there are some in the Leominster barrel.

Clinton people sent me a few in their box, I have some peas and beans.

The clock is striking twelve. Good night with much love from Hattie.

[P.S.] Your letter came a few days ago.

Shaw Collegiate Institute
Raleigh, N.C. March 11th
Saturday Evening

Dear Parents,

If you could see our front yard, shrubbery and flower-garden, you would think spring had come in earnest. Our peach-trees are in blossom; we have peas, radishes, and lettuce up in our vegetable-garden; the flowering-quince, a beautiful shrub with bright scarlet blossoms, is in full bloom, so is a shrub as large as the fragrant-currant, bearing bright yellow blossoms; we have crocuses, daffodils and quantities of hyacinth in blossom.

Our northern visitors left yesterday morning; we had a pleasant time with them; and they seemed to enjoy their stay south. Mrs. Shaw was interested in our School and thought it appeared better than many northern schools. I took the ladies round in the students' rooms, and they thought they were in good order, kept well, and the beds neatly made up; Mrs. Edwin Tupper said they made their beds up better than she could. It has taken line upon line, and precept upon precept to bring them up to this point, but I feel paid for all in the improvement I see them making. Never before have I been situated where I felt that I was doing the good I have the opportunity of doing here; there are so many ways in which we try to elevate this people, and in most of them our efforts are crowned with success. I believe many of our pupils would sacrifice their own life to save mine.

Monday Evening, March 13th

I have seen by the Watchman and Reflector that Rev. Mr. Russel of Leominster has lost his little boy, he was run over by the cars;—I suppose it was the same little boy who was at our house with his father and mother a few days before I left home, the paper stated that fears for Mrs. Russel's life were entertained; the shock was so severe, it overcame her.* Miss Hayes has finished writing, and is preparing for dreamland, Miss Lathrop is gaping, and I am sleepy, good night with love from Hattie.

Shaw Collegiate Institute
Raleigh, N.C. March 18th/71
Saturday Evening

Dear Parents,

I have written three letters this evening, and think this will only be commenced. When our students write letters north to the people aiding them, I generally write letters to accompany theirs; the three written to-night were of this class, one to South Dartmouth, Mass, one to Belmont, N.Y. and one to Wall Street, New York City. What would you say to see a person as white as ourselves, obliged to be considered of the negro race? We have one such, a young man nearly twenty-two, with brown hair and gray eyes; any where north he would pass for a white man. Mr. Tupper and I both thought him white when he came in October to seek admission to our School. I never had a kinder or more appreciative pupil, or one that would do more for me; I believe he would risk his own life any time to save mine. His roommate is one of our blackest ones; we have all shades between.

Monday Evening, March 20th

We are having spring, balmy spring, with flowers and fruit-trees in full bloom, and vegetables in our garden up and growing. I love the climate of the sunny south, or at least of some parts of it. Raleigh is a good place, as far as health is concerned; and long as I am in this work, I can be happy and contented here, with no society but the colored people, and the little circle we form of our own. Never have I felt it so forcibly impressed upon

*Rev. Thomas Clarkson Russell (1834–1919) and his wife, Helen (1837–1876), of Leominster, Massachusetts, lost their seven-year-old son, Alfred, on February 13, 1871.

my mind, that *this is my work and I must do it*, as I do here. I should almost fear to leave this field, lest evil should come upon me. The students begin earnestly to ask if I am going north this summer, and if I will not come back again.

The field daily becomes more interesting.

I ought to write to Lizzie and Abbie again; tell them I hope to get round to them by and by, after I have written a few more missionary letters. Love to all friends.

Good night, with much love from Hattie.

Shaw Collegiate Institute
Raleigh, N.C. Apr. 1st 1871
Saturday Evening

Dear Parents,

I have just finished the last of four Church letters, and shall only trace the introductory part of this tonight.

A letter from the Secretary of the Fitchburg Baptist Sewing Circle informs me this evening that another barrel from them is on its way to me. I think my Association of Churches has done well this year, and I believe they will do more and more every year as long as I stay in the field. I shall not get out of work very soon; the marking is no small item.

Our students have been hoeing potatoes the first time this week. It rains here pouringly every two or three days.

Monday Evening, Apr. 3rd

Is it settled weather and traveling north? What are Lizzie & Abbie employing their time about, sewing straw as fast as ever? We have new scholars every few days, four new ones came in this morning. Miss Lathrop has had a vacation of a week, and commenced again this morning with over fifty scholars. She is a good teacher, and is doing good here, not one white lady in one hundred would do better than she does, and very few would do as well. We all regard her as a superior woman; *our School* will probably be twice as large another year, and we hope to have her in that.

Miss Hayes has about 140 scholars in her school, she has a colored Assistant-Teacher. She was one of seven or eight girls, was brought up on a farm in Maine, they had no brother, and so the girls worked out-of-doors, doing boys' work.

I rather think she and I were brought up some alike; we get along beautifully rooming together. You would like her ever so much. We are a well-satisfied family-circle.

Gov. Holden has been impeached and put aside from office, impeached here in Raleigh, but we do not care, only to be glad of it. Many of the *so-called* Republican officers here in the south have been corrupt men—*a disgrace to the party.**

I dislike Grant now, and hope Sumner will carry the day.† Good night, with much love from Hattie.

*In December 1870, conservatives in the North Carolina House of Representatives impeached the Republican governor, William Woods Holden (1818–1892), for declaring martial law in two counties and using troops to arrest civilians, including a prominent Raleigh editor and leader of the Ku Klux Klan. Holden's trial in the state senate took place in 1871. He was found guilty of six of the eight charges against him and was removed from office.

†In 1870, Senator Charles Sumner, a Radical Republican from Massachusetts, led an effort to stop President Grant from annexing the Dominican Republic. In retaliation, Grant's administration worked to have Sumner lose his post as chairman of the Senate Committee on Foreign Relations in 1871. In 1872, Sumner opposed Grant's bid for reelection, instead supporting the Liberal Republican Horace Greeley.

Epilogue

HARRIET RETURNED to Massachusetts in June 1871. She likely decided to remain at home that fall to help care for her father, who died on October 8. She appears to have stayed in New England for the next two decades, until after her mother's death in 1887. She decided to return to Shaw University in September 1887. By then the institution had grown dramatically, with eight or ten departments, including literary, law, medical, pharmacy, industrial, teaching, and missionary training departments. Shaw's three hundred to four hundred students came from throughout the United States as well as from South America and Africa. Upon reaching Raleigh in December 1887, Harriet worked with Sarah Tupper to fundraise for and furnish the Leonard Medical School Hospital. She loved working with Mrs. Tupper, who, she wrote, "has always been like a sister to me." In the ensuing years she taught reading and elocution, as well as courses on "temperance and social purity" in the Missionary Training School. In 1891 she wrote the "Parting Song" for Shaw's commencement ceremony. When she died in 1895, the *Charlotte Observer* reported that she "was a teacher at Shaw University" "for 25 years," but that report probably just counted her time there from 1869 to 1895 and did not take into account her hiatus in Massachusetts.[1]

When Henry M. Tupper died on November 12, 1893, Harriet penned a heartfelt tribute for the *Baptist Home Mission Monthly*. Shaw University, she wrote, "is in deep mourning. Thousands of colored people grieve over the loss of a true and faithful friend; and numbers of white people in the South who have learned to respect and appreciate his noble character and grand work, truly lament his departure from the field of his labors." Harriet recalled Tupper's lifetime of Christian ministry and then described his final four days, during which he greeted each faculty member, taking them by the hand and wishing them a final farewell. "I have gained the crown," he told them. "All is happy with me. All is well with me. I have

Leonard Medical School, Shaw University, class of 1889. (Courtesy of Shaw University)

gained the victory. I have passed the final examination with thousands of others. I am so happy, praise the Lord. The grave is robbed of its victim. Death is pleasant. I am dying, but I am happy." Tupper "entered upon the rest of the Eternal Sabbath," Buss wrote, on a "beautiful Sabbath morn." Twelve students served as pallbearers, and according to one North Carolina magazine, it was "the largest funeral ever witnessed in Raleigh."[2] His and Sarah's graves now rest outside the Shaw University library building.

Toward the end of her life, Buss continued to return to Massachusetts for visits during breaks in the school year. In 1892 and 1893 the *Fitchburg Sentinel* reported when she was "in town for the summer" and when she returned to Raleigh.[3] In 1894 she attended a reunion of the class of 1851 of the Charlestown Seminary, but in September 1895 she was too ill to attend the upcoming reunion. The *Boston Journal* reported that she "has been laid aside from her work by reason of illness the entire summer, and is still confined in a hospital in that Southern city. Her absence was greatly deplored and the cause of sincere regret to every member of the class present. Expressions of sympathy were abundant, and all united in the hope that her recovery to health might be assured, and her useful life be still continued."[4]

Harriet died just over a month later, on October 10, 1895, following a twenty-one-week illness at Rex Hospital in Raleigh. The *Raleigh News and Observer* reported, "Miss Buss enjoyed the high esteem and friendship of teachers and pupils as well as a large circle of friends, and these are invited to be present at the funeral services, which will take place at 9 o'clock this morning in the University chapel." Her body was returned to Massachusetts for burial.[5] According to the terms of her will, she made several "private bequests" and the remainder of her estate was divided into five equal parts. The first two parts were given to relatives. The third was given to the Baptist State Convention of Massachusetts "to be applied toward the support of Baptist preaching in Sterling as long as such preaching shall continue in the town." If Baptist preaching "shall cease in Sterling," the same money "is to be used for some other needy Baptist church in the state." The fourth part was bequeathed to the American Baptist Home Mission Society of New York, the interest on which was to be used for the benefit of Shaw University. The fifth part was given to the Woman's Baptist Foreign Mission Society of New England.[6] Shaw applied its portion of her bequest to its endowment, creating the Harriet M. Buss Fund. In making appeals for further donations in the early twentieth century, Shaw's leadership wrote, "The good that can be done is almost incalculable, when we consider what has been done in the last thirty years with inadequate means. No safer investment can be made than in the training and development of human souls."[7]

Harriet M. Buss's long career as a teacher in the South sets her apart among the vast majority of white teachers of African Americans during the Civil War era and the Gilded Age. Most spent approximately two and a half years working in the South during and after the war.[8] Harriet's decision to return to Shaw University at the end of her life confirms her commitment to racial equality through education. She had always wanted to make a difference in the world, as she wrote in 1850: "If life and health are continued, the *world* shall know that I live in it, and in the *future ages* it shall know that I have lived in it, for I will leave mine impress deeply traced upon it." She continued, "I shall study my lifetime; something or nothing is yet my motto, I will have no halfway ground." In pursuing her vocation, she "accomplish[ed] something of usefulness" for her nation, just as she had said she wanted to in 1861.

NOTES

Foreword

1. Bradley D. Proctor, "White Supremacy in the Academy: The 1913 Meeting of the American Historical Association," November 6, 2019, https://activisthistory.com/2019/12/06/white-supremacy-in-the-academy-the-1913-meeting-of-the-american-historical-association/; Claude G. Bowers, *The Tragic Era: The Revolution after Lincoln* (Cambridge, MA: Houghton Mifflin, 1929); W. E. B. Du Bois, *Black Reconstruction in America, 1860–1880* (1935; with an introduction by David Levering Lewis, New York: Free Press, 1998), 637–67, 718–27; Jeffrey Aaron Snyder, *Making Black History: The Color Line, Culture, and Race in the Age of Jim Crow* (Athens: University of Georgia Press, 2018), 34–45.

Introduction

1. Arnold Gragston and Sarah Benjamin, WPA interviews; Ira Berlin, Marc Favreau, and Steven F. Miller, eds., *Remembering Slavery: African Americans Talk About Their Personal Experiences of Slavery and Emancipation* (New York: New Press, 1996), 2–6; Peter Irons, *Jim Crow's Children: The Broken Promise of the Brown Decision* (New York: Viking, 2002), chap. 1; Mark Flotow, ed., *In Their Letters, in Their Words: Illinois Civil War Soldiers Write Home* (Carbondale: Southern Illinois University Press, 2019), 147–48; Heather Andrea Williams, *Self-Taught: African American Education in Slavery and Freedom* (Chapel Hill: University of North Carolina Press, 2007), 17–35; James D. Anderson, *The Education of Blacks in the South, 1860–1935* (Chapel Hill: University of North Carolina Press, 1988), 16–17; Ronald E. Butchart, *Schooling the Freed People: Teaching, Learning, and the Struggle for Black Freedom, 1861–1876* (Chapel Hill: University of North Carolina Press, 2010), 1–7, 193n18; Amy Murrell Taylor, *Embattled Freedom: Journeys through the Civil War's Slave Refugee Camps* (Chapel Hill: University of North Carolina Press, 2018), 193–96.
2. Anderson, *Education of Blacks*, 18, 20–21; Mary Ames, *From a New England Woman's Diary in Dixie in 1865* (Springfield, MA: Plimpton, 1906), 16; Butchart, *Schooling the Freed People*, 2, 156; Hilary Green, *Educational Reconstruction: African American Schools in the Urban South, 1865–1890* (New York: Fordham University Press, 2016); Jonathan W. White, "Martial Law and the Expansion of Civil Liberties during the Civil War," in *Ex parte*

Milligan Reconsidered: Race and Civil Liberties from the Lincoln Administration to the War on Terror, ed. Stewart L. Winger and Jonathan W. White (Lawrence: University Press of Kansas, 2020), 66–67; Robert C. Morris, *Reading, 'Riting, and Reconstruction: The Education of Freedmen in the South, 1860–1870* (Chicago: University of Chicago Press, 1976), 177.

3. Anderson, *Education of Blacks,* 6–15; James M. McPherson, *The Struggle for Equality: Abolitionists and the Negro in the Civil War and Reconstruction* (Princeton, NJ: Princeton University Press, 1964), 158–77; Williams, *Self-Taught,* chap. 6; Taylor, *Embattled Freedom,* 192–200; Joseph O. Jewell, *Race, Social Reform, and the Making of a Middle Class: The American Missionary Association and Black Atlanta, 1870–1900* (Lanham, MD: Rowman & Littlefield, 2007), 2–3; Henry Lee Swint, *The Northern Teacher in the South, 1862–1870* (1941; reprint, New York: Octagon, 1967), 12; Amy F. Morsman, "Reporting from the South: Massachusetts Teachers and Freedmen's Education," in *Massachusetts and the Civil War: The Commonwealth and National Disunion,* ed. Matthew Mason, Katheryn P. Viens, and Conrad Edick Wright (Amherst: University of Massachusetts Press, 2015), 249–74.
4. W. E. B. Du Bois, *The Souls of Black Folk,* 3rd ed. (Chicago: A. C. McClurg, 1903), 25. Northern teachers had, in fact, been going into the South for many years before the war. See Michael T. Bernath, "Our Yankee: The Uncertain Fate of Northern Teachers in the Seceded South," *Civil War History* 64 (September 2018): 272–303.
5. Anderson, *Education of Blacks,* 6; Butchart, *Schooling the Freed People,* ix–xii. See also Thavolia Glymph, *The Women's Fight: The Civil War's Battles for Home, Freedom, and Nation* (Chapel Hill: University of North Carolina Press, 2020), chap. 5.
6. Butchart, *Schooling the Freed People,* xi–xii, 4–5, 19–20, 54–57, 79–87, 108–11, 118–19, 180; Williams, *Self-Taught,* 91–115; Clara Merritt DeBoer, *His Truth Is Marching On: African Americans Who Taught the Freedmen for the American Missionary Association, 1861–1877* (New York: Garland, 1995).
7. Eric Foner, *Reconstruction: America's Unfinished Revolution, 1863–1877* (New York: Harper & Row, 1988), 144–45.
8. W. E. B. Du Bois, "The Freedmen's Bureau," *Atlantic Monthly* 87 (March 1901): 361. On the joint work of the Freedmen's Bureau and the AMA, see E. Allen Richardson, "Architects of a Benevolent Empire: The Relationship between the American Missionary Association and the Freedmen's Bureau in Virginia, 18651872," in *The Freedmen's Bureau and Reconstruction: Reconsiderations,* ed. Paul A. Cimbala and Randall M. Miller (New York: Fordham University Press, 1999), 119–39.
9. US census production of agriculture schedule, 1850; HB to parents, March 12, 1850.
10. Massachusetts census of 1855; burial information at findagrave.com/.
11. HB, letter of February 18, 1870.

12. *A Catalogue of the Instructors and Members of the Teachers' Institute, at Fitchburg, November, 1845* (Fitchburg, MA: W. J. Merriam, 1845), 7.
13. *Catalogue of the Officers, Teachers and Pupils of the Charlestown Female Seminary, for the 50th Term, Ending November, 1847, with the Course of Study and Remarks* (Boston: J. Howe, 1847), 3–9.
14. Catharine N. Badger, *The Teacher's Last Lesson: A Memoir of Martha Whiting, Late of the Charlestown Female Seminary* (Boston: Gould & Lincoln, 1855), 274–76.
15. HB to parents, March 12, 1850, and undated scrap ca. June 1850, UPenn.
16. HB to parents, January 28, 1860, UPenn.
17. HB to parents, March 12, 1850, May 31, November 4, 1851, UPenn.
18. *Catalogue of the Officers, Teachers and Pupils of the Charlestown Female Seminary, for the 60th Term, Ending March, 1851, with the Course of Study, &c.* (Boston: J. Howe, 1851), 2, 12; HB to parents, December 2, 1850, UPenn.
19. HB to parents, December 18, 1851, February 27, 1852, UPenn.
20. HB to parents, February 25, 1854, UPenn; *Weekly Marysville (OH) Tribune*, January 10, 1855.
21. *First Annual Catalogue of the Officers and Students of the Ladies' Collegiate Institute in Worcester, Mass., for the Academic Year Ending July, 1857* (Boston: J. M. Hewes, 1857), 4–5; *Massachusetts Spy* (Worcester), July 22, 1857.
22. HB to parents, April 30, June 27, 1859, UPenn.
23. HB to parents, February 27, 1852, UPenn.
24. HB to parents, March 7, 1860, UPenn.
25. Butchart, *Schooling the Freed People*, 117.
26. HB to parents, January 27, 1860, UPenn, quotation written on January 30.
27. HB to parents, February 6, 1860, UPenn. Abraham Lincoln responded to Douglas in his famous Cooper Union Address in February 1860.
28. On the political activities of women in the antebellum and Civil War eras, see Elizabeth R. Varon, *We Mean to Be Counted: White Women and Politics in Antebellum Virginia* (Chapel Hill: University of North Carolina Press, 1998), chaps. 3–5; and Nina Silber, *Daughters of the Union: Northern Women Fight the Civil War* (Cambridge, MA: Harvard University Press, 2005), chap. 4.
29. HB to parents, March 8, 1860, UPenn; Butchart, *Schooling the Freed People*, 116.
30. HB to parents, September 14, 1861, UPenn.
31. HB to E. P. Stone, January 15, 1868, AMA Collection.
32. Horace Dutton to E. P. Stone, n.d. [ca. January 15, 1868], AMA Collection. Normal schools trained future teachers.
33. HB, letter of November 21, 1863.
34. On geographical movement by teachers, see Butchart, *Schooling the Freed People*, 99–100.
35. HB, letter of January 9, 1869; Butchart, *Schooling the Freed People*, 117.

36. HB to E. P. Stone, January 15, 1868, AMA Collection.
37. HB, letter of January 15, 1868, quotation from January 20.
38. HB, letter of January 16, 1869.
39. HB, letter of March 31, 1863, quotation from April 8.
40. Letters of June 15, 1869, February 4, 1870 (quotation from February 7), and March 7, 1870; HB to E. P. Stone, January 15, 1868, AMA Collection.
41. See, e.g., Henry L. Swint, ed., *Dear Ones at Home: Letters from Contraband Camps* (Nashville: Vanderbilt University Press, 1966); Wayne E. Reilly, ed., *Sarah Jane Foster, Teacher of the Freedmen; A Diary and Letters* (Charlottesville: University Press of Virginia, 1990); and James Robert Hester, ed., *A Yankee Scholar in Coastal South Carolina: William Francis Allen's Civil War Journals* (Columbia: University of South Carolina Press, 2015). For a related title, see Suzanne Stone Johnson and Robert Allison Johnson, eds., *Bitter Freedom: William Stone's Record of Service in the Freedmen's Bureau* (Columbia: University of South Carolina Press, 2008).
42. HB, letter of March 31, 1863 (quotations from April 1, 8). It is worth noting that HB's correspondence does not contain the stereotypical perceptions of darker-skinned freedpeople that were articulated by some teachers in South Carolina, such as the free black Philadelphian Charlotte Forten. See Charlotte Forten Grimke, *The Journals of Charlotte Forten Grimke*, ed. Brenda Stevenson (New York: Oxford University Press, 1988), 33–34.
43. See HB's monthly school reports in AMA Collection.
44. HB, letter of March 14, 1870.
45. Union nurses, by contrast, were expected to be docile and submissive. See Silber, *Daughters of the Union*, 213–14.

Epilogue

1. Shaw University annual catalogs, 1870–94, Shaw University Archives; "Home Mission Appointments," *Baptist Home Mission Monthly* 9 (November 1887): 296; "Good Words About a Worthy Man and His Worthy Wife," *Baptist Home Mission Monthly* 12 (August 1890): 228; Harriette M. Buss, "Items from Shaw University," *Baptist Home Mission Monthly* 17 (January 1895): 18–20; *Annual Report of the Mayor and Officers of the City of Raleigh for the Fiscal Year Ending April 30, 1888* (Raleigh, NC: Edwards & Broughton, 1888), 67–68; *Daily State Chronicle* (Raleigh), May 29, 1891; *Massachusetts Spy* (Worcester), June 18, 1875, July 15, 1878; *Fitchburg (MA) Sentinel*, June 16, 1875; *Charlotte (NC) Observer*, October 12, 1895.
2. Harriette M. Buss, "Henry Martin Tupper: Another Great Man Fallen," *Baptist Home Mission Monthly* 16 (February 1894): 58–61.
3. *Fitchburg (MA) Sentinel*, October 4, 1892, June 7, 1893.
4. *Boston Journal*, September 7, 1895.

5. *Raleigh News and Observer*, October 11, 1895; *Charlotte Observer*, October 12, 1895.
6. *Fitchburg (MA) Sentinel*, October 16, 1895.
7. *Thirty-seventh Annual Catalogue of the Officers and Students, Shaw University, Raleigh, N.C.* (Raleigh: Edwards & Broughton, 1911), 75.
8. Butchart, *Schooling the Freed People*, xiii–xiv, 81, 88, 113.

INDEX

Italicized page numbers refer to illustrations. HB refers to Harriet Buss.

RECENT BOOKS IN THE SERIES
A NATION DIVIDED: STUDIES IN THE CIVIL WAR ERA

The Cacophony of Politics: Northern Democrats and the American Civil War
J. MATTHEW GALLMAN

Colossal Ambitions: Confederate Planning for a Post–Civil War World
ADRIAN BRETTLE

Newest Born of Nations: European Nationalist Movements and the Making of the Confederacy
ANN L. TUCKER

The Worst Passions of Human Nature: White Supremacy in the Civil War North
PAUL D. ESCOTT

Preserving the White Man's Republic: Jacksonian Democracy, Race, and the Transformation of American Conservatism
JOSHUA A. LYNN

American Abolitionism: Its Direct Political Impact from Colonial Times into Reconstruction
STANLEY HARROLD

A Strife of Tongues: The Compromise of 1850 and the Ideological Foundations of the American Civil War
STEPHEN E. MAIZLISH

The First Republican Army: The Army of Virginia and the Radicalization of the Civil War
JOHN H. MATSUI

War upon Our Border: Two Ohio Valley Communities Navigate the Civil War
STEPHEN I. ROCKENBACH

Gold and Freedom: The Political Economy of Reconstruction
NICOLAS BARREYRE, TRANSLATED BY ARTHUR GOLDHAMMER

Daydreams and Nightmares: A Virginia Family Faces Secession and War
BRENT TARTER

Intimate Reconstructions: Children in Postemancipation Virginia
CATHERINE A. JONES

Lincoln's Dilemma: Blair, Sumner, and the Republican Struggle over Racism and Equality in the Civil War Era
PAUL D. ESCOTT